P9-CKC-535

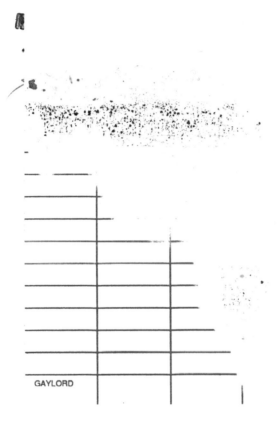

GAYLORD

# When Women Lead

# WHEN WOMEN LEAD

## Integrative Leadership in State Legislatures

Cindy Simon Rosenthal

New York   Oxford
Oxford University Press
1998

Riverside Community College
OCT '99        Library
4800 Magnolia Avenue
Riverside, CA  92506

HQ 1236.5 .U6 R67 1998

Rosenthal, Cindy Simon, 1950

When women lead

Oxford University Press

Oxford New York

Athens   Auckland   Bangkok   Bogotá   Buenos Aires
Calcutta   Cape Town   Chennai   Dar es Salaam
Delhi   Florence   Hong Kong   Istanbul   Karachi
Kuala Lumpur   Madrid   Melbourne   Mexico City
Mumbai   Nairobi   Paris   São Paulo   Singapore
Taipei   Tokyo   Toronto   Warsaw

and associated companies in
Berlin   Ibadan

Copyright © 1998 by Oxford University Press, Inc.

Published by Oxford University Press, Inc.
198 Madison Avenue, New York, New York 10016

Oxford is a registered trademark of Oxford University Press

All rights reserved. No part of this publication may be reproduced,
stored in a retrieval system, or transmitted, in any form or by any means,
electronic, mechanical, photocopying, recording, or otherwise,
without the prior permission of Oxford University Press.

Library of Congress Cataloging-in-Publication Data
Rosenthal, Cindy Simon, 1950–
When women lead : Integrative leadership in
State legislatures / Cindy Simon Rosenthal.
p. cm.
Includes bibliographical references and index.
ISBN 0-19-511540-6; ISBN 0-19-511541-4 (pbk)
1. Women in politics—United States—States.
2. Women legislators—United States—States.
3. Leadership in women—United States—States.
4. Legislative bodies—United States—States—
Leadership.   5. Legislative bodies—United States—
States—Committees.   I. Title.
HQ1236.5.U6R67   1998
306.2'3—dc21   97-53246

1   3   5   7   9   8   6   4   2

Printed in the United States of America
on acid-free paper

To Jim

# Preface

The adage "opportunity knocks" describes the serendipitous origins of this study. In 1992, in a graduate seminar on public organizational behavior, I wrote a research prospectus on examining the leadership behavior of women as chairs of state legislative committees. Like most graduate assignments, the prospectus was undertaken with a certain pragmatism on my part: I knew something about legislatures, committees, and legislative leadership from my years as director of legislative management at the National Conference of State Legislatures. What I did not appreciate at that time was that the study of legislative leadership borrowed very little from the theoretical insights of public administrationists and others who specialize in understanding organizations, leadership behavior, and gender. I also was unaware of the paucity of research on women as political leaders. As I connected these facts, a door opened and thus an opportunity presented itself.

Using gender as a lens for analysis and understanding, this book seeks to explore the nexus of representation, organizations, and leadership in state legislative bodies. Although these concepts are often given separate consideration, there is no extant study that examines their interrelationship both empirically and contextually. This study draws heavily on administrative and organization theories to inform an exposition of legislative leadership behavior, and in that sense, the project has been somewhat unique.

To date, much of what has been written about women as political leaders has been biographical or based on relatively small samples. To be sure, women as leaders of our major institutions of governance have been too few in number to allow for much analysis or comparison. As a result, many questions about women in institutional leadership roles have gone unanswered: Do women in positions of power and leadership in political institutions differ in background, behavior, and outlook from men? Are there gender-related leadership styles in political settings? What effect do institutional constraints and norms have on men and women holding similar positions of political leadership? What impact do women in leadership positions have on the institutions in which they serve?

State legislatures, and specifically legislative committees, provide an important venue in which to study gender and leadership. The professionalization of state legislatures over the past two decades makes them natural units of comparative analysis from which generalizations to other legislative bodies (including the U.S. Congress) can be made. More important, for scholars who wish to understand the impact of women as leaders of political institutions, sheer numbers argue for consideration of state legislatures and legislative committees. Simply put, there are many more women committee chairs than female speakers, majority leaders, or congresswomen. If, as some predict, women will cause a "feminization" of political leadership, then leadership in state legislative committees should provide some clues to this process.

Therefore, the principal goals of this study are (1) to make visible the perceptions, motivations, and behaviors of women and men who chair state legislative committees; (2) to assess the extent to which men and women differ in their leadership styles; and (3) to understand those differences in their gendered organizational context. It is my hope that this study's cross-fertilization of disciplinary approaches brings some freshness to the study of legislative leadership and some small insight to understanding gender, leadership, and organizations.

# Acknowledgments

This research is dedicated to the hundreds of women who are making a difference in political life. Being there matters. Articulating a vision of care, compassion, and community is, at this moment, the most important women's work to be done.

A book represents a journey that one does not travel alone, and I have accumulated many intellectual and personal debts along the way. First, I thank Ronald M. Peters Jr., director and curator of the Carl Albert Congressional Research and Studies Center at the University of Oklahoma and chair of Department of Political Science. He has been a thoughtful guide and mentor, a challenging intellect, and an insightful reader. I appreciate the intellectual contributions and professional advice of many at the University of Oklahoma, including Gary Copeland, Dave Morgan, David Carnevale, Craig St. John, Allen Hertzke, Ralph Hummel, Sally Coleman Selden, Larry Hill, and most especially James Rosenthal.

Over the past five years, I met a marvelous network of scholars engaged in research on women and politics. They have given freely of their time and ideas, have welcomed my questions, and have offered encouragement. I look forward to reciprocating in some small measure the intellectual support they extended to me. In particular, I am indebted to Rita Mae Kelly, Georgia Duerst-Lahti, Sue Thomas, Lyn Kathlene, and the staff and faculty at the Center for the American Woman and Politics.

In completing the manuscript, I am grateful to Jana Vogt who provided hours of valuable and competent research support in finalizing the notes, reading the manuscript, and assisting with the focus groups. Kellye Walker alleviated many administrative headaches by her able assistance. At Oxford University Press, I appreciate the encouragement and assistance of Thomas LeBien, Jessica Ryan, Susan Ferber, and Kathe Sweeney.

This project would not have been possible without the financial support of the Carl Albert Congressional Research and Studies Center at the University of Oklahoma and the National Science Foundation, which provided a dissertation improvement grant. The National Conference of State Legislatures (NCSL), particularly Nancy Rhyme and Annette Durlam, was extraordinarily helpful in providing mailing lists, writing letters of endorsement for the study, facilitating the scheduling of focus groups, and answering research questions. My debt to NCSL, however, is also personal. From Bill Pound, Carl Tubbesing, Diane Chaffin, Rich Jones, Karl Kurtz and many others, I have learned a great deal about state legislatures. Through NCSL, I also met Alan Rosenthal, whose perspective on legislative research reminds me that politics is about people and places, not statistics.

Most important, this project would not have been possible without the enormous commitment of time of the more than 360 state legislative committee chairs who completed a lengthy questionnaire, participated in focus groups, or consented to personal interviews. The Women's Network of the National Conference of State Legislatures, which State Representative Jane Maroney of Delaware chaired in 1993–1994, was particularly supportive. In addition, many legislative staff in Oklahoma, Ohio, and Colorado provided invaluable assistance, but in particular I appreciate the feedback given by Doug Brown, Tom Manuel, and George Humphreys on drafts of the chapters. I cannot thank all the others individually or adequately for their time and cooperation, but my gratitude is incalculable.

Finally, without the love, support, and patience of my family, Jim, Catie, and Aaron, I would be still far from my destination. Fellow travelers and partners in every possible way, they have inspired, challenged, encouraged, been with me, and put up with me all the way. To my parents, Clarence and Margarete, who survived the fireworks of heated dinnertime debates, and my four brothers, who were often my sparring partners, I owe many hours of challenging conversation that gave me confidence to tackle almost any project. In a conversation just a few weeks before his death, my brother Rourk provoked my thinking anew. To you, Rourk, a special thank you.

# Contents

List of Figures and Tables, xiii

1   Integrating Leadership in State Legislatures, 3

2   Gender, Leadership, and Legislatures: Theoretical Roots, 18

3   The Origins of Different Committee Styles, 32

4   The Components of Integrative Leadership:
    Motivation, Behavior, and Style, 54

5   The Constraints of Place on Leadership, 77

6   Oklahoma: Leadership in No-Woman's Land, 96

7   Ohio: Gender Power in a Time of Leadership Transition, 117

8   Colorado: Defining the Standards of Leadership, 137

9   A Vision of Integrative Leadership, 159

    Appendix: Methodology, 168

    Notes, 181

    References, 219

    Index, 233

# List of Figures and Tables

## Figures

Figure 1.1. Women in legislatures (1983–1997), 9

Figure 2.1. Integrative and aggregative dimensions in conflict situations, 24

Figure 2.2. Conflict-resolution behaviors and tactics, 25

Figure 5.1. Impact of women's power on integrative leadership styles of committee chairs, 91

## Tables

Table 1.1. Women's Representation in Specific States (1997), 11

Table 2.1. Integrative and Aggregative Leadership, 22

Table 3.1. Background Characteristics of Committee Chairs by Type of Legislature, 38

Table 3.2. Career Characteristics of Committee Chairs by Type of Legislature, 45

Table 3.3. Chairs' Perceptions of Their Role and Performance, 50

Table 4.1. Survey Items Associated with Different Motivations, 60

Table 4.2. Leadership Traits Associated with Different Personality Descriptions, 64

Table 4.3. Behaviors Associated with Conflict Management Styles, 68

Table 4.4. Patterns of Mentoring Among Committee Chairs, 73

Table 4.5. Influence of Female Mentoring on Men's Leadership Styles, 74

Table 5.1. Integrative Motivations and Behavior in Three Types of Legislatures, 88

Table 5.2.  Integrative Motivations and Behavior in Legislatures of Differing Sex Composition, 89

Table A.1.  Comparison of Overall Committee Population and Survey Respondents, 170

Table A.2.  Selected Characteristics of Colorado, Ohio and Oklahoma, 174

Table A.3.  Influence of Female Mentoring on Leadership Styles, 175

Table A.4.  Regression Models for Inclusive Behaviors, 175

Table A.5.  Regression Models for People Motivation, 176

Table A.6.  Regression Models for Policy Motivation, 176

Table A.7.  Regression Models for Collaborative Style, 177

Table A.8.  Regression for Competitive Style, 178

Table A.9.  Regression for Accommodative Style, 179

When Women Lead

# 1

## Integrating Leadership in
## State Legislatures

W hen Donna Sytek was elected by a unanimous vote to the speakership of the 400-member New Hampshire House in December 1996, she brought with her a reputation as a consensus builder who does her homework.[1] She developed the skills and reputation by following the usual path to leadership: She served as a committee chair (Ways and Means and later Criminal Justice), worked her way up, and paid her dues.

As a committee chair, Speaker Sytek learned and perfected a style of leadership that stresses community and collaboration. Though New Hampshire is a small (just under 1.2 million residents) and racially homogeneous (98 percent white) state, Sytek knows from experience that issues can be divisive. She believes that decisions are best made when all stakeholders get involved, when ownership of a policy develops among all the participants, and when people are persuaded of the merits of an issue. Sytek favors this approach for a simple reason: "It works."[2]

Even if she were inclined toward a more "command" style, the speaker has few perquisites to entice votes or enforce loyalty among her independent-minded Republican colleagues. Her most tangible rewards and punishments are the distribution or withholding of sixty Capitol-area parking spaces and the more comfortable aisle seats in the House's auditorium-like chamber.

Because her route to leadership was altogether traditional, Speaker Sytek rejects the idea that gender played a role in her ascension as the first woman ever to hold the speakership in her state. Indeed, if legislative behavior is best understood by studying a legislator's district and institution,[3] then gender seems tangential to her legislative career. Her thoroughly Yankee roots, traceable to the *Mayflower*, and Republican affiliation seem a good fit for Salem, the town of 28,000 in the hills bordering Massachusetts, which she has represented since 1977.

Moreover, New Hampshire's legislature, at first blush, seems defined by factors other than gender: Each of the 400 House members and 24 senators earns only $100 a year (the full-time speaker is paid $125), sessions are limited to forty-five legislative days, and staff support comes from a small cadre of employees. New Hampshire has traditionally ranked among the top ten states in number and percentage of female state legislators, but male legislators still outnumber the women more than two to one. The fact that other women have held leadership roles and chaired committees made the transition to "Madame Speaker" somewhat less dramatic than it might have been in another state.

Nonetheless, Speaker Sytek acknowledges that being a woman impinges upon many of the actions she takes and affects the way others see her. Being the first woman in a new role brings with it heightened visibility and scrutiny. When she sought the speakership, Sytek found herself subtly changing her wardrobe from conservatively tailored business suits to create a style that would be perceived by her male colleagues as a bit softer but still authoritative.[4] One of her first acts as presiding officer was to change the heavy draping behind the speaker's podium from red to blue—a less startling backdrop for one who favors clothes in pink, fuchsia, and purple rather than the traditional leadership uniform of gray pinstripes and navy blue. On the inauguration of New Hampshire's first female governor, Jeanne Shaheen, in the House chambers, Speaker Sytek selected a brown suit so as not to attract attention to herself on Governor Shaheen's historic day.[5]

Being a woman leader involves much more than wardrobe, however. The first few months of Speaker Sytek's term have been much like any other speaker except that gender mattered in a fundamental way: The novelty of two women in the top leadership roles of New Hampshire state government fed a continuing media story in which Sytek was assumed to be the counterpoint to Governor Shaheen—"the zag to her zig."[6]

In fact, three aspects of Speaker Sytek's experience are shared by a growing cohort of women who have acquired power and position in state legislatures. First, these women are "integrating" the ranks of the legislative hierarchy, a forum in which they have been largely absent. Second, the growing cohort of women leaders is "doing leadership" in an integrative style that subtly redefines what political leadership looks like and can mean. This integrative style emphasizes collaboration and consensus and sees politics as something more than satisfying particular interests. Third, leadership is performed in contexts and legislative organizations that are not gender neutral.

Gender permeates legislative organizational life. Though based on norms of theoretical equality among legislative members, legislatures are not experienced in the same way by all members. Just as minority party members receive different opportunities and play different institutional roles than do majority party members, those who do not fit the norm encounter legislative life in a different way. Even though the number of women in politics has steadily increased, legislatures have been historically and continue to be composed of and led primarily by men. In institutional leadership roles, women still comprise the "other" or "the second sex."

In a legislature as in any organization, the procedures, traditions, power dynamics, and norms shape behavior. In his theory of political leadership, James MacGregor Burns explains that the interaction between leader and followers involves both behavioral and structural variables, and "'structure' . . . is judged by its potential for constraining or blocking possible alternative courses by the leader."[7]

Missing to date from our understanding of legislative organizations and legislative leadership has been the impact of gender as a structural and behavioral influence.[8] All institutions have a distinctively gendered culture, and so too do legislatures.[9] As organizational scholar Joan Acker writes, "The term 'gendered institutions' means that gender is present in the processes, practices, images and ideologies, and distributions of power in the various sectors of social life."[10]

In this analysis of legislative leadership, I show that gender affects committee leadership and that legislative leadership is situated conduct that is not gender neutral. Three themes emerge from this study. First, women committee chairs come to their roles from different life experiences, and they report motivations and visions of leadership that differ in important ways from their male counterparts. Women's special understanding of committee leadership involves shared values and creative consensus. For many women, though not all, leadership style is shaped by the world of volunteerism, PTAs, community activism, family commitments, and church suppers. It is this style of leadership that I call integrative.[11]

Second, the fact that most formal positions in state legislatures have been and still are held by men has shaped our understanding of leadership behavior. Scholarly study of mostly male legislatures has reinforced a paradigmatic understanding of legislative leadership as transactional and aggregative. Indeed, political scientist James MacGregor Burns describes legislatures and legislative committees as "the classic seat of transactional leadership."[12]

However, a growing body of management studies suggests that women adopt leadership strategies closer to an integrative style: sharing power and empowering others, being noncompetitive and inclusive, seeking consensus and mutuality in relationships, and inviting participation rather than imposing dominance.[13] This study of committee chairs shows that although women employ aggregative strategies as do men, they differ in both modest and significant ways by bringing an integrative and collaborative dimension to leadership in state legislatures. Further, as more women occupy positions of leadership, they influence men to be more integrative through mentoring and role modeling.

Finally, I show that institutional factors matter a great deal: State legislative committee chairs "do leadership" in specific organizational, cultural, political, and gender contexts. In particular, the norms of professionalized legislatures, the percentage of women serving in leadership posts, and factors related to political culture mediate the tendencies of aggregative and integrative leadership. Some legislatures operate with procedures that make the most of integrative styles; others require and value skills of aggregative leaders.

Numbers constitute a critical influence in legislative organizations. When women serve a lonely leadership posting, they are perceived by others and hold self-perceptions that are subject to stereotyping. Women are paradoxically highly visible and yet sometimes never seen for whom they really are. As the proportion of women increases, they are freer to define their own political behavior but still must operate within gendered norms and boundaries. When women have been visible in substantial numbers over an extended period, they have greater ability to redefine the framework, assumptions, and definitions central to political leadership. But cautionary evidence suggests that increasing women's power does not always elicit cooperation and compliance from men.

## Legislative Leadership and Descriptive Representation

American legislative systems are based on representation, the linkage that "makes the people present in the actions of the governing power of the state."[14] Most discussions of the concept of representation focus on *what* is made present: We want our interests considered, our causes championed, our claims heard. This form of representation is what political theorist Hanna Fenichel Pitkin calls substantive representation (i.e., the acting for constituents' interests).[15] Pitkin's work also identifies another form of representation: descriptive (i.e., standing for constituents because of significant shared characteristics). The two are linked (and essentially codified in reapportionment case law[16]) by the assumption that when our representatives look like us they are better able to understand and transmit our interests into the political arena.

But representation is not just the *what* but also the *how* of governance; it is an "instrument of power"[17] and "an institutional technique by which power is structured."[18] Leaders act on behalf of others to fulfill special functions within an institution or society. In that sense, legislative leadership can be conceived as a special representational form based on trust and a relationship in which one party is empowered by another.

Just as a change in representatives affects *what* interests are present, one might expect that demographic diversity will also lead to procedural differences in *how* problems are handled and leadership exercised. At the time of the American Revolution, John Adams hinted at both the what and how of representation when he wrote to John Penn that a representative legislature "should be an exact portrait, in miniature, of the people at large, *as it should think, feel, reason and act like them* (emphasis added).[19] Similarly, political theorist Mary Hawkesworth argues that if sexual parity in membership composition were constitutionally mandated in a legislative assembly, the impact would not be simply substantive but procedural—"a means by which to incorporate concern with justice into the policymaking process."[20]

This study examines *how* leadership is practiced by female and male political representatives. Although I compare the motivations, self-perceptions, and practices of men and women who chair state legislative committees, the major focus is on the women and how their leadership styles are shaped by and understood within a specific place and time. Considerable attention previously has been focused on gender and policy representation, and scholars have established that women in politics pursue different priorities and issues.[21] Remarkably little is known about how elected women conceive of political leadership, what their leadership motivations are, how they behave in leadership roles, how organizational factors shape their experiences, and what impact their leadership has on the institutions in which they serve.

## Why Study Gender and Legislative Leadership?

There is a simple answer to the question, "Why study gender and legislative leadership?" As a practical matter, the study of legislative leadership until now has been the study of men. Congressional studies, which dominate the legislative literature, remain mostly about men. Might it be that male behavior has been conflated as institutional behavior? Other parts of the empirical canon of behavioral political science have been shown to be flawed because of the invisibility or lack of serious attention to women's experiences.[22] Thus, it is entirely possible the paradigmatic behavior understood to be typical or the norm among legislative leaders also derives from incomplete or gender-specific data. Because women increasingly occupy positions of legislative leadership at the state level, it now becomes possible to explore gender questions more authoritatively.

The history of women in legislative service has been one of slow steady progress, but the overwhelming reality of legislative life is that politics and power have been the province of men. In 1894 in Colorado, the first women to win election to state legislatures were Carrie C. Holly, Clara Cressingham, and Frances S. Klock. Their victories capped a twenty-five-year state struggle for equal voting rights and full participation in party nominating processes. Two years later, Utah elected the first woman state senator in the country, Dr. Martha Hughes Cannon, and two female House members. In 1898, Idaho followed suit with the election of three women state legislators. But not until 1936, when Louisiana elected a woman to the state legislature, had all of the then forty-eight states elected women lawmakers.[23] In 1917, Jeannette Rankin of Montana became the first woman to serve in the U.S. House, and in 1922, Rebecca Latimer Felton (D-Ga.) became the first woman to serve in the U.S. Senate. Felton was appointed and served for one day. Hattie Wyatt Caraway (D-Ark.) was the first women ever elected to the U.S. Senate after first being appointed to fill the vacancy caused by the death of her husband.[24]

Since 1969, the number of women winning state legislative seats has increased fivefold. After the 1992 election (the so-called Year of the Woman), the Center for the American Woman and Politics reported that women had reached record levels of representation in the U.S. House and the U.S. Senate and a new high of 20.5 percent of the 7,424 state legislative seats. The 1994 election saw no erosion of those gains, though the partisan composition was altered by the Republican electoral tide.[25] After the 1996 elections, 1,588 of the 7,424 state legislators were women, or 21.4 percent nationally.[26]

In terms of positions of institutional leadership, state legislatures are the venue in which women have made the greatest progress. Only former U.S. Senator Nancy L. Kassebaum ever chaired a major standing committee in the U.S. Congress, though Senator Caraway served as chair of the Committee on Enrolled Bills in the Seventy-third to Seventy-eighth congresses. A few women have chaired subcommittees in the U.S. House of Representatives, but none has chaired a standing committee. No woman ever held one of the top party leadership posts in the national legislature.

By contrast, in 1933, Minnie Craig of North Dakota became the first woman speaker in the nation.[27] That milestone, however, is a bit misleading: Fifty years later, when Representative Patricia "Tish" Kelly became North Dakota's second female speaker, only five other women held top party positions or served as presiding officers in the fifty states.[28] In 1997, among the top state legislative leadership positions, seven of the ninety-nine presiding officers were women and seventeen of ninety-eight majority and minority leaders were female.[29] Further, women in 1997 chaired 16.4 percent of all standing or joint committees among state legislatures.[30] The Center for the American Woman and Politics reported that between 1985 and 1993, women committee chairs increased in number from just under 10 percent to 16.4 percent of standing committee chairs.[31] Figure 1.1 shows the increasing percentages of women serving in legislatures and holding committee leadership posts and top legislative leadership positions between 1983 and 1997.

In politics, the ability to explore gender-related behavioral styles has been hampered by a paucity of women. Among the 370 studies in Eagly and Johnson's meta-analysis of gender and leadership, for example, only 19 were in governmental settings and all of those dealt with administrators rather than elected officials.[32] To date, research on women occupying positions of political leadership generally (not just legislative leadership) has been limited, and much of it is based on biographical or personal anecdotal insights.[33] Moreover, the most important leadership studies of women in politics involve relatively small samples from which it is difficult to generalize. For example, psychologists Dorothy W. Cantor and Toni Bernay explore the psychological development of twenty-five successful women leaders in politics and argue that women possess a distinctive style and approach to the use of power. Their sample includes women from a variety of offices including Congress, governorships, and large-city mayoralties. Their conceptualization of women's unique contribution to leadership emphasizes (1) a strong sense of self-worth, (2) an aggressive style of

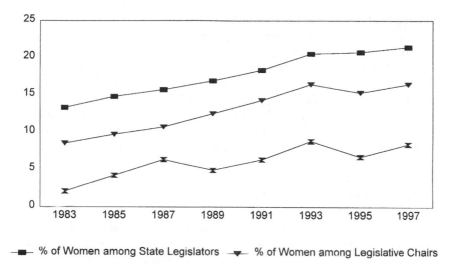

Figure 1.1. Women in legislatures (1983–1997).

taking initiative and speaking out, and (3) a caring kind of power that advances an agenda rather than personal reputation or career [34]

In another recent study, political scientists Malcolm Jewell and Marcia Whicker develop a typology of legislative leadership style constructed along two major dimensions: style (command, coordinating, and consensus) and goals (power, policy, and process).[35] They identify certain combinations as more "feminine" or "masculine" and found that their sample of fifty-four male and twenty-six female state legislative leaders met the expected gender differences. Specifically, women were more often classified with a consensus or coordinating type of leadership and men more often with a command or coordinating style.[36] The authors noted the unexpectedly high frequency of male leaders in the coordinating leadership type and concluded that today's legislators chafe under domineering leadership styles and expect the more "feminine styles" of consensus and participation. While contributing an important conceptual framework, Jewell and Whicker acknowledge the empirical limitations imposed on their findings by the relatively small numbers, the nonrandom nature of the sample, and the quite dissimilar leadership positions (from presiding officer to minority and majority party leaders to various assistant leaders or whips) that they compared.[37]

Although the aforementioned exploratory research hints at the same gender styles found in management studies, the limitations are evident. It is hazardous to extrapolate about the complexities of legislative leadership behavior from a nonrandom sample of different positions. Moreover, these studies are unable to attend to the defining institutional and contextual characteristics that are evident in shaping careers, experiences, and leadership styles.

In sum, gender is a relevant and critical variable to introduce into the study of legislative leadership, especially as most research uses male legislative leadership behavior to assert institutional norms of a transactional style. Until recently, a lack of women in legislative leadership positions made such investigations difficult to pursue. The increasing number of women committee chairs, however, makes it possible to conduct an organizational analysis that begins to deal with legislative leadership styles, contextual variables, and gender.

## Where to Study Gender and Political Leadership

For several reasons, women serving as committee chairs in state legislatures make a particularly interesting leadership cohort to study. First, there is a paucity of cross-jurisdictional political leadership research,[38] and the states provide an opportunity to explore gender similarities and differences within different institutional and cultural environments.

Second, state legislatures provide an opportunity to examine how the number of women and their share of institutional power affect institutional norms. Jewell and Whicker predict that the feminization of state legislative leadership is "likely to continue in the foreseeable future."[39] If, as political scientist Sue Thomas argues, the lack of parity in leadership positions has been an obstacle to women's impact, then procedural transformation should be more likely when women hold a substantial number of committee leadership positions.[40]

Among the ninety-nine state legislative chambers, the number and tenure of women legislators vary greatly, thus providing a natural setting in which to understand how a critical mass of female officeholders affects the legislative institution. For example, the percentage of women serving in state legislatures in 1997 ranges from a high of 39 percent in Washington to only 4 percent in Alabama. Theorists posit that numbers and proportions are a critical element of organizational life, and the sex composition of different legislatures is highly relevant to a gendered analysis. Table 1.1 shows state by state in 1997 the percentage of women legislators, committee chairs, and top leaders (majority and minority leaders or presiding officers).

Third, committees are an appropriate legislative structure in which to explore leadership behavior. Congressional scholar Leroy Rieselbach argues that "as discrete units of analysis, committees lend themselves to efforts to investigate power and leadership."[41] In effect, committee work is a middle-management level of legislative leadership. "Committee power lies at the heart of the whole transactional system of reciprocity, brokerage and exchange," which characterizes legislative leadership more broadly.[42]

Fourth, the committee setting offers the advantages of numbers of women and comparability of leadership duties. Both increase the possibility of greater generalizability of findings. There are simply more women committee chairs

Table 1.1. Women's Representation in Specific States (1997)

| State | % Female Members | % Female Chairs[a] | % Female Leaders[b] |
|---|---|---|---|
| AL | 4.3 | 0 | 0 |
| AK | 13.3 | 22.6 | 16.7 |
| AZ | 37.8 | 34.4 | 33.3 |
| AR | 17.0 | 10.0 | 0 |
| CA | 22.5 | 32.1 | 0 |
| CO | 35.0 | 50.0 | 33.3 |
| CT | 28.9 | 25.5 | 33.3 |
| DE | 25.8 | 24.2 | 16.7 |
| FL | 23.1 | 8.2 | 16.7 |
| GA | 16.5 | 6.9 | 0 |
| HI | 17.1 | 15.8 | 0 |
| ID | 23.8 | 20.8 | 16.7 |
| IL | 26.0 | 22.0 | 0 |
| IN | 18.7 | 10.0 | 0 |
| IA | 20.7 | 11.1 | 16.7 |
| KS | 29.7 | 29.0 | 0 |
| KY | 9.4 | 10.0 | 0 |
| LA | 11.1 | 5.3 | 0 |
| ME | 25.8 | 40.5 | 66.7 |
| MD | 29.8 | 18.8 | 0 |
| MA | 23.0 | 22.4 | 0 |
| MI | 23.0 | 23.3 | 0 |
| MN | 30.3 | 25.0 | 0 |
| MS | 11.5 | 3.0 | 0 |
| MO | 21.8 | 18.8 | 16.7 |
| MT | 23.3 | 6.3 | 16.7 |
| NB | 26.5 | 5.9 | 0 |
| NV | 33.3 | 28.6 | 16.7 |
| NH | 30.9 | 13.5 | 16.7 |
| NJ | 15.8 | 5.6 | 0 |
| NM | 26.8 | 15.4 | 0 |
| NY | 18.5 | 11.6 | 0 |
| NC | 17.1 | 17.2 | 0 |
| ND | 16.3 | 18.2 | 0 |
| OH | 22.0 | 19.4 | 16.7 |
| OK | 10.1 | 10.4 | 0 |
| OR | 25.6 | 21.9 | 0 |
| PA | 12.3 | 2.3 | 0 |
| RI | 26.0 | 23.1 | 0 |
| SC | 12.9 | 8.0 | 0 |
| SD | 17.1 | 12.5 | 0 |
| TN | 13.6 | 4.2 | 0 |
| TX | 18.2 | 9.3 | 0 |
| UT | 15.4 | 10.3 | 16.7 |
| VT | 32.2 | 38.5 | 0 |
| VA | 15.0 | 9.4 | 0 |
| WA | 39.5 | 31.2 | 16.7 |
| WV | 14.9 | 20.0 | 0 |
| WI | 23.5 | 15.1 | 0 |
| WY | 17.8 | 13.6 | 16.7 |

*Source:* Center for American Woman and Politics (1997), National Conference of State Legislatures (1997), and State Legislatures.

[a]Calculations are based on rosters from the states. At the time of calculation, some states reported a number of vacancies, particularly on joint statutory committees. The numbers do not include vacancies, and individuals who chair more than one committee are counted only once.

[b]Only the following leadership positions were considered: Speaker of the House, Senate President or Pro Tem, Majority and Minority Leaders.

than in any other higher political position. Furthermore, while the powers of state legislative leaders vary greatly by position and between states, committee chairs across the nation share many of the same duties and powers.[43] Committees study, screen, amend, defeat, and recommend bills. A chair generally controls the agenda, determines which bills will be heard and when, manages the allocation of time, and can direct the flow of discussion by granting recognition to speak. The chair is the focal point in dealing with members on the committee, bill sponsors, other committee chairs, the leadership, interest groups, and agency personnel. Certain qualities—flexibility, reliability, openness, firmness, tolerance, patience, and competence—are commonly cited by committee chairs as helpful in managing the committee.[44]

Finally, the fifty state legislatures serve as an important recruiting and training ground for candidates to higher elected offices. For example, almost half the members of Congress elected since 1978 once served in state legislatures.[45] As one of the most common formative political experiences of congressional members, state legislative service may predict future changes that could result as more women contend for congressional seats.

## Legislatures and Gender

Legislatures and legislative leadership are not gender neutral but rather reflect societal distributions of power, resources, and interests based on distinctions between male and female. To be sure, institutions do not have a biologically defined sex, hormones, or physical attributes associated with sex. What, then, is meant by the term "gendered institution" and how does that apply to legislatures?

Political scientist Sally Kenney offers three defining ways to think about the concept of gendered political institutions.[46] First, all people within the institution possess a gender. When a Kansas chair emphatically asserted, "I'm a legislator who happens to be a woman," she voiced her frustration with the fact that her sex and the role she holds are not always seen or treated as separate identities.[47] A male legislator may escape the identifying gender adjective because his sex and role status are not considered inconsistent and in fact have long been considered the norm. But both men and women bring gender to their roles.

A member's sex is not the only salient characteristic, but the scholarly preoccupation with counting the number of men and women who serve as legislators or chairs acknowledges the implicit connection that people make between gender and organizational life. In gendered institutions, it matters that the 289 respondents in this study serve on committees with a distinctive pattern of sex segregated work. The average woman chairs a committee that is 66 percent male, whereas the average man chairs a committee that is 81 percent male. The statistical probability of this difference occurring by chance is less than 1 in 1,000. Moreover, none of the respondents reported chairing an all-female committee, though thirty-one chairs reported chairing all-male committees. Only twenty-four chairs reported heading committees with a majority female membership, and most of these committees are engaged in "women's work," dealing with "softer" issues such as health, human services, children and families, education, consumer affairs, and the like.

Second, Kenney defines gendered institutions by noting that participants within the institution will have experiences that vary by gender. Typically, "not only will women most likely have fewer opportunities than men, but their perceptions of the obstacles and the existence of circumscribed opportunities will vary. . . ."[48] An example illustrates the point. The institution of major league professional baseball is gendered. Women can and do play baseball, but their roles within the major leagues are limited and often dependent—fans, wives, back-office staff, groupies, and, occasionally, as journalists and owners.[49] Men hold some of the same roles but also are the most visible actors—umpires, players, and coaches. When the first "female" reporters attempted to do their jobs and conduct locker-room interviews, gender was the defining concern; no similar consternation was expressed when "male" reporters conducted live broadcast interviews.

Until recently, women were not among the most visible actors on legislative committees. Thus, women committee chairs recount myriad examples of experiences that few if any of their male colleagues encounter. As the stories related in this study show, some women chairs have felt isolated from the social life of the legislature, embarrassed by "inappropriate" dress on the part of another female, chided into situations that involve flirting or have sexual overtones, blamed for the mistakes of other women, or felt an obligation to mentor other women. At other times, they simply feel invisible, as a Nebraska state senator did when she was introduced as one of "our legislators and their wives."[50] Invisibility leads to a widely held experience among female committee chairs: not being given credit for women-led policy initiatives. In the focus groups, women from Mississippi, Wisconsin, Colorado, Kansas, and California all shared tales in which a woman legislator's efforts went unrecognized or were attributed to a male colleague.

Personal role relationships are complicated by gender. As a North Carolina woman commented:

> "Many of my colleagues haven't known how to treat me, whether to treat me like their wife, their daughter or their secretary or their peer. By now [after 19 years in the legislature], they finally have figured it out."[51]

Women even experience the schedule of legislative life differently. Historically legislative sessions were organized around the assumption that legislators are men. The imperatives of their economic lives (e.g., cycles of planting, growing, and harvesting when the country was primarily an agricultural economy) drove the conduct of affairs of state into the fallow winter months. By contrast, women's work in the home and with the family is continuous with little seasonal variance. Even in contemporary times, as women participate in larger numbers in the paid labor force, the weight of household obligations continues to discourage women from legislative service. Women legislators are significantly more likely to serve in districts that are closer to the state capital, commuting daily to balance public and private duties.[52]

Finally, Kenney notes that gendered institutions produce and continually renegotiate gender meanings through language (e.g., formal interactions and everyday conversation) and images (e.g., appropriate dress, titles, symbols, and office decor). Gendered organizations code and recode competencies, for example, treating women as honorary males (e.g., "just one of the boys")[53] or coaching women to adopt a manly presence (e.g., the advice about dress and pitch of voice routinely offered and taken by female political candidates).[54] Even the simple fact of naming the role of committee chair reflects a coding of gender. In twenty-seven states, legislatures use gender-neutral language in their legislative rules (e.g., "The person who chairs . . .") and report that in everyday parlance, a chair may be addressed as chairwoman, chairperson, or chairman. In the remaining twenty-three states, "chairman" is routinely used for both men and women to signify the leader of a committee in published literature or legislative rules.[55]

As this brief introduction begins to suggest, legislatures are gendered. The full import of gender meanings does not begin to reveal itself, however, until one looks closely at legislative practices as illustrated by the women's stories and three case studies contained in this text. To say "gendered" does not mean that women and men cannot be fully effective legislators or leaders or that they are barred from full participation by overt discrimination or bias. Rather, a masculinist institution is simply embedded with vestiges of societal gender roles that implicitly (and sometimes explicitly) assume that men, not women, hold institutional roles and power. Women encounter such institutions differently than do those who possess the "normal" characteristics of membership.

## Matters of Method

To understand the individual behavior and attributes of leaders and to appreciate the organizational context in which they serve, a triangulated research strategy was used.[56] The research consisted of three complementary elements: (1) a 1994 mailed survey of male and female committee chairs from fifty state legislatures, (2) focused peer-group interviews with male and female committee chairs, and (3) interviews, fieldwork, and direct observation of committee chairs in three state legislatures.

The focus groups and field studies offer an opportunity to gain insight into leadership behaviors that cannot be readily captured through a survey instrument and to explore cross-jurisdictional leadership contexts and implications. The focus groups and state investigations also provide observed behavioral measures that mitigate against distortions due to social desirability in survey self-descriptions. The triangulated research strategy was intended to balance problems of external validity associated with survey data only.[57]

The questionnaire covers (1) demographic characteristics, and prepolitical and legislative career history; (2) self-assessment of leadership style; (3) committee operations, including sources of support, use of information, and approach to decision making in one's role as a chair; and (4) attitudes about conflict, power, ambition, and peer relationships.

The mail survey was sent to all women (353) and a random sample of 516 men who chaired standing, special, or statutory committees as of March 1994. Completed surveys were received from 135 women and 156 men. Respondents are generally representative of the population of committee chairs in terms of their committee assignments and different types of legislatures. With respect to race, state, party, and religious affiliation, the committee chair respondents match quite favorably the characteristics of state legislators generally. Details about the survey and sample are contained in the appendix.

The focus groups were conducted in conjunction with two annual conventions of the National Conference of State Legislatures, held July 1994 in New Orleans, Louisiana, and July 1996 in St. Louis, Missouri. In all, thirty-eight committee chairs participated in the focus groups. Convenience sampling was used to select the participants; nonetheless, the participants represented twenty-four different states, both parties (twenty-one Republicans and eighteen Democrats), and a range of legislative tenures (two to thirty years). Single-sex and mixed-sex groups were convened.

The three field states (Colorado, Ohio, and Oklahoma) were selected based on a number of factors. The states approximate political scientist Daniel Elazar's three dominant political cultures[58] and reflect important differences in the proportions of male and female lawmakers, sociopolitical environments, and types of legislative institutions. Table 1 in the appendix presents comparative data on the states. Ohio is the most professionalized legislature of the three and is historically and distinctly more urban and eastern, and women comprise about one-fifth of the legislative membership. Of the three states, Oklahoma is the least urbanized, has the smallest proportion of women legislators, and is the most culturally conservative as reflected by the high percentage of the state's population identified with conservative Protestant denominations. By contrast, Colorado has one of the highest percentages of women lawmakers and women in the labor force generally, a moralistic political culture, and a fast-growing metropolitan/suburban population. Colorado and Oklahoma have part-time, somewhat professionalized legislatures.

The state studies attempt to address a central theoretical puzzle that empirical data is not yet able to unravel. A central finding drawn from the study of gender in organizations is that "numbers affect power in institutions."[59] The feminist standpoint assumes that greater equality of women in politics will lead to a transformation of politics and institutions. The importance of numbers is taken as gospel, but the puzzle is how or in what way change is effected. Theorists argue that the impact of numbers can be seen (1) in individual-level psychological and performance pressures on the minority or token individual,[60] (2) in social relations and patterns of interaction among dominant and minority individuals,[61] and (3) in the distribution or redistribution of power as the dominant group reacts to intrusions by minority individuals.[62] Chapter 5 (in this volume) argues that the number of women legislators and women's power should be considered as separate influences and have differing effects on committee leaders. The case studies provide a further opportunity to tease out these theoretical propositions and new insights.[63]

Each of the three states received at least two field visits of one week each. In each state, interviews were conducted with at least eight committee chairs (four male and four female), staff, journalists, lobbyists, and scholars. The interviews were confidential, and all direct quotes come from open public forums or published reports or are used with the respondent's approval.

In sum, to probe beyond the most visible (and perhaps stereotypical) aspects of leadership behavior, a triangulated research strategy is employed. Like the study of icebergs from the ocean's surface, a single perspective may reveal that which is visible while most of the iceberg's mass is submerged below the water line.[64]

Chapter 2 (in this volume) provides a detailed discussion of the theory and hypotheses that guide this research, but some hypotheses should be noted here. First, based on prior research on state legislators and on cultural differences in socialization and societal roles, men and women committee chairs are expected to differ in background, motivations, and behaviors. Most important background differences are expected to move women toward a more integrative style of leadership.

Second, the central tendencies of leadership style are expected to differ in significant and substantive ways, but such differences are subtle rather than grossly deviant. Institutions reinforce behavior through powerful written and unwritten norms, through the selection and promotion of leaders who adopt those norms, and in daily processes, rules, and procedures. Ruth Mandel, director of the Eagleton Institute of Politics, notes, "Egregiously different women are unlikely to pass muster and pass by the customary gatekeepers. Slightly different women can slip through the gates."[65]

Third, leadership behavior is expected to have important gender content when placed in the context of specific organizations. Like an impressionist's canvas of color and image, human behavior is subject to interpretation, emotional response, and perceptual editing, and part of the response is based on societal notions of gender. Even though they may do similar things, a woman and a man may be interpreted as "doing leadership" and "doing gender" quite differently. Legislatures, like other organizations, are expected to have distinctively gendered cultures, meaning that "constructions of masculinity and femininity are intertwined in the daily culture of an institution rather than existing out in society or fixed within individuals."[66]

One caveat should be noted. This study is not evaluative and does not attempt to suggest that one particular leadership style is more effective, more appropriate, or preferable to another. No normative claim is made, implied, or intended by the discussion of gender and styles of leadership. Indeed, a legislature must be many things: a policymaking body and a representative body. Thus, different styles of leadership are required, and certain situations lend themselves to one approach as compared to another.

## The Road Ahead

Chapter 2 lays the theoretical groundwork for this study, drawing together leadership theory generally (and legislative leadership specifically), aspects of feminist understandings of gender and gendered organizations, and the organizational literature that highlights the importance of structural variables. I posit two types of leadership—aggregative and integrative—and argue that women are more likely to embrace integrative styles.

Chapter 3 looks at the people who chair state legislative committees, their backgrounds, legislative careers, ambitions, and attitudes about work, success, and satisfaction. I argue that socialization and background lead to leadership style; thus, differences between male and female committee chairs are highlighted. Background differences are compared briefly with the extant studies of male and female state legislators generally. The intent is not to generalize from committee chairs to all legislators but rather to suggest the durability of certain sex differences over time.

Chapter 4 focuses on the components of aggregative and integrative leadership styles including the motivations that committee chairs value most, the traits they see as characteristic of their leadership style, the behaviors they use in committee, and their preferences in resolving conflict. I also show that through mentoring, women chairs may influence their male colleagues' leadership orientations.

Chapter 5 focuses on the organizational constraints on leadership style. To the extent possible with these data, I examine the impact of the proportion of men and women in legislatures, of women's institutional power, of legislative professionalization, and of cultural variables—both political and social indicators of culture—on leadership behavior.

Chapters 6, 7, and 8 focus specifically on the experiences of committee leaders in Oklahoma, Ohio, and Colorado, respectively. These three cases illustrate that committee chairs "do gender" and "perform leadership" in settings that involve many relevant organizational influences. On the question of numbers, the social composition of legislatures affects leadership in two ways. First, the Oklahoma case reaffirms the extraordinary performance pressures women experience when they are few in number. Second, the Colorado and Ohio cases suggest that transforming norms of leadership depends not simply on proportions of male and female legislators but on the actual power of women to influence and change the institutional practice of leadership.

Chapter 9 reflects on the implications of the findings and reconsiders the theoretical distinction between integrative and aggregative leadership types. The empirical evidence suggests that women's contributions to legislative leadership necessitate a reconsideration of the transactional paradigm.

# 2

# Gender, Leadership, and Legislatures: Theoretical Roots

> The power of leadership is the power of
> integrating which creates community.
>
> —Mary Parker Follett

Aggregative or distributive theories have dominated the literature on legislative politics beginning with Lasswell's dictum of "who gets what" and its corollary "at whose expense."[1] This perspective assumes that legislators compete with each other to secure the advantages (principally electoral) of scarce policy goods.[2] In their simplest form, legislative decisions are "divide-the-dollar" competitions in which particular interests overshadow the broader common good and decision outcomes are reduced to three options: win, lose, or compromise to protect your interests.

The distributive paradigm applies not only to individual-level behavior but also to the logic of institutions.[3] March and Olsen call this dominant ideology "the logic of consequentiality" or rational calculation of preferences and consequences.[4] The kind of institution that results from this view is "aggregative," based on the processes of interests, power, and exchange.[5]

Modern legislatures are assumed to be aggregative, and the archetypal style of legislative leadership is what Burns describes as transactional—competitive bargaining and win-lose-or-compromise strategies. Indeed, he calls legislatures and legislative committees "the classic seat of transactional leadership."[6] The transactional leader facilitates the exchange of valued goods—"acts of reciprocal betterment"[7]—that are achieved by calculating interests, log rolling, competing, and maneuvering for strategic advantage. Necessary conditions of an aggregative system are conflict and competition.[8]

This picture of aggregative leadership emerges from legislative research based mostly on men, and thus this study of committee chairs poses the question: Has masculine behavior been conflated as institutional norms of conduct? Even Burns briefly entertains the possibility of a cultural gender bias in his leadership formulation:

> The male bias is reflected in the false conception of leadership as mere command or control. As leadership comes properly to be seen as a process of leaders engaging and mobilizing the human needs and aspirations of followers, women will be more readily recognized as leaders and men will change their own leadership styles.[9]

Other disciplines (e.g., management and organizational behavior) look more broadly at the phenomenon of leadership. I posit an alternative conceptualization of integrative leadership, a style that emphasizes mutuality and shared problem solving and collaborative win-win strategies. In this chapter, I argue that the integrative style becomes more visible when we examine gender differences among state legislative committee chairs. The integrative style is not uniquely feminine, but through socialization and traditional conceptions of social, family, and work roles, women are more likely to have learned and practiced integrative skills. In part, the underappreciation of integrative leadership comes from the gendered nature of legislative institutions. There may well be a correlation between legislatures, male behavior, and aggregative leadership, but one cannot assume that *all* legislative behavior is aggregative.

Four questions structure the discussion that follows:

1. *What is integrative leadership?* Drawing on the leadership literature broadly, on feminist critiques of that literature, and from organizational behavior theory, I define the integrative style of leadership
2. *Why don't we associate integrative leadership with legislative leadership?* Here I argue that the power of the distributive paradigm and the deeply embedded masculinity of politics and legislatures have combined to limit our understanding of legislative leadership.
3. *Why should we suspect that women committee chairs will be more integrative in their leadership style?* The primary rationale for hypothesizing a gender difference in integrative leadership comes from our understanding of social roles and socialization, the gender dimensions of the world of work generally, and evidence from other endeavors such as management.
4. *To what extent do context and situation have confounding influences on integrative leadership?* Again, theorists on leadership, gender, and organizations suggest that the practice of legislative leadership will be contextually situated and, therefore, must be understood in that light.

## Defining Integrative Leadership

No lack of scholarly effort is devoted to unraveling the mysteries of leadership. Scholars have focused on the *traits* that distinguish leaders as "great people"[10] or endow them with special attributes such as vision[11]; the *behaviors* of leaders that in turn effect a desired response by followers[12]; the *contingent* factors in a situation or environment that shape the interaction between leaders and followers[13]; the *intangible* qualities of vision, charisma, and theater[14]; the *political* dimensions of power, position, and authority[15]; the *culture* of the organization or institution[16]; the particular *institutional* forms of presidential, legislative, and managerial or executive leadership[17]; and some *synthesis* of perspectives.[18] The literature is often organized from one of four frameworks: (1) as individual-level traits or behavior, (2) as a property of interpersonal relationships, (3) as a situational phenomenon, or (4) as a complex of individual, structural, and organizational considerations that involve power and influence.[19] As this brief review suggests, the literature extends in diverse directions and clearly transcends institutional-level roles only, such as those found in the study of legislatures.

No shortage of definitions of leadership exist,[20] but despite all the theorizing and research some scholarly consensus has been reached. Leadership is *relational*. As management expert Peter Drucker notes, the only real requirement is that "a *leader* is someone who has *followers*."[21] Leadership also involves *activity*—doing as opposed to the accoutrements of office—"rank, privileges, titles or money."[22] In turn, the specific strategies of "doing leadership" are not fixed but instead are *contextually dependent* on the goals, available resources and power of a situation or organization. Finally, leadership has no small amount of *ideological* content about what constitutes an ideal leader, what goals and impulses motivate followers, and what ethics or values are conveyed.

One of the key criticisms of existing leadership theory by feminists is its unstated masculinist bias. Scholar Camilla Stivers argues in *Gender Images in Public Administration* that leadership exists not in empirical reality but as an important cultural and ideological myth that functions "to support and rationalize the continuation of existing political-economic, racial, and gender arrangements" and "to impart significance to organizational and political experience."[23] According to Stivers, the prevailing image of leadership "privileges masculine qualities over feminine ones and supports a distribution of labor in which people who are not white professional males are at a disadvantage."[24]

Similarly, Duerst-Lahti and Kelly note the ideological consequences of unspecified masculinism in leadership:

> Masculinism . . . has defined leadership and governance. As a result, women and feminism have been and remain particularly disadvantaged in these crucial domains of public life. One of the obvious disadvantages is that women have been forced to understand—even master—masculinism and its values if they are to move successfully into positions of public leadership. The converse for men is not true.[25]

This unspecified masculinism helps explain empirical results that suggest women adopt behaviors or styles that are "more male than the men,"[26] that organizations "clone" masculinity,[27] and that women try to avoid female stereotypes and embrace "antistereotypes."[28] Only by studying women in leadership roles can a more discriminative understanding of leadership be achieved.

What then is integrative leadership? The conceptualization is neither new nor solely my own but, rather, can be deduced from many other sources. Consider, for the purposes of definition, the constructs noted earlier. Integrative leadership, then, is a relational activity that is contextually dependent and infused with ideological content.

The relationships of integrative leadership are nonhierarchical, stressing mutuality and community. For example, the Chinese philosopher Lao-Tzu's Master is the penultimate leader, who leads the world not by conquering it but rather by becoming it.[29] Lao-Tzu's ideal of leadership is not competition, reciprocity, or pursuit of self-interest but, rather, mutuality and harmony.[30] Similarly, integrative leaders nurture community as management pioneer Mary Parker Follett envisioned[31] and are in relationship to others as "servants," a perspective articulated by former business executive, educator, and writer Robert K. Greenleaf.[32]

The "doing" of integrative leadership stands in stark contrast to bargaining, competition, and quid pro quo agreements. In contrast with domination (i.e., "victory for one side") or compromise (i.e., "each side gives up a little"), Follett favors "integration" as a preferred way of settling differences, "a way in which neither side has had to sacrifice anything."[33] March and Olsen argue that "integrative" institutions employ deliberation to discover what is best for the community based on shared social values.[34] The role of leaders in integrative institutions is that of "educator, stimulating and accepting changing world views, redefining meanings, and exciting commitments."[35] Distinguishing between integrative and aggregative, March and Olsen write:

> Integrative processes treat conflict of interest as the basis for deliberation and authoritative decision rather than bargaining. They are directed by a logic of unity, rather than a logic of exchange. They presume a process from which emerges mutual understanding, a collective will, trust, and sympathy. They seek synthesis and conversions rather than antithesis and concessions.[36]

Integrative leadership resembles what Burns calls "transformational" leadership but is perhaps more common in the humble "affairs of parents, teachers and peers."[37] In this sense, integrative leadership is about listening and engaging "with others . . . to raise one another to higher levels of motivation and morality."[38] Integrative leadership also stresses empowerment of others, a feminist conceptualization of power as support and cooperation rather than dominance. "'Power to' as characterized by energy, ability to get things done, and reciprocity takes the place of 'power over.'"[39]

In terms of its ideological content, integrative leadership contradicts existing structures or norms of leadership. The orthodox view of leadership qualities depicts a man who leads from a position of authority and hierarchy, who has vision, who can take charge and move others forward, who is the source of motivation for followers, and who tells others the meaning of their work. The antithesis of these qualities is the integrative leader who leads through interpersonal networks, who focuses on the ordinary, who empowers others, who relies on community as a source of motivation, and who participates with others in the discovery of meaning.[40] Table 2.1 summarizes the differences in structure, logic and behaviors associated with integrative and aggregative leadership.

## Distributive Leadership: The Power of a Paradigm

Why don't we associate integrative leadership with legislative leadership? Why does aggregative or distributive leadership have such a strong hold on students of legislatures?[41] The answers lie in the reinforcing dynamic of the distributive paradigm and the study of politics as the study of men.

A paradigm is a shared body of accepted theory that draws adherents away from competing modes of scientific inquiry and remains sufficiently open-ended to pose all sorts of questions to be investigated.[42] A paradigm helps to organize and explain our observations about the world. Paradigms, however, produce blind spots and cause us to reject data that just do not fit into the picture. Only when the evidence becomes too strong or weighty are contradictions recognized. The distributive paradigm presumes that leadership behavior is necessarily and typically aggregative. The distributive perspective is not hegemonic in political science, but challenges have not dented this dominant perspective.

The second part of why we do not associate the integrative perspective with legislative leadership is because politics has been largely a male experience. Instead of being gender neutral, leadership is inherently masculinist.[43] As political theorist Christine DiStefano notes, the concepts of power, reason,

Table 2.1. Integrative and Aggregative Leadership

|  | Integrative | Aggregative |
|---|---|---|
| Structure: | | |
| | Interpersonal networks | Hierarchy |
| | Cooperating parties | Competing interests |
| | Other-directed | Leader-centered |
| Leader Behaviors: | | |
| | Educate, listen, empower others | Direct, bargain with, exercise power over |
| | Facilitate discovery of shared goals | Broker exchange of valued goods |
| | Transformational | Transactional |
| Logic: | | |
| | Appropriateness of means and processes | Consequences of ends and outcomes |
| | Common purpose | Economic markets |

justice, history, interest, autonomy, and leadership have been produced by a political world of men and are imbued with masculine meanings and values.[44] The subfield of leadership in particular has been oriented around great men: princes, warriors, philosopher kings, founding fathers, heroes, and patriarchs. For example, leadership researcher Paula Johnson's reanalysis of early trait studies concluded that the only common factor among leaders was their sex.[45] Thus, conclude Duerst-Lahti and Kelly: "Using the gender lens, it is highly noticeable that we have been studying men and masculinity for some time in the arena of governance, even though we rarely acknowledge it as such."[46]

It is possible to illustrate how the distributive paradigm and the absence of gender as a relevant variable can have a limiting and reinforcing effect on legislative research. Let us begin with a theory that is less constrained by the distributive perspective. For example, organizational behavior theorist Kenneth Thomas posited that conflict-handling behavior represents more than the pursuit of self-interest. He argues that conflict produces outcomes with two dimensions: distributive and integrative.[47] The integrative component may be thought of as the total amount of satisfaction achieved by both parties in a dispute. The distributive component is the proportion of satisfaction going to each party. If the distributive dimension represents the way the pie gets divided up, then the integrative component represents the sum of the pie. Figure 2.1 represents the two outcome dimensions within Thomas's model.

Thomas uses his model to identify different conflict-handling behavior in which self-interest drives only the distributive dimension.[48] Conflict-resolution styles reflect two key attributes: (1) an individual's assertiveness in pursuing his or her own goals and priorities (e.g., self-interest) and (2) a person's willingness to cooperate in satisfying the other party's goals and concerns (e.g., other-directedness). Assertiveness and cooperativeness yield five behavioral predispositions toward conflict and give rise to different tactics of conflict resolution in any given situation. Figure 2.2 represents an adaptation of Thomas's model, noting the five dominant orientations in capital letters and the tactical manifestations of each in parentheses.

Using Thomas's model as a contrast, consider Christine DeGregorio's analysis of leadership styles and types of congressional committees.[49] She theorizes "a single continuum" of leadership approaches based on how chairs pursue "their own policy preferences."[50] She develops a typology of styles based on personal assertiveness over the committee agenda and witness testimony: *promoters*, who are aggressive in asserting personal control over issues and agenda; *accommodators*, who evidence very little personal egotism in their control over committee work; and *pragmatists*, who pick and choose among the issues over which they assert control. She then analyzes the chairs' style by three committee types, again assuming that self-interest will drive combinations of committee type and leadership style.[51] For example, chairs of power subcommittees are expected to be accommodators who grant and withhold favors "to establish indebtedness" that will enhance their status and visibility.[52] Her data come from interviews of a random selection of forty-three sub-

Figure 2.1. Integrative and aggregative dimensions in conflict situations. *Source:* Adapted from Kenneth Thomas, "Conflict and Conflict Management," in *The Handbook of Industrial and Organizational Psychology*, Marvin Dunnette, ed., Chicago, IL: Rand McNally, 1975.

committee staff directors and twelve subcommittee chairs of the Ninety-ninth Congress. None of her subcommittee chairs is a woman, not a surprising outcome because only 5 of 142 subcommittees in the Ninety-ninth Congress were chaired by women.[53] DeGregorio classifies the subcommittee chairs according to their personal assertiveness and finds evidence to support her typology but not to confirm the theoretical predictions by committee type.[54] DeGregorio's typology aligns closely with Thomas's styles of competing, accommodating, and compromising and reflects the transactional calculations envisioned in legislative politics—win, lose, or compromise when it serves self-interest. DeGregorio's important exploratory contribution to understanding committee leadership might have produced a different conclusion if she had had the possibility of including more women subcommittee chairs or had used Thomas's theoretical model rather than the more limited distributive paradigm.

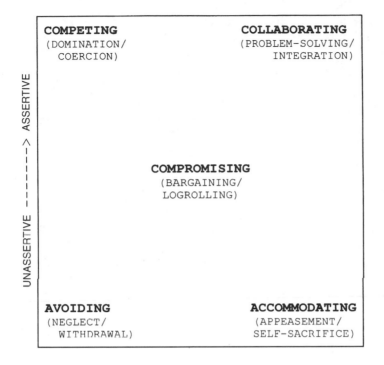

**COMPETING**
(DOMINATION/
    COERCION)

**COLLABORATING**
(PROBLEM-SOLVING/
    INTEGRATION)

**COMPROMISING**
(BARGAINING/
LOGROLLING)

**AVOIDING**
(NEGLECT/
    WITHDRAWAL)

**ACCOMMODATING**
(APPEASEMENT/
    SELF-SACRIFICE)

ASSERTIVE

UNASSERTIVE

UNCOOPERATIVE ------> COOPERATIVE

Figure 2.2. Conflict-resolution behaviors and tactics *Note.* Adapted from Thomas (1975), the model describes a person's conflict-management behavior along two basic dimensions: (1) assertiveness of one's own concerns and priorities and (2) cooperativeness in satisfying the concerns and priorities of others. The tactics associated with each behavioral style are indicated in parentheses. *Source:* Adapted from Kenneth Thomas, "Conflict and Conflict Management," in *The Handbook of Industrial and Organizational Psychology,* Marvin Dunnette, ed., Chicago, IL: Rand McNally, 1975.

By using gender and an interdisciplinary perspective of human communication behavior, research by political scientist Lyn Kathlene illustrates how distributive behavior may be gender behavior in legislative committees.[55] Analyzing speaking patterns in Colorado legislative committees, Kathlene found that women in committee speak less often than the male members, interrupt witnesses or other members less frequently, and exert a facilitative rather than a controlling influence over the flow of conversation in committees. Though she does not use Thomas's terminology, the patterns of more frequent interruptions and longer speaking time by men reflect more assertive, competitive male behavior whereas the facilitative nature of women's speech parallels a collaborative or integrative behavior.

Legislatures clearly deal with decisions that benefit from both aggregative and integrative approaches. Decisions that trade off one party's interests for another are usually zero sum; involve scarce resources; and are ideal for the accommodating, compromising, and competing styles.[56] Integrative problems (e.g., criminal justice sentencing guidelines, child health and welfare policies, or reproductive issues) are not typically zero sum and require more than simply calculating "gains from trades." When procedural fairness, communitarian values, or a desire simply to be heard motivates people, integrative strategies such as collaboration become important considerations.[57] In sum, breaking out of the distributive paradigm and treating gender as a crucial variable of analysis provide a fuller picture of what constitutes legislative behavior.

## Women and Integrative Leadership

Why should we suspect that integrative leadership might be more closely associated with female behavior? The simple answer is that women are more likely to be disposed to the application and practice of integrative leadership by cultural norms and socialization. The hypothesis that women will be more integrative also emerges from the gendered nature of work roles. In addition, other research from the fields of management and education suggests the association between integrative styles and women leaders.

Femininity and masculinity are not biological imperatives but are, to a great extent, socially constructed understandings of learned behavior that are reinforced by cultural norms. Boys learn to become men and acquire an understanding of what constitutes maleness, just as girls learn to become women and practice femaleness. Socialization theory posits that gender-role differentiation begins within the family.[58] Sociologist Talcott Parsons argues that women's biological role in childbearing carries over into childrearing responsibilities, with the result that women are likely to be relationship oriented and skilled in the socioemotional work of caregiving. Men, according to Parsons, are instrumental and task oriented as they manage the family's connection to larger social spheres. Parsons thought that these distinct male and female roles were passed through generations by socialization.

The cultural perspective of behavioral differences relies extensively on socialization processes but does not emphasize exclusively the role of family. Male and female norms are reinforced through sex-segregated peer groups of children and adults.[59] Society teaches gender roles through traditions of play, work, and spiritual development that are often carried out by same-sex groupings or dyads. For example, Western cultures reinforce some forms of gender roles and difference, whereas other cultures may instill another.[60]

These socially learned and culturally reinforced norms presage a correlation between the integrative style of leadership and female behavior. Because of patterns of parenting of children, feminist psychologist Nancy Chodorow argues that the feminine personality defines itself in relationship and connection to other people to a greater degree than the masculine personality does.[61] In her seminal study *In a Different Voice*, Carol Gilligan finds evidence to support a claim that women have a distinctive moral voice that embraces an ethic of care and responsibility for others rather than an ethic of rights based on principle detached from personal relationships.[62] According to sociolinguists who study same-sex play, this other-directedness on the part of young girls fosters cooperation and collaboration rather than rough-and-tumble competition and teaches facilitative rather than directive speech patterns.[63]

Sex-segregated work tends to reinforce and perpetuate gender styles learned through family and childhood experiences. Jobs and occupations are presumed to be gender neutral, but organizational theorist Joan Acker posits that society in fact divides labor, structures labor markets, and organizes the family and the state on the basis of gender roles.[64] Even though labor force participation, educational attainment, and employment opportunities for women have increased in the aggregate, the organized world of work is highly gendered.[65] Recent statistical data show that specific workplaces and jobs remain highly sex segregated, men routinely supervise women but the reverse is far less common, and earnings inequality persists (full-time working women in 1993 on average earned 28 percent less than their male counterparts).[66]

The gendered nature of work is relevant to the "doing" of leadership in two ways. First, women by and large specialize in what organizational psychologist Arlie Hochschild calls "emotional labor"—the management of feeling to produce a proper state of mind in others.[67] The modern service economy, rather than being based on physical labor, is based increasingly on emotion management (e.g., services in large part are purchased and evaluated based on the feelings they elicit), and women are overrepresented in jobs calling for emotional labor while men are underrepresented.[68] When they perform emotional work, men and women tend to specialize—men in the hard-edged, aggressive, even threatening tasks such as bill collecting and insurance adjusting and women in the soft, empathetic, "being nice" work of flight attending, secretarial support, and library assistance.[69] Because integrative leadership is attentive to the feelings of others and values collaboration and mutual satisfaction, women are more likely to have experience in this kind of emotional labor and thus to call on these skills when performing as leaders.

The gendered world of work is related to integrative leadership in a second way. Most work has some gender content, and so too does leadership. Some occupational roles are so deeply embedded with gender that they require qualifying adjectives when the role occupant does not fit the standard model—examples include "female doctor," "male nurse," "female firefighter," and "male secretary." Gender is also part of the performance of work. For instance, sociologist Elaine Hall documents how different restaurants engender the work of table service: A *formal*, dignified style characteristic of high-prestige and higher-paying restaurants is gendered as masculine and performed by male waiters or women garbed in pants, shirt, and tie. By contrast, a *familial*, casual style found in lower-paying coffee shops and family restaurants is gendered as feminine and performed almost exclusively by women.[70] Individuals also "do" gender to negotiate conflicts between their gender role and the display or performance required to fit the structural conditions of different social settings. For example, male nurses distance themselves from a female-gendered work role by developing a "masculine" style of nursing that emphasizes the physical tasks of lifting and moving patients.[71]

The classic images of aggregative leadership—brokering and deal making, conflict and competition—are male. But the picture of modern leadership and management is clearly changing with the advent of downsizing, total quality management, and participatory management, and integrative leadership evokes more feminine images. The point is not that men or women are better suited for one style or the other but that one's sex and the implied gender content of a style may interact or cause conflicts. Sociologists West and Zimmerman argue that "doing gender" involves gender as performed and gender as subsequently interpreted.[72] Performance and interpretation potentially may conflict, and such conflicts often require an individual to invest considerable effort in negotiating gender behavior.

Finally, extant research in the fields of business and education suggests gender differences in management and leadership behavior that resemble the integrative-aggregative distinction. Management researchers have found that men conceive of management as rules, roles, and controls, whereas women managers focus on relationships and "connectedness without hierarchy."[73] Others have found that women employ power for the purpose of nurturing rather than controlling and are committed to openness and sensitivity to all points of view.[74] Business researcher Judy Rosener finds that women in business are more likely than men to encourage participation, empower others, and celebrate the worth of others.[75] Women view power as a means to promote change, whereas men view power as a means of having influence over other people.[76] Similarly, women managers are more likely to use and share power while men base power on position or ability to reward or punish.[77] Human behavior expert David McClelland concludes that the expression of an individual's psychological need for power is shaped by sex roles. Women, he argues, view power as highly interdependent, interpersonal, indirect, and contextual, whereas men are more likely to see power in personal, direct, analytical, and aggressive terms.[78]

In sum, socialization and social roles, the gendered nature of work, and research from other disciplines all give rise to the hypothesis that women committee chairs will be more integrative in their leadership style.

## The Context of "Doing" Legislative Leadership

Why should we be concerned about the gender context in which legislative leadership is performed? Attention to organizational and institutional setting is not new. Contingency theorists such as Fred Fiedler argue that leaders must adapt their behavior to situational factors to be effective.[79] Neoinstitutionalists say that institutions are not merely passive "arenas for contending social forces" but also collections of procedures and structures that "define and defend values, norms, interests, identities, and beliefs."[80] These concepts are not foreign to students of bureaucratic behavior but seldom appear in legislative studies. "Those who study legislatures or the policy process seldom treat committees or the institution as organizations," write Duerst-Lahti and Kelly, "nonetheless, legislative settings and their policymaking activities operate every bit as much in an organized context as bureaucracies. So knowledge about gender power and leadership derived from other organizations applies to legislatures as well."[81]

Gender and leadership are not fixed solely in an individual or individuals but, rather, are the product of social understandings rooted in a specific organizational context. Organizations operate within the larger culture and also contain many situational factors that affect behavior.[82] For these reasons, political culture and the extent of legislative professionalization are considered key constraints in the analysis of contextual influences on leadership style (see chapter 5, in this volume). However, two organizational realities warrant particular note here: (1) the extent of power held by socially differentiated groups, and (2) the social composition of groups.

The important variable that emerges from organizational analyses, argue Duerst-Lahti and Kelly, is gender power, particularly who has it, who does not, and how organizations embody and recreate maldistributions of societal power.[83] Who would not agree that mothers exercise powerful influences in family life, yet women in other organizational settings are not always so empowered. Recall that as illustrated in figure 1.1, women in legislatures do not hold either committee chairs or top leadership positions in proportion to their share of the overall membership. Thus, "[w]hile both women and men have access to gender power . . . that access is highly differential."[84]

In her seminal work, *Men and Women of the Corporation*, Rosabeth Moss Kanter documents the importance of power in corporate life.[85] Kanter devotes several chapters to distinctive and common female corporate experiences as secretaries and wives of executives and argues that women managers in large corporations generally face a lack of opportunity and a lack of power. Kanter also notes that people often do not want to work for women bosses because they are seen as less powerful organizational players.[86] Cynthia Fuchs Epstein detects this lack of power among women in law. While documenting the considerable progress made by women attorneys, she writes:

> It is one thing to be employed, and even paid well, and another to be a true working partner in the camaraderie of the legal community. The structure of the profession and the cultural views about the nature of men and women often prevent women from becoming fully integrated into the legal profession.[87]

The importance of gender power has been documented in the absence of women's influence on reproductive policies in Congress[88]; in the demographic makeup of state bureaucracies[89]; in the roles of doctors, nurses, and First Lady

Hillary Clinton in the debate over health care reform[90]; and in the political spectacle surrounding the Senate Judiciary Committee hearings involving Anita Hill and Clarence Thomas.[91] The practice of committee leadership similarly must be considered within the larger picture of gender power in legislatures and undoubtedly will be influenced by the presence or absence of gender power.

The sex composition of an organization is also a central influence. In addition to focusing on power and opportunity, Kanter's work documented the importance of numerical proportions that tend to isolate and stereotype the performance of "token" individuals.[92] Kanter's work spawned so many analyses of group composition that in 1983, *Sociological Abstracts* made "tokenism" a separate subject category.

Tokenism and its attendant performance pressures apply to women and other minorities who find themselves in numerically skewed groups. Kanter's detailed case study of a Fortune 500 multinational company, dubbed Indsco, drew attention to three particular experiences.[93] The women she studied experience high levels of stress because they were highly visible, isolated from informal and professional networks, and judged by others in gender stereotypical ways. Clearly, most women committee chairs serve in institutions of numerically skewed proportions and lead committees that are predominantly male. Thus, certain aspects of their leadership styles may be judged stereotypically.

A substantial body of empirical research confirms Kanter's original findings, especially in settings in which token numbers of women are engaged in male-dominated occupations.[94] But whereas Kanter views numerical minority status (not sex per se) as the defining variable, other scholars place greater emphasis on societal and organizational sexism. Research has shown that men who are a numerical minority within a group find that the visibility accorded their token status is advantageous rather than stressful.[95] Organizational behavior expert Janice Yoder argues that gender status, norms of gender-inappropriate occupations, and a reaction to intruders are distinct and important confounding factors in the token experience.[96] The theory of intrusiveness refers to the reaction of the dominant group to lower-status tokens whose presence threatens the majority's pay and social standing.[97] Intrusiveness, for example, provides a powerful explanation of why some craft unions resisted racial integration in the 1970s. Scholar Judith Long Laws aptly describes the interplay between tokenism and intrusiveness:

> The Token is a member of an underrepresented group, who is operating on the turf of the dominant group, under license from it. The institution of tokenism has advantages both for the dominant group and for the individual who is chosen to serve as Token. These advantages obtain, however, only when the defining constraints are respected: the flow of outsiders into the dominant group must be restricted numerically, and they must not change the system they enter.[98]

Intrusiveness provides an explanation, which tokenism alone cannot, for stepped-up sexual harassment, blocked mobility, and wage inequities that are organizational forms of discrimination, according to Yoder. The proposition of intrusiveness builds on sociologist Peter M. Blau's theorems and corollaries explaining the nature of intergroup contact, association, discrimination, and inequality.[99] Blau deduces that in circumstances with few minorities, the token individuals have the most contact with and thus the best conditions for support from the dominant group. Blau argues that increasing the size of a minority group only decreases individual opportunities for social interaction and increases the likelihood of majority discrimination against a minority.

The numerical proportion of women committee chairs is clearly a fundamental part of understanding leadership experiences and styles. But Yoder, Blau, and Duerst-Lahti and Kelly add critical theoretical nuances that can be summarized in a simple point: Numbers alone do not explain how institutions and organizations respond to new leaders and different styles of leadership. If, as surmised, integrative styles of leadership are more strongly associated with women, then resistance to the integrative mode or to the intrusion by women leaders themselves might well be expected. These theoretical propositions are most clearly illuminated in the case studies.

## Conclusion

Several hypotheses guide this research. Because of differences in socialization and background experiences, women committee chairs are expected to differ from their male colleagues in terms of motivation, background, and leadership style. Women committee chairs are expected, as a consequence of different life paths, to be more integrative in their leadership style.

Because legislatures have been historically gendered in masculine terms, women's experiences as committee chairs are likely to differ from those of their male colleagues. Masculinity is also evident through institutional factors that affect leadership style; thus, committee styles are expected to reflect not only how chairs "do leadership" but also how they "do gender." Institutional factors mitigate gender differences and reinforce organizational norms of leadership behavior.

The numerical proportions of men and women in legislatures are expected to have an impact on committee leadership behavior. As occupants of roles that have been traditionally defined by and dominated by men, women committee chairs are likely to experience the performance pressures, isolation, and gender stereotyping associated with tokenism. At the same time, I expect intrusiveness to be evident, particularly when women are few in number and their gender power is limited. Only when both significant numbers and gender power exist will women's leadership styles show their potential to transform leadership within legislatures.

# 3

## *The Origins of Different Committee Styles*

Jane Maroney and Liane Sorenson were once seatmates in the Delaware House of Representatives, and they now chair important legislative committees. But their legislative careers are hardly carbon copies. For one thing, Jane Maroney was first elected in 1978 and Liane Sorenson won her first election in 1992. Much like bookends, the careers of Jane Maroney and Liane Sorenson mark how much *and* how little things have changed over three decades for women in legislatures. They do share the characteristics of older age when first elected, family background, and community commitments that define the legislative careers of women committee chairs generally and are associated with integrative leadership styles. These characteristics also represent the differences that distinguish the careers of women and men committee chairs and create social distance among presumed equals.

Jane Maroney had an early career in corporate public relations and a stint with the Central Intelligence Agency, but she spent her middle years organizing her life around her children and husband. Married to a pediatrician who built a practice in the days of house calls, Maroney ruled out a two-career household while her children were at home. Instead she served as a hospital volunteer, charity organizer and fund raiser, and museum docent. After her two children left for college, Representative Maroney felt unfulfilled by bridge, gardening, and charity work. At the age of fifty-six, she turned to politics and ran successfully for the legislature.

If political ambition had been her goal, age and no small amount of male chauvinism stood as obstacles. Representative Maroney requested but did not get appointments to the House's most powerful committees; instead, she found herself on the House Human Needs Committee, where few men wanted to serve and seniority was not an issue. Almost by default, she later became chair of the committee because none of her male colleagues were interested. As health, social services, and family issues rose in prominence on the policy agenda, however, she found herself a powerful player on some of the most contentious and financially important issues of state government.

At forty-seven, Liane Sorenson was almost ten years younger than Jane Maroney when she first ran for the legislature. A working mother and college administrator in a women's studies program at the University of Delaware, she too did not consider a political career until her children were older—out of elementary school. In her first term, Representative Sorenson was named chair of the House Education Committee because of her professional background and the relatively lesser status of the committee. Like Maroney, Sorenson found her male colleagues less concerned about "soft issues" such as education.

Sorenson chafed under some of the chauvinistic traditions of the House. Her certificate of election read "Liane Sorenson (Mrs.)," whereas her male colleagues had no such marital label. When she questioned why the directory of offices listed House members by "Mr." and "Mrs.," she was told, "We have to know who are the women." When she persisted and suggested the use of "Representative," she was asked, "Aren't you happily married?" After one House term, she set her sights on a state Senate seat, which she won in November 1994. Further ambitions are not out of the question.

As illustrated by Maroney and Sorenson, the experiences and political paths of women lawmakers have become somewhat more varied in recent years. Women today enter politics at a slightly younger age and are more likely to be juggling, rather than sequencing, the demands of family and career. At least some women still encounter resistance as intruders into traditionally male institutions. Their background characteristics not only shape their institutional experiences but also presage their leadership style.

This chapter, therefore, turns to the question of differences between male and female chairs. Do men and women chairs differ in important ways? What experiences do chairs bring to their leadership roles?

I begin with a brief review of prior studies of women legislators because there is no comparable study of state legislative chairs with which to compare these data. These other studies provide a picture of change and continuity in legislative life and legislators' careers. The chapter then compares careers and backgrounds of male and female committee chairs and highlights differences that might lead to a more integrative style.

## Women as Legislators

Scholars have offered various reasons to explain the underrepresentation of women as political officeholders. Among the most important is the notion that women traditionally were not viewed as "political" because they were less positively oriented toward politics than men or less advantageously placed to pursue electoral opportunities.[1] Thus, in 1974, Jeane Kirkpatrick felt it necessary to declare as her most important finding about women state legislators that "political woman exists." Kirkpatrick's political women were not overtly masculine or "grossly deviant" from other women.[2] Later studies, however, compared male and female lawmakers and found them to be cut from a different cloth. Among the differences, background, life factors, political ambition, and ambivalence about aspects of legislative life loomed large.[3] Some but not all differences have disappeared over the years.[4]

Background differences have always been relevant factors in a political career. A candidate's viability for political office often depends on his or her educational qualifications. Networks and connections, whether professional or volunteer, launch political ambitions. Social background also influences the likelihood of political life because of the types of people a candidate meets as a youth, the choice of college and career, the circle of associates and advisers, and access to resources. Family background, education, and social status also are critical to leadership styles because they influence leadership philosophy, provide leadership training, and shape valuable social skills.

## Politics and Family

Women legislators serving in the 1990s are different from women who served in the 1970s, but although women's backgrounds have changed, male legislators in the 1990s share the characteristics of their predecessors.[5]

A key difference is age when first elected. In the 1970s, compared with their male peers, female legislators were older when first elected to office and were more likely to have postponed their political careers until their children were in school.[6] Men were three times more likely to have been elected before the age of forty than were women.[7] In the 1980s, age differences persisted.[8] That gap appears to be closing though it has not disappeared. Women serving in 1992 were somewhat younger than their sisters from 1972 whereas the average age of men has not changed.[9]

Historically, the vast majority of state legislators have been married, but women legislators of the 1970s and 1980s were less likely to be married than the men.[10] Comparing cohorts from 1972, 1982, and 1992, Dolan and Ford found a significant increase in the percentage of married women (68 percent to 81 percent) serving as legislators, but again the significant differences in marital status between men and women have not disappeared.[11]

## Education and Jobs

Since the 1960s, growing numbers of women have pursued higher education, entered the paid work force, and joined the ranks of nontraditional occupations from firefighter to physician.[12] Women legislators reflect these same trends.

Early studies of women legislators revealed that women lagged behind their male colleagues in terms of educational attainment, especially beyond a college undergraduate degree.[13] More women lawmakers today than in 1972 have a post–college education (now on a par with their male colleagues), but the number of women lawmakers with a law school education remains less than that of the men.[14]

Paralleling a societal trend, women legislators are today more likely to be in the paid work force and in nontraditional roles. In the 1980s, Thomas found that a large proportion (41 percent) of female legislators still came from fairly traditional backgrounds (e.g., homemakers, clerical workers, or teachers), and female state legislators did not equal men in the business or professional categories.[15] Between 1972 and 1992, however, the percentage of women who identified themselves as homemakers dropped from 25 percent to 8 percent, whereas the percentage of women citing business or professional occupations rose from 21 percent to 35 percent, a level now on a par with men.[16]

## Social Status, Family Background, and Networks

Mary Guy and Lois Lovelace Duke argue that women develop alternative organizational and social networks to compensate for their exclusion from the "Old Boys' Club."[17] During the 1970s, one such alternative path to electoral office was through party work and civic leadership, where female state legislators honed their abilities and reputations through long apprenticeships.[18] Dolan and Ford find significant declines in both party and civic memberships when comparing women legislators from 1972, 1982, and 1992. Among male legislators, the trend away from party activities does not hold, but the decline in civic memberships does.[19]

The importance of social class was evident in the early studies of women officeholders. For women, as Guy and Duke point out, middle- and upper-middle-class families are more likely to foster higher expectations for achievement for young girls and are less likely to experience sex-role differentiation in childhood than are working-class families.[20] Thus, highly educated women from affluent backgrounds comprised the primary pool from which female candidates for state legislatures were recruited during the 1970s.[21] In six state surveys comparing male and female public managers in the late 1980s, women consistently reported higher childhood socioeconomic status, more parental education at the college level or beyond, and parents in professional or managerial occupations.[22]

Besides the socialization benefits, there is a pragmatic reason to expect a more affluent socioeconomic background among women in elective politics: "Money enables women to hire babysitters and other people to do the chores around the house that they would otherwise have to do."[23]

## Legislative Career Contours

If women state legislators of the 1970s did not come from the same backgrounds as their male peers, they also experienced legislative service differently. Early studies of the typical female lawmaker describe "an obsession with being well prepared, doing her homework, and being known for speaking only when she has something to say."[24] Even with the emphasis on hard work and conscientiousness, the majority of women legislators did not feel well prepared for legislative life or as influential or successful as their male colleagues.[25] Some women in the 1970s felt channeled into committee assignments based on stereotypical expectations about women's special aptitudes or interests in people problems and "care" issues.[26] By the 1980s, women were no longer confined to certain types of committees and any residual ghettoization of women into health and human services committees occurred as a result of self-selection rather than coercion or discrimination.[27] By the 1990s, Dolan and Ford found more women serving in all committee subject areas with no change in the committee assignments of men.[28]

## Ambition

In the 1970s, female legislators expressed considerable ambivalence toward seeking higher office. Kirkpatrick noted the absence of a "female equivalent . . . of Barber's 'advertisers,' young men on the make, bent on using a stint in the legislature to advance a career."[29] Whether employed outside the home or not, women were significantly less interested in higher office than were their male colleagues. Diamond concluded that in part, the lower levels of ambition resulted from a lack of the skills and advantages that make progressive ambitions realistic.[30]

In the 1980s, the gender gap in political ambition had virtually disappeared.[31] Scholars attributed the shift to "increased acceptance of women in public life and the increased opportunities that flow from acceptance."[32]

## Attitudes about Work, Success, and Satisfaction

In the 1970s and 1980s, women lawmakers often experienced feelings of inadequacy, frustration, and ambivalence in their legislative service. In their 1977 study, political scientists Marianne Githens and Jewel Prestage argued that female politicians experienced acute role conflict and marginality resulting from the multiple roles of mother, wife, and politician:

> Much time, effort and energy goes into seeking some reconciliation of the roles of woman and politician. Political women want to be respected by their male colleagues; yet they also feel the need to serve dinner on time, clean the house and so forth.[33]

In keeping with the paradigms of legislative behavior, scholars of the 1970s and 1980s asked whether women legislators deviated from "normal" aggregative bargaining. In the 1970s, they found female legislators more averse to legislative bargaining than their male peers and less active in bill introductions and committee interactions. If in the 1970s women felt on the margins of legislative life,[34] their 1980s' sisters "joined in the fray and adapted to ongoing norms and procedures."[35] Women in the 1980s showed little ambivalence over legislative bargaining and no difference in legislative and committee activity and success than their male colleagues; they made a "dramatic reversal . . . and began to perceive of themselves as highly effective legislators."[36]

## A Profile of Committee Chairs

In this sample, the prototypical committee chair is white (94.5 percent), Protestant (57.3 percent) or Catholic (19.6 percent), married (79.2 percent), from a middle-class or working-class background (75.1 percent), well educated (80.6 percent with at least an undergraduate college degree), and 53.6 years old. A few more Democrats (57.4 percent) than Republicans comprise the sample of chairs.

Looking beyond the prototypical chair, the data explored here suggest that gender often defines a different experience in the legislature for women than for men and creates the potential for barriers and social distance among presumed equals. Like the research on legislators generally, male and female chairs differ in terms of age, family circumstances, prepolitical leadership experiences, and legislative career characteristics. They do not differ in terms of race, party, or religion.

Female committee chairs are more likely to be older than their male colleagues, to wait until their children are older before entering politics, and to postpone electoral ambitions until after the prime years of domestic or marital responsibilities. In general, women chairs are more likely to come from backgrounds hypothesized as important to integrative leadership. These differences, however, vary somewhat by the kind of legislature in which a lawmaker serves. Table 3.1[37] reports the background characteristics of legislative committee chairs in this study for the whole sample and by three types of legislatures:[38]

- "Professionalized" legislatures, such as California's, meeting virtually year-round with large professional staffs and relatively generous pay and benefits for members.[39]
- "Hybrid" legislatures, such as in Oklahoma and Colorado, with limited legislative sessions, more modest staff resources, and part-time pay and benefits for members.[40]
- "Citizen" legislatures, as in New Hampshire, with short legislative sessions, limited professional staff resources, and minimal pay and benefits for members.[41]

Table 3.1. Background Characteristics of Committee Chairs by Type of Legislature

| | Whole Sample | | Citizen Legislatures | | Hybrid Legislatures | | Professional Legislatures | |
|---|---|---|---|---|---|---|---|---|
| | Women | Men | Women | Men | Women | Men | Women | Men |
| Age When First Elected | 43.7 | 39.8**** | 41.6 | 41.0 | 45.1 | 39.4**** | 44.0 | 39.1*** |
| % with Children under 18 Home | 20.0 | 42.5**** | 23.9 | 47.3** | 19.4 | 43.1*** | 14.8 | 35.0** |
| % Currently Married | 74.6 | 84.9** | 80.0 | 85.5 | 75.8 | 86.2 | 63.0 | 82.1* |
| Level of Education(%) | | **** | | ** | | * | | *** |
| High School Diploma/Some College | 23.1 | 16.6 | 24.4 | 9.1 | 25.8 | 17.2 | 14.8 | 26.3 |
| College Degree | 34.3 | 30.5 | 24.4 | 30.9 | 38.7 | 34.5 | 40.7 | 23.7 |
| Master's Degree | 26.9 | 14.6 | 35.6 | 14.5 | 22.6 | 15.5 | 22.2 | 13.2 |
| Professional Degree | 15.7 | 38.4 | 15.6 | 44.5 | 12.9 | 32.8 | 22.2 | 36.8 |
| Family Social Class (%) | | ** | | | | | | *** |
| Upper/Upper Middle | 26.7 | 16.8 | 22.7 | 18.9 | 29.5 | 24.6 | 26.0 | 2.6 |
| Middle | 48.1 | 42.3 | 47.7 | 50.9 | 49.2 | 36.8 | 46.2 | 38.5 |
| Working/Lower | 25.2 | 40.9 | 29.5 | 30.2 | 21.3 | 38.6 | 26.9 | 59.0 |
| % Employed outside Home Prior to Legislature | 78.5 | 96.1**** | 82.6 | 94.5* | 77.4 | 94.9*** | 74.1 | 100.0*** |
| Most Important Preparation for Role as a Chair (%) | | | | | | | | |
| Professional | 49.0 | 54.5 | 42.9 | 54.8 | 47.9 | 53.5 | 66.7 | 55.6 |
| Government/Political | 33.7 | 18.8** | 22.9 | 14.3 | 37.5 | 25.6 | 46.7 | 14.8** |
| Civic/Volunteer | 53.1 | 14.3**** | 48.6 | 21.4** | 58.3 | 14.0**** | 46.7 | 3.7**** |

*p <.10, **p<.05, ***p<.01, ****p<.001.

Note. Significance levels for education and social class are based on Pearson's chi-square statistic. For all other variables, significance levels are based on t-tests.

## Politics and Family

On average, male committee chairs are four years younger than their female colleagues when first elected to the legislature. Less than one-third of female chairs were elected before their fortieth birthday, whereas more than half of the men came into legislative service by that age. Statistically, this difference would occur by chance less than 1 time in 1,000.

Male chairs are slightly more likely to be married and twice as likely to have children under the age of eighteen at home. By contrast, young children are rare among female chairs. Consider, for example, Ohio: Even though more than 100 women have served in the Ohio General Assembly since 1922, childbirth has not been remotely associated with their lives as legislators. In 1985, Jane Campbell, who served as a chair and later as House assistant minority leader, became the first woman ever to be pregnant while serving in the legislature. Since that time, only one other woman has given birth while serving in the legislature.

These data underscore two points. First, rearing young children is a significant deterrent for mothers from pursuing political careers, more so than for fathers. Most women choose to raise their children first, then enter politics. In addition, the press of household duties constitute a "second shift" that has been documented as a barrier to women's professional pursuits in other arenas as well.[42] For those women who do not delay their political careers, the competing demands of home and legislative service can be especially daunting. One Nevada woman chair, in returning her uncompleted 1994 survey, wrote:

> "I'm a single mother working a full-time job, with myriad legislative and community responsibilities, and now running for my fifth term. I race around seven days a week and have *no* discretionary time. I wish you well but this is not a priority for me."[43]

Such experiences are not unique. Representative Peggy Kerns, former minority leader of the Colorado House, points out that only recently has her caucus been joined by younger women who are balancing legislative service, careers, and young families.[44] Representative Campbell notes that younger women are seeking office, "But it's still relative. Lots of the guys run at twenty-two when they are first out of college. The youngest woman in Ohio ever to run was twenty-nine."[45]

The second key point is that motherhood is an excellent training ground for integrative leadership skills. As one management writer notes:

> "Motherhood is being recognized as an excellent school for managers, demanding many of the same skills: organization, pacing, the balancing of conflicting claims, teaching, guiding, leading, monitoring, handling disturbances, imparting information. . . . "If you can figure out which one gets the gumdrop, the four-year-old or the six-year-old, you can negotiate any contract in the world."[46]

## Education and Jobs

State legislative committee chairs are a well-educated group, but the women differ significantly from their male colleagues in terms of higher education beyond the undergraduate level. Although 53 percent of the male committee chairs hold college degrees beyond a baccalaureate, only 43 percent of the women do. By a margin of more than two to one, male committee chairs are more likely to have acquired an advanced professional degree in law, medicine, or business.

In terms of occupations, better than half of the chairs (54 percent of women and 57 percent of men) claim a professional or managerial background. But women in professional and managerial occupations are more likely to list experiences in small business, government, or the nonprofit sector rather than in large corporations. The percentage of chairs who are educators is similar (17 percent of women; 16 percent of men), but most of the men indicated administrative positions or jobs in higher education as opposed to the classroom positions cited by the women. Two and a half times as many men as women chairs listed their occupation as attorney. The women committee chairs are eight times more likely to report clerical occupations, and men are five times more likely to report occupations in agriculture, ranching, skilled trades, labor, or transport. Women chairs are six times more likely to report no employment outside the home. The picture that one draws from the occupational data is one of sex-segregated work experiences and quite different leadership preparation.

Two points should be underscored about educational and professional differences. First, the committee chairs who participated in the focus groups considered occupational background important in establishing their credibility. Nonetheless, female chairs report that often they are assumed to be homemakers and as a consequence not taken seriously by their colleagues, members of the press, or lobbyists. A Kansas state senator noted that she worked full time and came from a professional background, but still she encountered male colleagues who assumed that she was a "housewife."[47] Consider, too, the frustrations expressed by a veteran Wisconsin legislator who was not working outside the home prior to her election:

> "It's hard to describe. There's a lack of deference. The press doesn't give you as much attention. I've said things in debate, and a man moments later said something similar and he got quoted. I've expressed ideas in committees that others get credited with."[48]

A Mississippi chair related that she had little problem with her all-male committee but had encountered problems in being recognized by the insurance industry for her substantive knowledge even though she had professional experience in banking and insurance. These comments illustrate how societal gender meanings get translated into legislative experience and how few women escape untouched.

Second, the educational and professional backgrounds of women chairs are much more likely to be in areas that Hochschild calls emotional labor, which is fundamental to integrative skills. Hochschild stresses that especially in the middle class, women specialize in "emotion work that affirms, enhances, and celebrates the well-being and status of others."[49] Fewer women than men come to committee leadership with the kind of adversarial training common to the study and practice of law or the emphasis on competition found in the corporate business world. Instead, more women chairs come to the legislature from the classroom, the social service sector, small business, and community work. In New Hampshire Speaker Donna Sytek's experience, those chairs who are retired military or executives of large corporations have a difficult time developing the skills needed to build consensus; those chairs, more often the women, who have been active as scout leaders, United Way volunteers, community activists, and local government officials have integrative experience.[50] One Colorado committee chair captured the essence of integrative values when she joked that serving in a state legislature was a lot like her church experiences: "You're working with people you can't get rid of."[51]

## Social Status, Family Background, and Social Networks

Among committee chairs, important sex differences in family social strata are found. Three-quarters of the female chairs compared with a little more than half the men come from middle- or upper-middle-class backgrounds. Significantly more of the women have fathers who were college educated or employed in professional or managerial occupations.

Community and volunteer associations remain an important avenue into politics. An Ohio woman noted:

> "The League of Women Voters has been absolutely critical to everything I've ever done . . . the issues I've followed and the network of supporters who have helped me along the way."[52]

More important, community and volunteer work are valued as formative leadership training much more by women committee chairs than by men. Committee chairs were asked in an open-ended survey question to identify the "experience, either professional, volunteer or otherwise, [that] has most prepared you for being a committee chair." The responses were coded into six categories reflecting a range of experiences including volunteer and community involvement, prior government or political experience, professional background, legislative service, and personal factors.[53]

More than half the women cited the importance of volunteer and community work compared with only one out of seven men. Both men and women committee chairs identified some kind of professional experience more frequently than any other type of preparatory leadership experience. Male committee chairs, however, were much more likely to cite only professional experience, whereas women typically cited professional background in combination with other experiences. As one Minnesota woman wrote on her survey:

> "Being a parent, active in the League of Women Voters, my volunteer work with teenage parents and my teaching all gave me a background in understanding issues and I learned how to build consensus and make sound use of time."

In personal interviews, four times as many women committee chairs as men mentioned skills learned through church work, fraternal groups, and such organizations as PTAs, the League of Women Voters, or the American Association of University Women. These represent precisely the kind of civic organizations that political scientist Robert Putnam argues create social capital.[54]

For Putnam, civic engagement produces "past success at collaboration, which serves as a cultural template for future collaboration."[55] When Putnam speaks of the benefits of "social capital," he uses the explicit language of integrative leadership and notes that less hierarchical networks, more consensual norms, and social trust "facilitate coordination and cooperation for mutual benefit."[56] Thus, community and volunteer experiences may well be antecedents to the integrative style of leadership.[57] Although Verba, Schlozman, and Brady make the point that "those who enter the higher levels of politics . . . have almost always developed civic skills at work, in non-political organizations, or in church,"[58] the survey of committee chairs suggests that women (much more so than men) consciously connect these experiences with leadership approaches and skills.

## Differences among Legislatures

The literature on legislative professionalization shows that different types of legislatures attract different kinds of members.[59] The committee chair survey, however, suggests that demographic characteristics vary more for men than for women between citizen and more professionalized legislatures. No statistically significant differences exist among women by type of legislature.[60]

The male chairs show differences in social background and educational attainment by category of legislature. In professionalized legislatures, 59 percent report growing up in working-class families compared with only 31 percent of the male chairs in citizen legislatures. Also the percentage of male chairs with less than a bachelor's degree is three times greater in professional legislatures than in citizen legislatures. (See table 3.1.)

Professionalized legislatures are thought to be more open to service by individuals from working- and lower-class backgrounds because of the higher pay. In fact, advocates of legislative modernization couched their support for longer legislative sessions and increased pay in part on the belief that a broader segment of society might be able to serve if higher compensation was provided.[61] This pattern does not hold for women chairs, however, who come from similar family backgrounds across all three types of legislatures.

Indeed, to serve in a full-time professional legislature, a woman chair seems to bring every possible resource of education, social class, and prior professional, community, and political experience to her role. Women chairs on average report middle- and upper-middle-class family backgrounds in all three types of legislatures and greater levels of formal education in professional legislatures.[62] At the same time, they are the least likely to have children under eighteen at home or to be married—both competing pressures for their time and energy. These results confound the logic of professionalization by suggesting that, for a woman, service in a professional legislative body requires more resources (i.e., education, profession, and social class) and fewer disadvantages (i.e., young children and personal commitments) to serve.

These differences by type of legislature suggest the social distance between male and female chairs is likely to vary from state to state. In citizen legislatures, women chairs attain significantly lower levels of formal education compared to their male colleagues. In professionalized legislatures, educational backgrounds are more similar, but women come to the legislature from significantly higher social strata than do most of their male peers. In all but citizen legislatures, women on average are significantly older when first elected.

The background experiences that chairs value as leadership preparation also vary by type of legislature. Civic and volunteer experiences are valued by a majority of women chairs regardless of the kind of legislature in which they serve. A different pattern is apparent among men: Professional legislatures show a distinct decline in the number of male chairs who cite community service as an important preparatory experience. In the most professionalized legislatures, civic and voluntary commitments seem to be remarkably absent from backgrounds of male chairs, or at least are not considered important enough to mention. The strong association between community experience and sex has the probability of occurring by chance less than 1 in 10,000 times.[63]

At the same time, professional experiences and prior government or political service appear to become more important for women chairs serving in professional legislatures. For men, the importance of professional or prior government service does not vary by type of legislature.[64] Certainly these data suggest that women chairs value and identify more diverse leadership development experiences than their male colleagues, particularly in professional legislatures.

Two explanations of these differences are possible. First, women may be reticent to step into leadership roles until they have acquired considerable experience. Alternatively, men may feel less encumbered by any gaps in their experience. An exchange in one focus group hints at both points[65]:

"Before I decided to run for office, I felt like I needed a whole series of credentials, a resume to run on. Some guys just say, 'You know, I think I'll run.'" (West Virginia female)

"I think that we often have the perception that we [women] have to work harder, that we have to lay all these credentials on the table to equal their credentials." (Missouri female)

"Yes, I think women are less likely to step forward and say, 'I want to be chairman of that.' We feel we have to pay our dues. We have to develop the expertise, learn the rules, and work our way up. I mean, a guy isn't encumbered by that. He steps in and says, 'I'll figure it out when I get there.' I think women are much less likely to expect to be named chairman until they've developed their expertise and paid their dues." (New Hampshire female)

"That's not me. I wanted to make sure that I had experience in the community, that I could do this, or that I brought with me some level of competency." (New Hampshire male)

"Yes, but everybody knows you're a 'New Age' kind of guy." (New Hampshire female)

## Legislative Committee Careers

The typical legislative committee chair (male or female) has served almost twelve years in the legislature and four years in his or her present position as chair. The chairs generally profess little ambition for higher office and feel well satisfied and successful.

Again, however, there are some significant differences in the legislative careers of women and men chairs. Women as committee chairs have fewer years of experience. Women are more likely to chair committees dealing with social services, education, and family issues, and they think they have been appointed for slightly different reasons than do their male colleagues. Furthermore, women feel less included by the leadership in the flow of information and perceive that they work and lobby harder to be effective and recognized.

### Experience and Position

Women chairs have fewer total years of experience chairing a committee (5.2 years compared to 7 years for men) and have less overall tenure on the committee that they currently chair (6.1 years compared with 8.3 years for the men). When controlling for the total years of legislative service, the significant sex difference in the number of years as committee chair disappears.[66] Simply put, women have fewer years of experience as committee chairs because they have been in the legislature for a shorter amount of time. Women are appointed chair after fewer years of committee and overall legislative service and are more likely to perceive their sex as a factor in their appointment. Table 3.2 reports the legislative tenure and career characteristics of committee chairs.

Legislative leaders consider many factors when appointing committee chairs, and with rare exceptions, most state legislatures do not utilize a formal seniority system such as that found in the U.S. Congress.[67] In the survey, chairs were asked to rate eleven different factors that might have been "important in

Table 3.2. Career Characteristics of Committee Chairs by Type of Legislature

| | Whole Sample | | Citizen Legislatures | | Hybrid Legislatures | | Professional Legislatures | |
|---|---|---|---|---|---|---|---|---|
| | Women | Men | Women | Men | Women | Men | Women | Men |
| Total Years in Legislature | 10.2 | 13.1**** | 10.5 | 12.5 | 10.0 | 12.0* | 10.2 | 15.6**** |
| Total Years on Current Committee | 6.1 | 8.3**** | 6.5 | 7.5 | 6.0 | 8.5** | 5.4 | 9.0** |
| Total Years as Chair | 5.2 | 7.0**** | 5.5 | 5.9 | 5.2 | 7.4** | 4.6 | 8.1**** |
| Years Before Becoming Chair | 5.1 | 6.1* | 5.0 | 6.6* | 4.8 | 4.7 | 5.8 | 7.6 |
| % Who are Full-time Legislators | 64.9 | 37.3**** | 40.0 | 13.2**** | 67.7 | 26.3**** | 100.0 | 85.0** |
| % Expect to Seek Higher Office | 26.0 | 25.5 | 28.9 | 27.3 | 19.7 | 34.5* | 36.0 | 10.0*** |
| % Would Take Policy Job If Offered | 44.1 | 44.0 | 54.3 | 45.3 | 43.9 | 41.4 | 25.0 | 46.2* |
| Reasons for Appointment as Chair | | | | | | | | |
| % "Extremely Important" | | | | | | | | |
| Willingness to Spend Time | 58.5 | 35.8*** | 60.0 | 34.6** | 58.3 | 35.7** | 56.0 | 37.5* |
| Gender | 31.4 | 10.9**** | 28.8 | 14.3* | 37.6 | 7.3**** | 24.0 | 00.0 |

*b <.10, **p<.05, ***p<.01, ****p<.001

your appointment as chair." Rated on a five-point scale of importance were criteria such as: reputation with various groups and other members, relations with and loyalty to the leadership, ability, willingness to commit time, seniority, sex, race, and geographic factors. Out of all the appointment criteria, committee chairs rated race and sex the least important; ability and relations with leaders were most important.

Only three of the factors were rated significantly different by the men and the women. Three times as many women chairs as men (31.4 percent compared with 10.9 percent) identified sex as "important" to "extremely important," a difference that would occur by chance less than 1 time in 1,000. Almost 60 percent of the women compared with one-third of the men rated "willingness to spend time" as an "extremely important" factor, again a difference that would occur by chance less than 1 time in 1,000. "Ability to get things done" was rated "extremely important" by half the women and a little more than one-third of the men, a difference that would occur by chance less than 1 time in 100.

In focus groups, women legislators also emphasized "commitment of time" and "task accomplishment" as reasons women emerge as committee chairs. In the words of a Texas representative:

> "We're fortunate, because even though he's a 'good ol' boy' from West Texas, the Speaker's very much a feminist. You know when there's work to be done, he gives it to the women. We're not the showhorses; we're the workhorses. Anymore, those smoke-filled backrooms in the Texas capitol are filled with women."[68]

An Idaho chairwoman added this comment:

> "I have chaired the committee for sixteen years and have always had a wonderful working relationship with my co-chairman. I have worked and served with just two men from the Senate side in that whole time. In my opinion, I have had great gentlemen to work with, very cooperative, *and very glad to let me do the work.*"[69] (Emphasis added.)

Making a similar point, an Ohio state senator said: "We are more willing to take on committees that require more work. But I don't really feel we work harder; it is just that we don't shy away from the heavy committees."[70]

Commenting about the relative importance of sex as an appointment factor, one Missouri chairwoman wrote the following on her survey: "This Speaker was asked one time how come he had so many women as chairs. He was really surprised that he did but upon considering it, he said, 'I was just looking for people who would do the work.'"

In the 1993–1994 biennium, women could be found chairing virtually every type of committee, including traditionally male domains of business and agriculture committees. Nonetheless, women were still concentrated among the "care" committees of human services, health, education and children's issues (27.8 percent of all such committees). The female respondents to the 1994 survey reflect both the full range of women's committee interests as well as the continuing concentration of women among human services committees.

The opportunity to chair more traditionally male committees appears to be a direct consequence of numbers. When there are fewer women in a legislature, the draw of human services issues looms over other policy concerns. The comments of a Kansas state senator make the point:

> "When I went into the legislature I thought, 'I don't want to get labeled with traditional women's issues.' But I found out quickly that they were important issues and that if we [women] weren't taking them on, they weren't being addressed. My goal [to avoid women's issues] got quickly shoved aside. But what is curious now . . .is we are at a point where those traditional women's or 'soft' issues are now the issues that are driving policy."[71]

As the number of women lawmakers grows, opportunities arise to pursue other interests. In the focus groups, an Arizona chairwoman stressed the liberating importance and luxury of a greater number of women:

> "We have had such a long tradition of so many women in the Arizona legislature that lobbyists, staff, and fellow legislators are really used to it. We have had women doing the commerce committee and the banking committee. They always talk about women and the 'soft' issues, but women are all over the board in terms of interests and experience."[72]

As this comment suggests, when the proportion of women reaches some "critical mass," the potential exists to change culturally embedded attitudes and to alter distributions of political power.

Finally, the diversification of committee interests among women chairs may reflect an integrative perspective that appreciates the interconnectedness of public policy concerns. As an Ohio state representative commented about her new assignment on the agriculture and economic development subcommittee of appropriations:

> "I have done the human services bit but I was tired of pulling bodies out of the river downstream and I decided I needed to go up river and see who is throwing the bodies in. I thought I'd try to find out why economic development programs do not seem to work for women . . . but it's easier to make the move now because I know [two other women in the caucus] will carry the issues in human services."[73]

## Ambition and Service

Political ambition and full-time legislative commitments are two prominent features of contemporary legislative life. State legislatures vary in terms of their different career and institutional reward structures and thus attract members with either internal or external ambitions.[74] How might sex and type of legislature be related when it comes to a committee chair's ambition?

Overall, the responses for men and women chairs with regard to ambition are quite similar. Only one in four chairs expects to seek higher political office; less than half would forsake politics if offered an influential policy job.[75]

The percentage of male and female chairs who express interest in running for higher office varies markedly by type of legislature.[76] In professional legislatures, women are more likely to indicate ambitions for higher office than are men, but the reverse is true in hybrid legislatures. Another distinction in professional legislatures is that the men were more likely to consider leaving their electoral careers if an influential policy job becomes available. Interpretation of these results is speculative but suggests a need to revisit assumptions about ambition in light of gender and institutional type.

Striking and statistically significant differences are apparent in the number of men and women who identify themselves as full-time legislators. Overall and by every category of legislature, women chairs are significantly more likely to describe themselves as full-time lawmakers. In his case study of the Colorado General Assembly, Alan Ehrenhalt argues that women are more willing to commit full time to their legislative service because fewer of them are full-time breadwinners and therefore a modest legislative salary is not a household sacrifice.[77] Ehrenhalt's argument may have some relevance. For example, three-fourths of women chairs were employed outside the home prior to running for office, and two out of three of them opt to make legislative service a full-time calling. Only one out of three men forsake full-time employment for full-time legislative service. Among part-time legislators, men also are less likely than women to look favorably on an opportunity to pursue a policy job outside the legislature.[78] Stated differently, men whether full-time or part-time legislators are less likely to abandon their careers to pursue legislative policy interests.

By contrast, women chairs articulate a form of ambition that emphasizes policy goals. The comments of a woman state senator from Kansas, where the legislature meets for ninety calendar days each year, bear on this point:

> "Women are not as personally ambitious in the process as men. Our ambition is to move forward in an agenda that we care about and get the job done. As I look at the women in our legislature, that would be pretty much the case. It is not personal political ambition that motivates us."[79]

Similarly, an Arizona committee chair related the personal dilemma posed when she and another woman had the opportunity to run for a leadership position: "We both had agendas we wanted to accomplish as committee chairmen."[80]

## Attitudes about Work, Success, and Satisfaction

The current survey reveals no differences on questions asking chairs to evaluate their overall feelings of success and satisfaction with their committee experience. The mean scores are very high (5.6 to 6.1 on a seven-point scale) and virtually identical for men and women. Moreover, when asked to compare themselves with other committee chairs, women and men do not differ at all in the frequency with which they felt (1) taken seriously, (2) sought out for advice, or (3) more effective. Nonetheless, significant sex differences are found on some aspects of legislative life.

Women are significantly more likely to describe themselves as working harder and lobbying harder than the average chair. However, no significant difference exists in the average number of hours per week that male and female chairs report spending on committee work.[81]

Most of the perception of harder work comes among those chairs who describe themselves as part-time rather than full-time lawmakers and among those in citizen legislatures. Among the women who consider themselves part time, 78.7 percent feel they work harder than other committee chairs whereas only 52.1 percent of the part-time male chairs feel that way. This result has a statistical probability of occurring by chance 1 time in 500. The full-time legislators demonstrate no difference. But even among part-time legislators, committee chairs report the same number of hours spent on committee work.

The fact that male and female chairs report roughly the same number of work hours may mask a qualitative distinction of how work is approached. In comments made in the focus groups, some women emphasized their attention to detail, thoroughness of preparation, and efforts to understand all sides of an issue. An Oklahoma state senator explained this ambiguity with an analogy to private sphere responsibilities:

> "It's just our way of life. We organize. We take care of the details. We feel like we have to work twice as hard. I don't even know if the men know that we feel this way. We all worked just as hard to get here. We're all elected the same way. But I think we [women] do it to ourselves."[82]

Some of the chairwomen in the focus groups, however, were quite critical of the work ethic of some male colleagues. An Arizona House chairwoman commented:

> "The women are more likely to read the bills than the men. The men don't even bother reading the bills. They are the least prepared on my committee generally, unless a lobbyist has gotten to them and given them some amendments to write."[83]

A veteran Missouri woman legislator added:

> "We go to the floor debates better prepared; the women do. We go in with our notebooks full of the details, and we get asked detailed questions. We ask detailed questions. The men go in and maybe they have a few notes, but don't ask them very many questions."[84]

In an all-male focus group, members drew no distinctions between work effort; however, a focus group with both men and women chairs generally agreed that women as a group were harder working.

Some of the survey responses suggest a small residue of feelings of marginality by some women politicians. Specifically, the women are less likely to feel that strategic information is shared with them, that they are included as often as other chairs, or that their advice is sought by leaders (see table 3.3).

Table 3.3. Chairs' Perceptions of Their Role and Performance

|  | Women | Men |
|---|---|---|
| Compared with other chairs, On average I: | % responding YES | |
| work harder[a] | 70.4% | 56.9% |
| am included more[a] | 47.4% | 58.8% |
| lobby harder [c] | 40.0% | 22.2% |
| How frequently are you: | % Responding OFTEN or ALMOST ALWAYS | |
| included in important leadership discussions[a] | 58.5% | 70.1 |
| provided timely strategic information by leadership[a] | 55.5% | 68.2% |
| sought out to advise leaders on issues outside the committee | 43.2% | 51.0% |

[a]$p <.05$, [b]$p<.01$, [c]$p<.001$

These feelings, however, appear to reflect instances in which women are few in number, less experienced, and feel outside the circles of power or unable to crack the "good ol' boys network." When control variables are included, the significant sex difference disappears. Specifically, when controlling for the number of women in the legislature and their positions of power and a committee chair's years of experience, female committee chairs are no less likely to feel included than are their male peers.[85]

The gendered nature of legislatures leaves some female chairs feeling marginalized. In the focus groups, women chairs voiced complaints about sexist attitudes, ideological barriers, and feelings of isolation. A Delaware state representative, for example, shared her frustration over being taken seriously as a policy leader:

> "The House is very chauvinistic. Women chair traditional committees. They rarely ever chair anything, but if they are chairs at all it's committees like education and human needs. That's the way it has always been. I have had to fight to get them to see education as something more than a women's committee. I am constantly reminding them that it [education] is the biggest share of the state's budget. In other states the education committee is a powerful committee, and it is amazing with the dollars that go into it that they don't see it that way."[86]

A North Dakota representative saw her role in the legislative process as an ideological outsider who also wanted to be a team player:

> "I find myself walking a fine line between wanting to be a team player with the leadership and pushing the issues I'm concerned about. My party has not been very enthusiastic about programs for children, domestic violence, welfare reform, and women's issues; their favorite ploy is to put me in a box. But I've learned that you have to pick your battles and go along once in a while to demonstrate that you are a team player. Other times I say, 'I can't do it.' My strategy is for the long term. I'll outlast the bastards. I try to get

credibility and not give them a reason to replace me. It's more important for me to be there in the long run to fight the battles."[87]

An Ohio committee chair identified the simple frustrations of being the only woman among many men. When she served on the county commission, she often found it frustrating that the other commissioners (all men) would continue to discuss county business in the restroom during meeting breaks. She attributed the incidents to benign insensitivity more than overt exclusion, but with eight women in the forty-member Ohio Senate, she added:

> "Now we kid the guys that we're going to take a bathroom break. When we recently organized a luncheon for all of the women, some of the men got worried about what we were up to. I think it was quite unsettling for some of them."[88]

Representative Maxine Berman, author of a book about her experiences in the Michigan Legislature,[89] articulates a more critical view of women's continuing marginality in state legislatures. Representative Berman chronicles a long list of offenses against what she calls the male legislative "comitatus," a modern-day version of the Anglo-Saxon, nobleman–warrior ruling fraternity that excludes women. She concludes:

> "Because our common background is inevitably one of being an outsider and because so many elected men attempt to perpetuate that once we're in office, we remain both insider and outsider forever. Few women ever forget that, no matter how powerful they become."[90]

## Conclusion

Women committee chairs share many characteristics with their male colleagues; nonetheless, important and unique public-private dimensions separate women and men in politics. First, women serving as committee chairs on average defer their public commitments in favor of private responsibilities. Sue Thomas wrote in *How Women Legislate*:

> Trends in marriage rates and number and ages of children illuminate the difficulty women have had in maintaining professional and private careers. Because women were responsible for home and hearth, political careers for them have often been an either-or choice—or, at least, a life cycle-dependent choice.[91]

Nothing in these data suggests a resolution of women's struggle with these choices.

For the most part, female committee chairs are women who already have established their families, negotiated marriage and major career choices, and invested heavily in community life. When they turn to politics, they often make a full-time commitment that focuses on issues of family, community, and well-being.

Women chairs bring to politics unique contributions and special experiences from their family lives and community experiences. The management training of motherhood and the leadership experience of community service are clearly precursors to and consistent with an integrative style. As Jean Bethke Elshtain has written so eloquently in *Public Man, Private Woman*:

> To affirm a vision of the private-familial sphere as having its own dignity and purpose is to insist that particular experiences and spheres of social relations exude their own values and purposes, and have ends not attainable by, or within, other spheres.[92]

The background differences between male and female committee chairs, however, suggest a second important conclusion: Men and women chairs often possess and value different leadership preparation. Men are twice as likely to have acquired an advanced professional degree in law, medicine, or business, and women chairs are three times more likely to be schooled in the more integrative modes of community and volunteer leadership. Coming from occupations in traditionally sex-segregated fields means committee chairs have not honed their interpersonal skills in situations with the same gender relationships or dynamics.

While explicitly describing an aggregative style of leadership, an Iowa senator in an all-male focus group saw women ill-prepared for committee leadership because of these background differences:

> "My personal motto is: Never compromise until you absolutely have to. I don't compromise readily unless I know I have to. From my experience, they [the women chairs] are not very good at that. In Iowa, you tend to get a lot of women legislators who came in later in life. They've raised their kids, and their kids are out of the home now. So they're a little bit older than I was, I came in when I was 33. So my sense is the women can compromise or they can force their way through, but they're not really very good at judging which time to do what. Is this the time to force or is this the time to give in?"[93]

As the previous comment suggests, background differences not only hone different leadership styles but also are a source of social distance. Managing gender relations is difficult enough, but the task is compounded by significant dissimilarity in occupational status, educational attainment, social class, age, legislative career characteristics, or future ambition. These differences play out in interesting ways in various types of legislatures. Consider, for example, the potential barriers that might occur in a professional legislature when negotiations bring together a well-educated, upper-middle-class, Junior League–trained woman chair and a male labor leader from a working-class background. Or, consider the not-unusual-scenario (in Iowa perhaps) of a chairwoman leading a committee of much younger males who have more legislative and paid work experience than she. The role of chair is one of presumptive equality, but societal inequalities are attached to ascriptive characteristics such as sex or race and to achieved status of education, profession, and socioeconomic class.

As legislators bring these differences into the legislative institution, social barriers can arise.

Finally, these data suggest that marginality depends on the gendered aspects of legislatures, particularly the number of women in an institution. Women chairs today feel as successful, as satisfied, and, to a great extent, as involved as men in the legislative process. This sense of inclusion contrasts with the marginality expressed by women in the studies of the 1970s. Nonetheless, residual feelings of marginality persist, particularly when women serve without benefit of other female colleagues or leaders.

# 4

## The Components of Integrative Leadership: Motivation, Behavior, and Style

Vera Katz gives voice and substance to integrative leadership. The current mayor of Portland and former speaker of the Oregon House of Representatives believes she and other women lead by emphasizing collaboration and partnership rather than competition and self-interest.

Katz was not always perceived as a consensus builder. Early in her career, she earned a reputation as the aggressive chair of the Ways and Means Committee who eschewed a "give-and-take style" in favor of a "take-it-or-take-it" approach to issues she cared about.[1] Her detractors saw a legislator with little patience for those who disagreed with her; supporters, however, saw a caring, perceptive person who could "tune into precisely that thing that rings someone else's bell."[2] During her Ways and Means Committee tenure, Katz began a metamorphosis from Kennedy liberal to a more centrist, fiscal pragmatist. While shedding the sharp ideological edges, she also began to hone the skills of integrative leadership.

In 1985, after a seventeen-hour caucus and 101 ballots, she became the first woman in Oregon history to become speaker.[3] During her three terms as speaker, she made consensus building and collaboration the hallmark of her approach.[4] At one point she contrasted her consensus approach with more classically aggregative norms of legislatures:

> Traditionally, legislatures have fostered the spontaneous generation of conflict and competition. Members are taught to look out for themselves. Protocol and titles are considered of central importance. The "victor" in any given struggle is often the one who pushes the hardest and the longest.[5]

After being elected mayor of Portland, Katz continued with that style and developed "an unusually fruitful experiment in local-government inter-

jurisdictional cooperation."[6] In 1994, she was cited, along with her former legislative seatmate and now county administrator Beverly Stein, as "public officials of the year" for their unique efforts to end turf battles and find creative
solutions to city and county problems.[7] Part of that effort involves a strategy
known as community benchmarking, which advocates see as a revolutionary
strategy to reinvent government.

From her perspective, Katz sees women bringing about nothing short of a
fundamental "feminization of leadership," transforming a male model of competitive gamesmanship into a shared, inclusive style. She once told a veteran
political reporter:

> I think women view power differently. We view rules differently and the
> purpose of rules. For males, the purpose of rules is to control. For me, I
> would change the rules just to make it easier to get something done, rather
> than control somebody to make sure they are thwarted.[8]

Katz's assertion of a female style of leadership seems quite consistent with
the integrative form posited in the second chapter, but her early years as a
committee chair also suggest a leadership approach that initially conformed to
the legislative norms of an aggregative style—dominant, hard bargaining, and
competitive. Whether or not Katz is correct in her prediction of feminine leadership, she illustrates the interplay of gender and leadership style in her public
service commitments.

This chapter explores the motivations, behaviors, and traits of state legislative committee chairs to discover whether there are more women whose
style resembles Katz's. I rely on survey data, focus groups and interviews with
state legislative committee chairs to describe differences between and among
women and men. What emerges is a picture of female committee chairs who
are on average more inclusive and people oriented, more collaborative and
policy motivated. Male chairs who are mentored by female leaders are more
integrative than other men. In short, a clear gender dimension seems to underlie
the aggregative-integrative typology.

## Women Chairs: A Difference in Leadership?

Powerful reasons underlie the belief that female political leaders manifest different orientations than men. Sex-role differences stem from socialization,
educational and career experiences, work environments, and family and social roles; thus, men and women chairs are drawn toward different agendas
and concerns.[9] By extension, their leadership style may be expected to differ as
well.

Other scholars have established that women legislators pursue different
policy goals and handle official duties differently from men. The evidence
suggests that women differ in terms of their policy priorities,[10] their vision of
policy as needs based rather than rights oriented,[11] their emphasis on constitu-

ency service,[12] their perceptions of power relationships with colleagues,[13] their more liberal and more feminist voting records,[14] their view of themselves as representatives of women's concerns,[15] their conceptualization of policy problems,[16] and their communication patterns in committees.[17]

Because of differences in background and socialization and an emphasis on community and volunteer experience (see chapter 3, in this volume), women chairs are expected to hold motivations and to adopt strategies that are more integrative than their male colleagues. Simultaneously, as participants in organizations that have norms of bargaining, men and women are expected to be quite similar in many aspects of the transactional leadership style. As a consequence of these countervailing influences, the magnitude of sex differences is expected to be clearly discernible but not necessarily dramatic.

This chapter explores several facets of leadership style, including (1) personal motivation and goals of being a committee chair, (2) traits characteristic of one's style, and (3) interpersonal behaviors such as sharing power, including others in decision making, and resolving conflicts. To balance against overreliance on potentially biased or culturally stereotypical responses in self-report survey data,[18] I also consider one indirect measure of interpersonal behavior and analyze focus group data. Finally, I consider the effects and patterns of mentoring on the leadership styles of committee chairs. If women on average are more integrative, then those whom they mentor might also develop such skills.

## Theoretical Roots

Before turning to the evidence from the study, consider first how integrative and aggregative leaders might differ in terms of motivations, traits, and behaviors. Also, what connection if any might these differences have with gender?

### Leadership Motivations

Integrative committee chairs are likely to stress quite different goals than are classically aggregative committee chairs. Specifically, the integrative style should be associated with (1) a greater emphasis on people and their involvement in the process, (2) on policy as a collective and educational enterprise, (3) on power as a means to other goals rather than as a personal asset in and of itself, and (4) on legislative work as something more than simple aggregation of pluralistic interests.

Scholars have linked these integrative motivations with women more than men. Gilligan argues that women's goals are driven by relationships, personal commitments, and an orientation that focuses on others rather than self.[19] In contrast, men's goals tend to emphasize authority, control, personal achievement, and dominance. For example, Loden notes that men talk about business teamwork in terms of sports rules and competitive analogies, role clarity, and tight controls, whereas women managers focus on relationships—autonomy of individuals, empowering others, and "connectedness without hierarchy."[20] Lunneborg describes women managers' "morality of responsibility," which assumes a commitment to do the following:

> (1) put our responsibilities to people above what is officially "right," (2) use any power we have to be nurturant, (3) change rules to preserve relationships, (4) not let some people's successes mean other people's failures, and (5) be open and sensitive to everyone's point of view.[21]

Research has also shown that power motivates men and women differently.[22] Women are much more likely to share power and to use it to promote change, whereas men use power based on position or ability to reward, punish, or have influence over others.[23] Women's sense of power emphasizes self-enhancement or self-control rather than societal definitions of power as control over others and resources.[24]

Aggregative leaders are motivated by a desire to represent constituent interests in the legislative process. The aggregative impulse is clearly more instrumental (i.e., a means to accomplish a discrete purpose); the integrative motive is often expressive (i.e., having emotional or affective purposes separate from specific outcomes). Using Vera Katz's terms, aggregative politicians compete for personal victory and titles, whereas integrative leaders strive for trust.[25]

On the surface, nothing about the aggregative motive seems inherently "male." Societal expectations about role behavior, however, tend to predict that men display instrumental or agentic behaviors and women display expressive or communal behaviors. In small-group research, men are more likely to emerge as task-oriented leaders and women are more likely to emerge as social leaders.[26] Eagly argues that such differences are not innate but rather determined by social expectations; in other words, men and women are motivated to act according to the roles assigned in a given situation and the gender-role expectations held by others.[27]

## Characteristic Leadership Traits

Integrative and aggregative leaders are likely to manifest different traits. The aggregative style should be associated with dominance, competitiveness, ambition, a drive to control, and opportunism. An integrative style, by contrast, should be reflected in such traits as trust, affection, a team orientation, moderation, and a commitment to process and task. Traits such as interpersonal skill, managerial acumen, procedural discipline, and analytical ability have gendered connotations but do not explicitly fall into either the aggregative or the integrative style.

No one personality trait defines a person's approach to leadership. Research has shown that women and men leaders differ little on specific personality traits; however, they combine those traits in distinctive gendered combinations.[28] Using factor analysis of self-reported behavioral traits, Kelly and

colleagues find strong sex-specific interactions between such traits as dominance, intimidation, affection, risk taking, predictability, and attractiveness.[29]
In describing the traits of effective and ineffective managers, Quinn reports
sex differences: No women were found in a conservative, rigid, controlling
type or in a bureaucratic, command-control, technically oriented style. Women
clustered in two categories: the first is distinguished by over sensitivity to criticism, inability to delegate, tendency to become bogged in detail, and very
formal relations with subordinates; the second includes "master managers,"
who reflect a balanced and comprehensive capacity for management.[30]

## Leadership Behaviors

The integrative style of leadership implies a commitment to sharing power
and empowering others, to being noncompetitive and inclusive, and to seeking moderation and mutuality. The aggregative style of leadership connotes
other behaviors such as classic bargaining, log rolling, competing, and maneuvering for strategic advantage. Integrative leaders are likely to favor collaborative conflict resolution styles, whereas aggregative leaders are more likely
to adopt win-lose-or-compromise strategies (see figure 2.1 and discussion in
chapter 2, in this volume).

Other research demonstrates that women adopt more participatory or con-
sultative styles whereas men tend toward more autocratic styles. In legislatures,
Jewell and Whicker find the most common style for men is not a "command"
style but a "coordinating" one; however, for women, the most common style is
also the most participatory approach, a "consensus" style.[31] Women leaders are
described as encouraging participation, empowering others, and emphasizing
the self-worth of others. The terms applied to these notions vary slightly: democratic versus autocratic[32]; interactive leadership as opposed to command and
control[33]; collaboration, conciliation, and accommodation as means of problem
solving versus competitive and conflictual styles[34]; and seeing one's leadership
role at the center of "a web of inclusion" as opposed to atop a hierarchy.[35] Behavioral theories of leadership distinguish between task behaviors (e.g., planning,
organizing, and structuring) and interpersonal behaviors (e.g., counseling, coaching, and teaching). Eagly and Johnson found that women leaders emphasize
*both* behaviors (rather than one over the other) to a greater extent than do men.[36]

## Differences among Committee Chairs

### Motivations

I used two methods to determine the motivations of committee chairs: open-
ended interviews in the three field states and the survey of chairs. The survey
questionnaire included thirteen items prefaced by the following statement:

Being a committee chair affords tremendous opportunities to affect policy, work with people, or wield power. Some of these opportunities may be more or less important motivations for you.

The thirteen items were designed to assess various motivations, for example, to move up the ladder, to better represent constituency interests, to be a policy spokesperson, and to involve more people in the process. Respondents answered each individual item using a five-point scale from "not at all important" to "extremely important." Factor analysis, a statistical technique, was used to evaluate the interrelatedness of items and then weight them into composite scores. As expected, the thirteen items converge into four global motivations: (1) an orientation to personal status and greater power, (2) a desire to get people involved and bring them together, (3) a focus on policy leadership, and (4) classic legislative goals (i.e., representing constituency interests in policymaking).

Male and female committee chairs report considerably different motivations. On average, women committee chairs rated higher the importance of all the individual motivations except the item "exercise power." The differences in the mean scores of men and women are significant on seven of the thirteen items. By margins of three to two or two to one, women were more likely to select the response "extremely important" on the following items: "make process work," 62.7 percent of women compared to 45.5 percent of men; "get people involved," 29.1 percent compared to 16.9 percent; "get people together," 35.1 percent compared to 17.5 percent; "build issue coalitions," 26.1 percent compared to 12.4 percent; and "develop creative approaches," 48.5 percent compared to 27.9 percent.

The factor scores also reflect significant differences between women and men[37] (see table 4.1). Consistent with Gilligan's arguments and previous research,[38] women committee chairs are more motivated by people and relationships. They score significantly higher than the men on the "people-oriented" factor. In all, 60.4 percent of the women scored above the mean on the people oriented factor compared with only 43.1 percent of the men. As suming normal distributions of scale scores, the average woman scored higher than 64 out of 100 men, the sixty-fifth percentile of men's scores on the people-oriented factor.[39]

A story by a Colorado woman chair illustrates the women's motivational emphasis on involving people in legislative deliberations:

"I sent letters to all the 'ordinary' citizens who had testified in front of my committee to get suggestions, asking them if the procedures of the committee made them feel comfortable, what they would like to see done differently, what they didn't understand when they were in the process. There was an amazing number of people who responded to the letters. And I got all of these comments from the committee chairmen who were men. They couldn't figure out why I had wasted my time. One of the men commented to me: 'I will never waste my time trying to figure out what they don't understand. Who cares?' And to me that was very important to figure out. That is

Table 4.1. Survey Items Associated with Different Motivations

| Policy Oriented | People Oriented | Power and Status | Constituent Interests |
|---|---|---|---|
| Be a spokesperson on the issues | **Pull people together** | Achieve greater status | Serve my constituents better |
| **Develop creative approaches** | **Get people involved** | **Move up the leadership ladder** | **Make good policy** |
| Get my ideas into law | **Build issue coalitions** | Exercise power | Make the process work |
| | | Control the policy agenda | |

*Note.* **Boldface type** indicates the overall motivational factors or individual items on which women on average scored significantly higher than the men (p < .05). Motivations are listed in order of the strength of their correlation with the factor, and all motivations correlated with the factor at .50 or stronger.

why I think I am there—to help citizens feel like their government works for them, not that it works for me."[40]

The policy leadership motivation factor captures elements of advocacy and activism—for example, being "a spokesperson on the issues" and developing "creative approaches." Women committee chairs score significantly higher on the "policy leadership" motivation. Among the women in the sample, 55.2 percent scored above the mean on the "policy leadership" factor compared to only 43.7 percent of the men. Assuming normal distributions of the scale scores, the average woman scored higher than 62 out of 100 men, the sixty-third percentile of men's scores on the "policy leadership" factor.[41]

Activism and advocacy in policy leadership may be a necessity because women find that traditional legislative policy and career paths do not always coincide with their own goals. For example, former Missouri Representative Kaye Steinmetz's policy commitments required her to first convince her presiding officer of the need for a committee dedicated to issues affecting families and children. She overcame that hurdle by quietly mobilizing a network of interest groups to advocate and lobby the speaker for a committee. In 1983, she was appointed the first chair of the House Committee on Children, Youth, and Families, a position she held until her retirement eleven years later. During her tenure, children's issues gained a level of visibility not previously seen in Missouri and she spearheaded legislation to establish a family court system, to improve the regulation of child-care facilities, and to create programs to prevent child abuse.[42]

Women are no more or less motivated by the opportunity to achieve greater status and to move up the leadership ladder. On the factor measuring power and status motivation, women on average differ little from their male colleagues; however, the *only* motivation item on which women scored lower than the men on average is the desire to "exercise power." Thus, the opportunity to enhance one's status seems less power driven for women. This conclusion reflects other research that suggests women seek power not purely for the sake of "power-over" but as a means or "power-to" effect change or influence others. It may also reflect women's unequal access to power resources in legislatures.[43]

The use of power for advancing policy goals, rather than for enhancing one's political reputation, is evident in the comments of an Arizona chairwoman who told of a conversation she had with a younger male colleague:

> "He said to me, 'You ought to just run for Congress because you are never going to be in leadership here.' I have chaired a committee since my second term, and I said to him, 'You know, maybe I am not going to be in leadership, but I don't think that is the goal here. The goal is: Are you successful in getting your agenda completed? All the bills that I sponsor, that I care about, I get passed. That is what I am here to do.'"[44]

Finally, the constituent-interests motivation raises some questions even though on average women and men do not appear to differ significantly. The constituent-interests factor is the only one for which there is a significant interaction effect when controlling for years of experience as a committee chair.[45] An interaction means simply that men and women chairs show distinctly different patterns of association between two variables. For women, the importance of serving constituents' interests declines significantly as a motivating force with more years of experience as a committee chair.[46] In other words, women chairs with more committee experience are less motivated by classically distributive goals. For men, the same motivation increases slightly in importance among those who have served for longer as committee chairs.

Because these data are cross-sectional rather than longitudinal, interpretation of the results is speculative at best. The absence of similar correlations of the constituent-interests motivation with age, total years of service in the legislature, or year elected suggests that the phenomenon is not generational or merely a function of age. Rather, one might interpret these results to suggest that for women chairs the aggregative norms (i.e., brokering exchanges on behalf of constituent interests) become less important the longer they serve as legislative committee chairs. This pattern parallels the maturation of Vera Katz's style from the give-and-take exchanges of the Ways and Means Committee to an overtly collaborative manner of speaker and then mayor.

Under what conditions might this evolution take place? The presence of other women in the legislature may provide women with greater confidence and support to eschew the traditional give-and-take. Also, women serving in male-dominated institutions may gain confidence over time in their skills as committee chairs and, as a consequence, may see possibilities to pursue a less aggregative course. These data do not by themselves offer a clear explanation but do point to the need for examining career differences for men and women lawmakers over time.

The traditional processes of legislative bargaining may disadvantage women chairs who do not share these aggregative motives. In an all-male focus group, an Iowa chairman related a story illustrating the point:

"We were passing the lottery [bill] a dozen years ago in Iowa, and there was a woman legislator who hated it. She wasn't going to vote for it no matter what. It was a close vote. The entire session had been spent twisting arms to get up enough votes to pass this thing. She had a couple other issues that were real important to her, and I said, 'Why don't you offer them as amendments.' This bill had kind of become a Christmas tree bill. 'Oh no, I hate the lottery,' she said. I told her, 'Don't vote for the lottery, but that's a freight train that's going to pass through here before the session is over. There is no reason why you shouldn't attach one of your boxcars to it.' But she couldn't bring herself to do that."[47]

In summary, clear motivational differences distinguish male and female committee chairs. Although the differences are not great, they are statistically significant and substantively consistent with the integrative leadership style. Female committee chairs are more strongly motivated by a desire to involve people in the legislative process and to serve as a policy catalyst for the issues they champion. Taken together, the motivations of female committee chairs resemble what McClelland describes as a socialized power motive rather than a personalized power motive.[48] Socialized power places greater emphasis on group goals and empowerment of the group to achieve those goals. A personalized power motive tends to emphasize personal goals and dominance. McClelland concluded that many leaders "balance on a knife edge" between the two motives,[49] but clearly these data align women's motives more on the side of socialized power. At the same time, these results strongly resonate the kind of interpersonal care and common purpose implied by the integrative style. Evidence exists to believe that women's motivations may become less aggregative (i.e., less focused on bargaining for constitutent interests,) over time. The exact causes of or reasons behind the transformation cannot be unraveled with these data.

## Characteristic Leadership Traits

The survey asked legislative committee chairs to weigh "the extent to which you think the following traits characterize *your* style." In all, the respondents ranked twenty-two traits on a scale ranging from one for "not very characteristic" to five for "extremely characteristic." The purpose of the question was to probe for different perceptions of key personality traits and, through the use of factor analysis, to identify those clusters of traits that constitute legislative committee chairs' self-conceptions. In turn, these clusters can be analyzed for sex differences and their fit with the aggregative-integrative dimension. The specific question used in the survey has served the same purpose in surveys of state administrators in at least six states.[50]

Results reveal sex differences that are statistically significant on eleven of the twenty-two items and approach significance on two other items. Among those traits that show significant differences, the women on average see themselves as characteristically more process oriented, task oriented, managerial, assertive, attractive, affectionate, risk taking, skilled at interpersonal dealings, frank and direct, and team oriented. On all these traits, the percentage of women choosing the category "extremely characteristic" was one and one-half to two times greater than for men. The "opportunistic" trait is the only one the men, on average, ranked significantly more characteristic than did the women. Almost 51 percent of the men identified the trait "opportunistic" as "characteristic" or "extremely characteristic" of their behavior, compared to only 30 percent of the women.

The factor analysis produced six clusters of leadership traits that were strongly associated with each other.[51] Each cluster is given a name reflecting the traits that correlated most heavily with that factor (see table 4.2).[52] Only one set of traits ("the dependable") showed no gender difference. Female and male committee chairs differed most markedly on "the dominator," the "nurturer," and "the competent." In all, 65.7 percent of the women scored above the sample mean on the factor labeled "the competent" compared with 45.7 percent of the men. Some 57.5 percent of the women compared with only 39.7 percent of the men scored above the sample mean for the cluster of traits labeled "the nurturer." On "the dominator" traits, 59.6 percent of the men compared to only 44.4 percent of the women scored above the sample mean. Assuming normal distributions on the score, the average woman scored higher than only 36 out of 100 men, the thirty-seventh percentile of men's scores, on the "dominant" traits, at the sixty-fifth percentile of men's scores on the "nurturing" traits and at the sixty-seventh percentile of men's scores on "competent" traits.[53] Although the traits associated with "the innovator" were statistically significant (i.e., would occur by chance less than 2 times in 100), the effect is smaller.

The survey also included one indirect measure of the traits associated with committee leadership style—Fiedler's "least preferred coworker" instrument.[54] The instrument has proven to be a reliable means of assessing a person's underlying predisposition toward task behaviors (e.g., controlling, structuring, and directing) versus interpersonal behaviors (e.g., supporting, empathy, and consideration).[55] The instrument is useful because it provides an indirect measure of task versus interpersonal attentiveness that avoids gendered stereotypes and balances out self-report data.[56] For example, a chair who is hard driving, ambitious, and competitive may nonetheless describe herself as team oriented, nurturing, and good at interpersonal skills because of a desire to present herself in a more socially acceptable light.

As a group, committee chairs are more task oriented than other people,[57] and on average, the women chairs had more task-oriented scores than the men, though the difference falls just short of the usual standard of statistical significance.[58] Scores on the instrument are often grouped into three categories: a high score represents an orientation to personal relationships, a low score reflects task motivation, and a middle score is interpreted as flexible with regard to task and less concerned about opinions of others. In the sample, 55.3

Table 4.2. Leadership Traits Associated with Different Personality Descriptions

| *Dominator* | Innovator | Nurturer | Processor | Competent | Dependable |
|---|---|---|---|---|---|
| **Opportunistic** | **Risk-taking** | **Affectionate** | "By the book" | **Task oriented** | Trusting |
| Willing to intimidate | Creative | Attractive | **Process oriented** | Independent | Loyal |
| Ambitious | Analytical | Interpersonal Skills | Analytical | Managerial | Predictable |
| Dominant | **Assertive** | | **Team oriented** | Assertive | **Frank and direct** |
| Competitive | **Interpersonal Skills** | | | | |
| | | | | | |
| Factor means: | Factor means: | Factor means: | Factor means: | Factor means: | Factor means: |
| Men, .149; | Men, −.128; | Men, −.183; | Men, −.093; | Men, −.209; | Men, .026; |
| Women, −.168** | Women, .145* | Women, .207*** | Women, .104 | Women, .235*** | Women, −.030*** |

*Note.* **Boldface type** indicates the clusters of traits or individual items on which women on average scored significantly higher than the men. ***Boldface italic*** type indicates items which the men ranked significantly more characteristic of their leadership style. Traits are listed in order of the strength of their correlation with the factor, and all traits correlated with the factor at .40 or stronger.
*p < .05, **p < .01, ***p < .001.

percent of the women were in the task-oriented category compared to 42.7 percent of the men.[59]

At first glance, the task orientation seems at odds with theory and other evidence arguing that women are more oriented toward relationships and people.[60] However, task and competence might be considered alternatives necessitated by the realities of power and gender. Goodchilds argues that power can be thought of as three "gettings": getting one's way, getting along with others, and getting things done.[61] If the first two "gettings" pose a stylistic or psychological conflict for a leader, the third—an emphasis on task—offers the possibility of resolving the conflict. If a leader is uncomfortable using power to command or direct others or is only marginally integrated into a group, he or she may be more successful emphasizing a group effort aimed at solving a problem or achieving a desired outcome.[62]

The focus groups and individual interviews lend distinctive interpretations to men's and women's task orientation. For example, a North Dakota chairman described the main tasks of committee management in strictly instrumental terms: developing a plan, managing time, arranging seating strategically, and "spreading baby oil on burnt butts" when necessary to mollify individual members.[63] By contrast, a Colorado chairwoman emphasized the collective nature of committee decision making and the expressive task of "setting a goal, seeing it through and making sure that everybody else is brought along."[64]

The women chairs tended to emphasize a selfless quality to task. For example, showing extraordinary persistence over eight years of work, a Colorado chairwoman won acceptance of legislation creating a statewide medical-trauma, emergency-care network. Media reports credited her patience and tenacity for bringing together "the ungainly collection of feuding interests to agree on a plan."[65] In a focus group discussion, a California assemblywoman, similarly highlighted task commitment:

> "I think . . . women are more task-oriented, trying to get the job done. I think you see that some of our male counterparts, much more so than the women legislators, really pursue the media. I have seen women legislators forego publicity to get something passed or to get something done."[66]

Speaker Jo Ann Davidson of the Ohio House of Representatives sees task commitment as a barrier preventing women from seeking leadership positions:

> "If you have ever tried to recruit women to the legislature, you know what I mean. . . . There is a good illustration in the audience today. When I first tried to get her to run for the legislature she was mayor of her community and she had to finish that job. I think many of the women in the legislature came in with an agenda and they have to finish that. They really have not focused as much on seeking leadership positions."[67]

Two Arizona women had a similar experience of being hesitant to pursue a legislative leadership position until they finished work on issues within their committees.[68]

Not all men, however, see task commitment as a positive value, particularly when it may violate norms of aggregative behavior. In a focus group of all men, a Connecticut senator had this complaint:

> "My experience has been that the women chairs are less willing to work to the compromise and work out the details. They feel as though their view of the bill or what they want to do is the way it's got to be. They are less willing to do the compromise. . . . Males that I've dealt with, and I've dealt with chairs on both sides of the aisle, come to you and say, 'You want a bill through my committee? You better take care of mine.' . . . I've found the women less willing to do that. 'Oh no, I can't. You've got to get mine through because it's good, but I don't really like your bill.'"[69]

In sum, men and women chairs describe their leadership style using different traits. To some extent, the self-descriptions reflect stereotypical evaluations. The indirect measure of task and interpersonal orientations, however, may suggest an alternative power strategy (i.e., power achieved through task accomplishment) for women who might otherwise be unwilling or unable to exercise "power over" others.

## Leadership Behaviors

Two aspects of leadership behavior—inclusiveness and conflict resolution—were included in the survey. Six questions examined the frequency or preference for including others in committeee activities or decisions. A second set of questions measured five different styles of conflict resolution along the lines posited by Thomas (see discussion of conflict styles in chapter 2, in this volume).

Participation and inclusiveness have several dimensions. Committee chairs answered five questions regarding how often they consult with their vice chairs, share strategic and political information with the committee, let other committee members take the lead on important bills, let others chair meetings, and work closely with other chairs. A sixth question asked the committee chairs whether they "like to share power with others."[70]

Differences are evident on three of the six items. The women chairs reported more frequent sharing of strategic information with committee members[71] and more frequent work with other chairs on issues of mutual concern.[72] Women also expressed a stronger preference for sharing power with others.[73] Women chairs were twice as likely to say they "almost always" share strategic information or "strongly agree" they like to share power. Several chairs commented that letting other members chair meetings or take the lead on an issue is not typically done in their state. Indeed, when contextual factors are considered, patterns of participatory behavior vary a great deal (see chapter 5, in this volume). Combining the individual items into an overall scale of inclusive behaviors, women on average are more participatory.[74] Of all women chairs, 59.3 percent scored at or above the mean on the scale of inclusive behaviors, compared with only 48.3 percent of the men. Assuming normal distribution of scale scores, the average woman chair scored higher than 59 out of 100 men, the sixtieth percentile of men's scores on the scale.[75]

The questions dealing with different styles of conflict resolution are adapted from the Thomas-Kilmann Conflict Mode Instrument.[76] The Thomas-Kilmann instrument was chosen in part because of its utility in more distinctly defining five styles of conflict resolution:

- *Avoidance*, which involves postponing decisions or avoiding disagreement in the face of conflict.
- *Accommodation*, which involves subordinating one's own wishes to those of others.
- *Competing*, which describes the primary pursuit of one's own goals in the face of opposition.
- *Compromising*, which denotes a classic log-rolling dynamic of finding some middle point between opposing positions.
- *Collaborating*, which is a process of discovering a solution through discussion and shared problem solving.

On eleven of the fourteen individual items, male and female committee chairs differ little (see table 4.3), but three items produced significant differences. Women were twice as likely to say they "almost always" stress direct discussion of issues of conflict (38.1 percent compared to 17.9 percent of men). Women were also significantly more likely to say they "almost always" seek a fair combination of gains and "almost never" or "rarely" avoid controversial positions. The factor analysis produced five conflict resolution styles generally consistent with those posited by Thomas-Kilmann.[77] Analysis of these results suggests that the competitive style for women includes a significant element of discussion and persuasion and not merely an attempt to dominate. Alternatively, competitive men seem to be less concerned about efforts to "convince others of the merits" of their position, and the item that best captures competition for men is "I make every effort to get my way."

On two of the conflict resolution styles (avoidance and collaboration), sex differences emerged. It is important to recall that these two styles anchor the ends of the integrative dimension in Thomas's model (see figure 2.2). Men were significantly more likely to indicate an avoidance style (the low end of the integrative dimension), and women were significantly more likely than men to identify with the collaborative style (the high end of the integrative dimension). On the three styles along the distributive dimension (compete, compromise, accommodate), men and women chairs did not differ significantly. In all, 57.1 percent of the women scored above the mean of the collaboration scale compared to only 40.1 percent of the men. Assuming normal distributions of scale scores, the average woman scored higher than 65 out of 100 men, the sixty-sixth percentile of men's scores on the collaborating style.

Table 4.3. Behaviors Associated with Conflict Management Styles

| Compete | Avoid | Compromise | Accommodate | Collaborate |
|---|---|---|---|---|
| Make every effort to get my way | *Avoid controversial positions* | Trade points in exchange for others | Meet others' wishes | **Stress direct discussion** |
| Try hard to convince others of my position | Do what is necessary to avoid tensions | Seek middle ground between me and others | Try to satisfy all | Share problems to work things out |
| Firm in pursuit of my goals | Postpone when emotions are high. | Postpone when emotions are high | Willingly sacrifice my wishes | **Find fair combination of gains/losses for all** |
|  |  |  |  | Firm in pursuit of my goals |
| Factor Means: Men, .058; Women, −.068 | Factor Means: Men, .103; Women, −.120* | Factor Means: Men, −.021; Women, .025 | Factor Means: Men, .005; Women, −.006 | Factor Means: Men, −.189; Women, .221*** |

*Note.* **Boldface type** indicates the conflict resolution approach and items on which women on average scored significantly higher than the men. ***Boldface italic*** type indicates items on which the men ranked significantly higher than the women. Behaviors are listed in order of the strength of their correlation with the factor, and all behaviors correlated with the factor at .40 or stronger. $^*p < .05$, $^{***}p < .001$.

Chairs are distributed fairly evenly among the five styles, but women were almost twice as likely to present the collaborative style as their dominant style as compared to men chairs (29.4 percent compared with 15.6 percent). Among the men, the collaborative style is the least common conflict approach, whereas for women the avoidance style is the least common conflict approach.[78]

Again, the focus groups and individual interviews resonate with confirmation that collaborative and inclusive behaviors are more frequently embraced by women. Not that male committee chairs are inattentive to personal relationships or unconcerned about open discussion, but some give more emphasis to the technical process of formulating legislation than to collective choice and deliberation. The comments of an Ohio chairman illustrate the point and also suggest the tendency to avoid conflict situations.

> We get some pretty partisan issues in my committee. When that happens I try to separate the two sides and avoid head-to-head conflict. I'll recess if necessary when emotions are high. In my opinion, that's not the best way to do public policy. I feel like I need to run the committee in a very business-like manner to try to find a balance between running it efficiently and with enough control but also so that people are at ease with the process. I don't want to limit debate if it is germane. I hope to give everyone who wants an opportunity a say. But it's my responsibility to make sure that the bills coming out of my committee are improved by our review; so that a committee bill is in the best technical shape as far as correctness.[79]

By contrast, collaborative strategies attempt to accomplish more than technical improvements in legislation and the avoidance of controversy and conflict. The emphasis is on participation that ultimately leads to ownership.

Participation may be as simple as the Colorado chairwoman who routinely invites all the witnesses to take a place at the committee table during a lively hearing. Or, it may be as orchestrated as the chairwoman who uses trained mediators to negotiate agreements among contending interest groups. Even on the most controversial issues, women are likely to seek consensus (see, e.g., the discussion of an abortion bill in Ohio, in chapter 7, in this volume). At its source, participation features a commitment to sharing power. As a Wisconsin chairwoman stated:

> "We're willing to share more of the decision making, more of the power. We let go a piece at a time. First one piece and then another piece. We can share in the decision making in the interest of getting things done. Some times we luck out and we share a piece that we didn't care if we let go in the first place." (*Laughs*)[80]

Or, as a veteran North Carolina chairwoman remarked:

> "I haven't seen very many bills that go through the process the way that they are introduced. So my way of operating is just getting people around the table. I figure I can't be too committed to a particular piece of legislation. No one can be! What you have to be is committed to the process and to teamwork."[81]

A Delaware chairwoman commented:

> "Women want to make everybody a winner. If a bill comes and there are people in support of it, and groups opposed to it, I think we are more apt to try to get everybody to sit down around a table or put it in a subcommittee and try to work out the differences. . . . Women go in with that win-win, keep-the-peace kind of attitude."[82]

Underlying the emphasis on participation and collaboration, a longtime legislative staffer sees another important quality—listening. He described the quality this way:

> "If I had to say that there is a difference [between the styles of men and women] it would be that the women listen to what the other members say and try to find out where the rub is. The best women are real good listeners. . . . Representative . . . would talk to anybody, anywhere, anytime. She would engage others, listen and then try to meet their concerns."[83]

In three focus groups (one of only men, a second only women, and the third a mixed group), the participants were asked to describe the conduct of committee business and provide a definition of consensus. The comments were coded as either aggregative (i.e., framed in terms of winning and losing, interest group competition, bargaining, and majority votes) or integrative (i.e., framed in terms of deliberation, discussion, and overall participant satisfaction in the outcome). In the group of men, aggregative comments outnumbered integrative comments by two to one, whereas the opposite pattern was the case in the all-female group. The mixed group had roughly equal comments. Typical of the aggregative comments were stories of winning votes and sufficient support for a committee product that would withstand questions or challenge on the floor. For example, an Iowa Senate chairman commented:

> "When we dealt with gambling legislation, we had three days of subcommittee meetings, as long as the critics wanted. . . . I made sure I had the votes to get it out of subcommittee, but I made sure it was a balanced subcommittee—that it had two critics, one from each party, and it had three members who were supportive. We sat through three days of two and a half hour meetings to go over the details of that bill to make sure that nobody felt like they were being snuck up on."[84]

By contrast, a typical integrative comment did not center around a vote or a winning outcome but on participant satisfaction. A Maryland House chairwoman offered this comment:

> "I think ideally that consensus is a process, but also the product of a process in which all members feel that they have a stake. Whether they like every little bit of [the final decision] or whether it was their idea, they all have a stake. You have a feeling, it's not unanimity, but of comfort. . . . I served once with an ideal chairman . . . who went around the committee and by the end everyone honestly felt that they had a stake in the project, that it was their baby even though you knew that the product was what the guy

had in mind in the very beginning. Everyone was cooperative. That, to me, was the ideal, but as you know, there is a range of abilities."[85]

Noting that consensus has become an accepted part of the legislative process, a Texas chairwoman added:

"Consensus is now a part of the procedure, whereas when I first got involved [sixteen years ago]: 'The big dog ate and everybody else just lost.' Bills would get introduced, they wouldn't get amended, they would come out like they were introduced. If you had the power, you got the bill passed, and if you lost—well, tough. I got used to losing and it was pretty frustrating. Both the times and having more women involved, I think, are what make consensus seem positive and desirable as opposed to just winning. . . . The downside, though, is that you do lose some enthusiasm in the process. . . . Now every bill is a consensus bill. . . . Nobody walks away feeling like they've really taken the cake and won a major victory over the opposition. I feel more comfortable with that."[86]

In sum, women committee chairs are more likely to emphasize participation, shared power, and collaborative problem solving through direct discussion. Overall, the women chairs do not describe themselves as distinctly less competitive than their male colleagues; however, men and women manifest competition in different ways. For the men, a competitive style of resolving conflict means getting their way, but for the women getting their way involves persuading others of the merits of a particular position. Men and women differ distinctly on the least and most integrative strategies of conflict resolution.


## Replicating Integrative Leadership Through Legislative Mentoring

If integrative leadership exists as a style of behavior and if women are more likely to bring such behavior to the legislature, then modeling and mentoring by women should have an impact. The mentor-protege relationship is recognized as an important conduit through which behaviors are learned or passed on. Thus, mentoring relationships offer the possibility to consider whether the sex differences uncovered thus far are principally self-perceived or are actual practices. If women are indeed more inclusive and more collaborative, then these aspects of leadership behavior should be more evident among those men who have learned their committee leadership skills from women.

Much of the research on mentoring tends to emphasize career planning and progress, developing collegial networks, and navigating organizational structure and politics.[87] Mentoring, however, also helps proteges learn the norms and values of the organization, provides them with guidance and training in necessary skills, and serves a coaching function by suggesting strategies for accomplishing work.[88] In the absence of mentoring relationships, Hale points out that "one's participation and achievement in organizations can be severely limited."[89]

Not only are women less likely to develop mentoring relationships, but they also tend to have different types of relationships. Traditionally, women face a chronic lack of access to mentors because of a paucity of other women to act as mentors and an unwillingness of some men to mentor women. As a result, women turn to peers for mentoring more frequently than do men. Organizational barriers also work against opposite-sex mentorships. For example, opposite-sex relationships may invite heightened public scrutiny, provoke questions about potential sexual involvement, arouse peer resentment and jealousy, and stir up sex-role stereotypes and biases.[90] To be sure, no claim is proffered that only men can or should mentor other men or only women can or should have female proteges. Rather, these problems suggest how mentoring is a gendered process that may reinforce differential power and opportunities of men and women.

Such barriers are evident in state legislatures where few senior women are available to serve as mentors and male colleagues may be unwilling or unavailable as mentors. As one Delaware woman wrote on her questionnaire:

> "There was no buddy system when I was elected. I just learned it the hard way on my own and then earned the respect of the leadership and my peers. It is different today [for women in the legislature] but has always been available to men through "the good ole boy" network."

Despite the barriers, however, mentoring can and does take place within state legislatures. Among the chairs who completed surveys, distinct patterns of mentoring emerged[91] (see table 4.4[92]). Clearly, women committee chairs do not lack for mentors overall, and they are just as likely as the men to report having a senior male legislator or leader advising and guiding them. Nonetheless, women's experiences with mentoring are quite different from those of their male colleagues. Women are two to three times more likely to identify female mentors in every category except top leadership positions. To find other women as mentors, women must turn to their peers rather than women with greater seniority or leadership authority. Men committee chairs almost never lack for other males to serve as mentors, but almost 60 percent of the men report having no experience with a woman as a significant mentor. In the sample, ninety-one men reported no female mentors and sixty-two men identified at least one female mentor. By contrast, only nine female committee chairs reported having only other women as mentors. Women are more than eight times more likely than the men to have no same-sex mentor. These patterns of mentoring are similar to that reported for women managers in state government.[93]

The effects of mentoring should be evident in leadership styles and behaviors. In other words, integrative styles, which seem more prevalent among women, should be replicated among their male proteges, and aggregative styles, which are associated with men, should be passed on to their proteges. Because so few women identify no male mentors, this second proposition cannot be tested with these data. Although it is not possible to isolate the effects of male

Table 4.4. Patterns of Mentoring among Committee Chairs

|  | Women | Men |
| --- | --- | --- |
| % Identifying a Female Mentor |  |  |
| As speaker/party leader | 8.9% | 5.2% |
| As senior legislator** | 17.0% | 7.1% |
| As legislator peer*** | 57.8% | 26.0% |
| As professional colleague*** | 20.0% | 6.5% |
| As friend/political adviser*** | 47.4% | 15.6% |
| % Identifying a Male Mentor |  |  |
| As speaker/party leader | 57.8% | 63.0% |
| As senior legislator | 33.3% | 32.5% |
| As legislator peer | 58.5% | 63.6% |
| As professional colleague | 24.4% | 19.5% |
| As friend/political adviser | 45.2% | 53.9% |
| % Reporting |  |  |
| No opposite-sex mentors*** | 6.7% | 59.1% |
| No same-sex mentors*** | 21.5% | 2.6% |

$*p < .05, **p < .010, ***p < .001.$

mentors on female proteges, the differences in women's leadership behavior discovered thus far are all the more striking. In effect, female committee chairs embrace different leadership strategies in spite of their predominantly male tutelage.

Three groups were compared on all the scales or factors that differed significantly by sex. These groups include men who identified female mentors, men with no female mentors, and the women in the sample. Female mentoring has the expected effect on eight of the ten measures[94] (see table 4.5 for the general pattern of results and appendix table 2 for full results).

Two major points may be drawn from the data. First, the contrast between women committee chairs and men who do not identify any female mentors is more stark than the data in the whole sample. For example, on the key integrative measures of collaborative style and inclusive behavior, the average women scores five standard deviations higher than the average man with no female mentors. On the other measures, the average woman scores three to four standard deviations higher than the average male chair without a female mentor. The data suggest that if legislatures had no female members, integrative leadership would be all the more rare.

Second, female mentoring may foster more integrative leadership in men. Male committee chairs who have had a significant female mentor in the legislature are significantly more collaborative, inclusive, and people oriented than other male committee colleagues. At the same time they are less likely to characterize themselves with dominant traits and more likely to characterize themselves with nurturer and innovator traits.

In sum, female mentoring is positively linked with integrative leadership among men. But a cautionary note is necessary. It may be that men who have

Table 4.5. Influence of Female Mentoring on Men's Leadership Styles

| | % of Chairs Scoring above the Mean on Selected Leadership Measures | | |
| | Women (N = 134) | Men Identifying 1+ Female Mentors (N = 62) | Men Identifying No Female Mentors (N = 91) |
| --- | --- | --- | --- |
| Policy motivation | 55.2% | 40.3% | 45.1% |
| People motivation | 60.4 | 58.1 | 33.0 |
| Inclusive behavior | 59.3 | 54.2 | 44.4 |
| Collaborative style | 57.1 | 39.7 | 33.3 |
| Competent traits | 65.9 | 41.0 | 48.9 |
| Innovator traits | 59.7 | 42.6 | 51.1 |
| Nurturer traits | 57.3 | 42.6 | 37.8 |
| Dominator traits | 44.4 | 55.7 | 62.2 |

Note. Only those leadership measures that show a significant linear trend or significant between group differences using the .05 level of statistical significance are shown.

had female legislative mentors differ in some significant way from their colleagues and are thus predisposed to more integrative leadership. That assertion was voiced by several chairs in the focus groups who felt that younger men were more likely to have worked with and for women in professional settings. A comparison of the men with and without female mentors reveals no difference in age, education, or year of election, but some other factor may be involved.

These results may be attributable to a larger societal shift or special circumstances that have influenced some committee chairs but not others. Noting a transition from a "command" style of leadership to one emphasizing consensus in her legislature, a Maryland chairwoman commented in one focus group:

> "To some extent there is a societal change. There are men coming into leadership positions now who are more used to thinking of trying to build a consensus. They can't rely on simply telling people what to do or giving orders . . .the chain of command is simply not as clear as it used to be. In our House, our previous speaker came from a different school and was forced by economic conditions and other things to assume a leadership role in which he felt it was his responsibility to tell people what to do. . . . Some of the guys, committee chairmen, didn't like that and they became more sensitized." [95]

## An Integrative Style of Leadership?
## Putting It All Together

The data seem to affirm Vera Katz's description of a female style of leadership. But do the integrative factors clearly distinguish the men from the women committee chairs? The differences on the individual measures are statistically significant but relatively modest. Certainly some of the participants in the focus groups (both men and women) emphatically see differences, and the fact that women differ even after mentoring by their male colleagues suggests something more than self-perception. Do these differences remain significant when key demographic variables are included? (Note: The next chapter introduces contextual variables into the analysis.)

One way to test the results is to determine whether the traits, behaviors, and motivations found to be significantly associated with male and female committee chairs remain important when controlling for other differences such as age, mentorship, or legislative experience. The statistical technique known as logistic regression is a method of analysis that uses other variables to predict a dichotomous variable such as sex. In other words, if we know a chair's score or response on several key variables, does that information improve our chances of guessing a respondent's sex more than would be the case by chance?[96]

Knowing a chair's score with regard to integrative motivations, traits and behaviors and controlling for female mentorship, age when first elected and years of legislative service, it is possible to correctly predict a chair's sex almost 79 percent of the time. Given that the makeup of the sample is 56 percent male and 44 percent female, these traits provide substantial predictive power and link integrative leadership with women committee chairs.

## Conclusion

Men and women who chair state legislative committees are alike in many respects. The participants in the focus groups emphasized that skills such as managing time, planning, and running effective meetings are not sex specific but rather the mark of a good chair. They saw these traits as a reflection of personal competence more than sex. Nonetheless on matters such as consensus and decision-making approach, differences do emerge.

This chapter provides evidence that the theoretical distinctions between aggregative and integrative leadership have a significant link to gender. This evidence supports the hypothesis of a more integrative style of leadership practiced by women. Thus, the "feminization of leadership" proclaimed by Vera Katz seems to be affirmed by a subtle but important shift in leadership traits, motivation, and behaviors.

Several major findings emerge from this chapter. First, women chairs are far more motivated by people and policy goals than are male committee chairs. Moreover, women talk about their policy motivations in terms of personal commitments and connectedness. Citing her own experiences, a California chairwoman noted, "They [women] care about the bills that they are willing to sponsor, and they think in terms of how [a bill] affects their loved ones."[97]

Second, as they gain more experience as committee chairs, women also seem to be less motivated by the classic and most aggregative goal of serving constituent interests in policymaking. Women committee chairs also articulated a view of policy detached from particular interests. For example, a Missouri representative distinguished between a woman's perspective on issues and a more traditional conception of women's interests:

"Outside of the Equal Rights Amendment, that was an issue for women, I don't see any issue that isn't a women's issue. The economy is a women's issue, the environment is a women's issue, education. I think there are some issues that we consider soft issues, but not women's issues."[98]

When women chairs do advocate on behalf of "interests," it is often for those who are frequently less able to marshal political resources or organize a lobby. As one senior Delaware legislator wrote on her survey:

"Early [in my career] . . .the agenda for 'the lame, the weak, the halt and the blind' was not a dominant concern. That has been turned around after a long struggle to raise its importance in the legislative ranking process. I have succeeded in bringing to the attention of my colleagues the significance of the issues I pay attention to. I am therefore now looked to by members of my caucus and the Speaker as the definitive person in that public policy arena."

Third, women characterize their leadership style with different attributes, most notably an orientation that emphasizes *both* task and interpersonal relationships.[99] These female self-assessments persist in spite of male-dominated legislative institutions, mostly male mentoring, and leadership selection processes that would tend to encourage and stress conformity and homogeneity.

Fourth, the men and women in this study also report different leadership behaviors. Affirming other research, women chairs more frequently consult others, share strategic information about matters under committee review, and say they like to share power. In making decision and resolving conflicts, women embrace collaborative strategies, stressing discussion of alternatives, sharing problems, and finding creative solutions.

Finally, these behavioral and motivational differences are manifest indirectly through mentoring. Not only do women *say* they are participatory, inclusive, and collaborative, but their male proteges report the same behaviors. Men who have had important female mentors also indicate stronger motivations to involve people in legislative deliberations and report less dominating, more nurturing traits than men without female mentors.[100]

The next chapter looks more closely at how organizational context, legislative norms, the presence of more women in the legislature, or state factors have an impact on leadership styles.

# 5

## The Constraints of Place on Leadership

California State Senator Diane Watson and Utah Representative Beverly Evans live in very different political worlds. There are the obvious contrasts of size and demographics between their home states and their districts: Senator Watson represents some 750,000 residents of a Los Angeles district that is 40 percent white and 60 percent minority with growing Asian and Hispanic populations. Representative Evans represents two rural counties and some 28,000 residents in racially homogeneous (93 percent white) Utah.

Their legislatures also differ. California dwarfs other states in terms of the number of staff, the year-round legislative session, legislator compensation ($75,600 a year), and the funds required to wage a successful electoral campaign. Utah lawmakers, by contrast, meet forty-five calendar days every year, earn $100 per diem salary, and have no personal staff or offices.[1] As a result, Senator Watson finds she has much more in common with her California male colleagues than with many other women legislators: "Where you are has great meaning; geography is destiny."[2]

Both chairs, however, have had common experiences related to being one of the few women in their legislatures. Both have encountered doubts about their abilities and have developed strategies to manage the visibility that comes from being different. In 1986, many people laughed when Evans first ran in a race against eight men, but her hard work and personal reputation in the rural areas have discouraged potential rivals in subsequent elections. She has won over the skeptics. Even the president of her local stake (a Mormon geographic jurisdiction comprising several smaller church units) has come around: He confided once to Evans's husband that he never imagined he would vote for a woman candidate.[3] Evans notes:

In our state, we're ultra-conservative. It's been a tradition of our religion that has a very patriarchal order. . . . If you are going to be in there and you are going to be effective as a woman, you've got to have the information. You've got to become a specialist in those areas of water, transportation, the oil and gas industry—whatever you represent. When men have to start coming to you and asking you for information, that seems to change the attitudes.[4]

Watson also has won acceptance over time. Her first electoral office was on the Los Angeles school board, where she was a high-profile advocate of forced busing. When she was first elected to the Senate in 1978, she avoided busing and education issues in an effort not be button-holed as a single-issue legislator. Furthermore, she befriended those Senate colleagues who were most likely to be her ideological opponents. She, too, did her homework: "I burned a lot of midnight oil. I was a loud-mouth black female who had led the charge on busing which was a very polarizing issue. I had to prove that I was capable and could do the job."[5]

In addition to experiences shaped by gender, these two committee chairs also share a leadership style that fits the integrative model. Both describe themselves as problem solvers, strongly focused on the policy task, and committed to involving people in the legislative process. In managing committee decision making, Evans and Watson tend to emphasize strategies of collaboration and listening. Watson notes, "I hear the bills out. I do not expedite them. I let the opposition take their time, ask the questions that they need to, and get their concerns on the table."[6]

On what was expected to be the most controversial child welfare bill in 1995, Evans won unanimous approval of the legislation by bringing together all the contending groups. "I gave everyone an opportunity to have input and then pulled them altogether. I don't believe there was anyone in the state who I didn't take the time to listen to."[7] She attributes her emphasis on teamwork to growing up on an Idaho sugar beet farm where everyone's help was required and her mediating ability to skills learned as a mother.[8]

The similarities and differences of these two women's experiences raise fundamental questions: Is their leadership style more a reflection of the different realities of *where* they serve? Or, is being a woman in a predominantly male institution a more significant and central influence? To understand who a legislator is and what it means to legislate and to lead, scholars have argued that one must understand a legislator's political geography and the multiple constituencies at home and in the institution.[9] Less well understood is how gender is part of the organizational reality of legislatures.

The organizational reality Representative Evans confronts means being willing to accept the state's dominant religious culture, not taking offense at sexist remarks that inevitably occur, avoiding women's issues, and focusing on getting things done rather than being in the limelight. "I don't have an agenda, I just try to get problems solved," she says.[10]

By contrast, as the state's first black female state senator, Watson feels an organizational responsibility to be an outspoken advocate for "human and humane issues" and a conscience on behalf of women and people of color. She feels a broad spectrum of voters look to and trust an African American woman to be their presence in government.[11] She has worked to appoint an office staff that reflects diversity and serves as a "threshold [into state government] for people of color."[12] Her first three staff directors were female—an Asian followed by a Hispanic and then an African American. She notes with a laugh that as an equal opportunity employer she has also had a white male chief-of-staff.

As the experiences of Representative Evans and Senator Watson suggest, women committee chairs are not cut from a single pattern. A critical determinant of behavior involves where and under what circumstances a leader serves. Institutional rules and procedures, cultural influences such as race and religion, and the presence of other women all make a difference. This chapter explores how context shapes committee leadership behavior. In particular, place matters in three ways:

- The sex composition of an organization has as impact on leadership styles of male and female committee chairs, but more than numbers is the importance of gender power. When women have more power, men may be resistant to adapting the more integrative styles of leadership.
- Both political culture and social variables exert influence on committee leadership styles. As indicated by the experiences of Evans and Watson, cultural influences may constrain integrative leadership styles or direct them in situationally appropriate forms.
- Professional legislatures advance and reward certain kinds of behaviors and motivations at the expense of others. In terms of integrative leadership, professional legislatures are friendly environs for competitive, policy-oriented chairs but less conducive to inclusive behaviors and accommodating styles of conflict resolution.

In this chapter and in the appendix tables in this volume, I show how gender differences fare once personality and contextual variables are added to the analysis. I demonstrate that leadership motivations and behaviors differ from place to place. Third, I try to unravel how key contextual variables affect men's and women's leadership styles in different ways.

To understand how this plait of factors comes together, chapters 7, 8, and 9 (in this volume) explore, in more nuanced terms, how integrative leadership is influenced by state political culture, sex composition, and institutional practices. These subsequent state studies help account for differing norms and practices that cannot be adequately captured in a quantitative analysis. Not all committee systems are created the same: other actors—the leadership, the party caucus, individual members—vie with chairs for policy control[13]; basic committee structure—number of members, jurisdictional scope, workload, staff, frequency and length of meetings, session length and deadlines, and procedural rules for notice, voting and amending—limits or increases a chair's discretion.[14] Furthermore, state legislative norms of comity and respect affect behavior among individual members.[15] As with any organization, these rules of the game, behavioral regularities, dominant values, and institutional traditions give rise to a distinctive culture that cannot be reduced to a single variable.[16]

## Does Place Matter? Insights from Theory and Research

Scholars of bureaucratic behavior have noted that personal style does not spring solely from personality but rather depends on organizational position and culture.[17] Legislative behavior is no different. As in any organization, the procedures, traditions, power dynamics, and norms of the legislature in which one serves are determinants of behavior. As Burns explains in his theory of political leadership, the interaction between leader and followers involves both behavioral and structural variables, and "'structure' . . . is judged by its potential for constraining or blocking possible alternative courses by the leader."[18]

Before turning to the analysis, it is helpful to reflect on how context affects behavior. What can we learn from existing theory and research?

### The Impact of Sex Composition

As only the second woman in the California State Senator, Senator Watson understands that being virtually alone in an organization not only brings heightened scrutiny but also leads paradoxically to invisibility. She remembers that in the early 1980s the legislature's $59 million renovation project of the state capital building proceeded for months and millions before she and the Senate's only other female member discovered there were no plans for a restroom for female senators.[19] Early in her career, she experienced difficulty getting recognized to speak on the floor. When she did get noticed, her legislation on children's and women's issues was laughed at as frivolous by her male colleagues.[20]

As noted in chapter 2 (in this volume), one of the key structural determinants of organizational behavior is the proportionate size of subgroups based on ascriptive characteristics of race, sex, or ethnicity.[21] Social composition affects both the individual's experience and the interactions between socially different groups within an organization.

Chapter 2 highlighted a conflict in theory about how changing proportions affect norms of behavior. In 1977, two different theories emerged to explain the effects of relative numbers on individual behavior within an organization. Drawing on a detailed case study, business scholar Rosabeth Moss Kanter specifically examined skewed sex ratios and the experience of "token" women.[22] Using a deductive approach, sociologist Peter M. Blau outlined a set of theorems and corollaries to explain the nature of intergroup contact, association, discrimination, and inequality.[23]

The implications for the minority individual in organizations differ distinctly in Blau and Kanter's theories. Kanter argues that tokens are subject to disproportionate visibility, differences from the dominant group are perceived as exaggerated, and behavior is stereotyped as "larger-than-life caricatures," such as mother figures, seductresses, iron maidens, or one of the guys.[24] Tokens tend to be isolated and marginalized because they are seen and treated as "representatives of their category rather than independent individuals."[25] Moreover, the conditions of tokenism impose systemic pressures on individuals who feel required to internalize distinct roles.

Kanter focuses primarily on the conditions experienced under tokenism, but she gives some hints about the dynamics of tilted groups (where minorities number more than 15 percent) and balanced groups (where the minority proportion exceeds 35 percent). In tilted groups, "individuals [become] differentiated from each other as well as a type differentiated from the majority."[26] Compared to tokens, individuals in tilted groups gain greater status, form coalitions for increased power, begin to affect the dominant organizational culture, and develop alliances for the purpose of acquiring tangible gains.[27] When subgroups become balanced, an organization's culture and interpersonal interaction reflect the balance. At that point, the systemic constraints of tokenism disappear; individuals are judged on personal, not group, factors.

By contrast, Blau suggests a different dynamic. In circumstances with very few minorities, the token individuals have the most contact with and thus the best conditions for support from the dominant group. Blau argues that increasing the size of a minority group only decreases individual opportunities for social interaction and increases the likelihood of majority discrimination against a minority.[28]

Blau and Kanter may both be right, but resolving this contradiction in theory requires focusing not simply on numbers but on another variable — power. Organizational psychologist Janice Yoder makes the point that numbers are only one part of the processes of minority segregation and integration. She notes that individual performance pressures are mitigated by the presence of others who share token characteristics, but a growing minority may also provoke a reaction from the dominant group that feels its privileged status threatened. Indeed, she asserts that a "dominant group can effectively restructure the workplace to reduce the competitive threat posed by the growing minority."[29] Yoder calls this phenomenon the intrusiveness hypothesis: the dominant group resists intruders and "reacts with defensive strategies aimed at containing the advances made by the intrusive minority."[30]

Political scientists Duerst-Lahti and Kelly also demonstrate that gender power, not numbers alone, is the variable of interest in understanding leadership and governance.[31] Numbers and power, although related, are not necessarily the same thing. In a legislature, that distinction can be easily made. If most women legislators are members of the minority party, their impact may be felt on interpersonal relationships but not on organizational norms. There is no reason to expect that more women in a legislature represent more like-minded women who will act in unison. Indeed, the opposite may be true: As more women enter legislative service, greater diversity of perspectives might be expected. Many women who ran for state legislative seats in the 1970s were drawn from among supporters of the Equal Rights Amendment. In the 1980s and 1990s, religious conservatives also recruited and elected women candidates.

If, however, women hold a significant share of power positions — leadership and committee chairs — their presence may be felt more profoundly. When women gain a greater share of institutional power, their presence also may be more threatening to norms.[32]

The literature on proportions, therefore, informs this analysis in three ways. First, the competing theories dictate that some effort be made to control separately for both the proportion of women in legislatures and their share of power as measured by the percentage of committee chairs and leadership positions. Second, the literature suggests that numbers and power proportions may have different effects on men and women chairs: Women are expected to capitalize on opportunities for coalition building and collaborative work when their institutional power increases. As the number of women legislators increases, men may adopt certain aspects of integrative leadership because of the dynamics of tilted and balanced groups that Kanter describes. However, because power represents a clear intrusion into an established structure, we should not be surprised to find that men may resist these same behaviors as women's power increases.

## Legislative Institutions and Professional Norms

As the stories of Representative Evans and Senator Watson suggest, legislative institutions also impose constraints on committee leadership behaviors. States provide very different institutional contexts. The Virginia delegate's committee career can only be understood in the context of that state's formal seniority system. A committee chair in the Florida House of Representatives is necessarily the product of a unique system of speakership rotation and a process of policy innovation crafted through interim studies. The Nebraska state senator is sure to preface her description of committee duties by noting that legislature's unicameral and nonpartisan makeup.

In addition, legislatures differ considerably in terms of their levels of institutionalization.[33] Institutionalized legislatures are characterized by boundedness — "separation of the institution from its environment" — and norms that differentiate members from nonmembers.[34] Institutions and bureaucracies tend to perpetuate themselves by promoting and advancing leaders who fit into a preferred organizational model. Organization scholar Natasha Josefowitz calls this phenomenon the "clonal effect,"[35] an organization's ability to replicate its norms and values by selecting a certain type of middle- and upper-level manager.

Of particular interest are norms of legislative professionalization. Legislators in professional legislatures are more likely to identify themselves as full time, to have no other employment or substantial interests outside the legislature, and to have access to large staffs to develop policy expertise.[36]

A profession is not a neutral form of organization but, rather, values a certain like-mindedness, enshrines technical know-how and expert competencies, and develops a culture that sets the professional apart from the rest of society.[37] Feminist public administration scholar Camilla Stivers points out that professions grew out of brotherhoods that historically resisted diversity:

> [P]rofessionals have a perennial tendency to promote their unique perspective, mystifying their subject matter to veil the intuition and guess work that inevitably supplement "scientific" judgement; exclusivity helps ensure that those who are uninitiated in the uncertainties of practice remain that way. . . .[38]

In many ways, the ideal of the modern, institutionalized legislature enshrines the values of professionalism — the autonomous institution, the importance of objective expertise and authoritative knowledge, the emphasis on capabilities, and the need for decisive leaders to bring order out of disorder.[39] In professionalized legislatures, committees answer "technical questions," function efficiently in processing legislation, and "enable the legislature to break up its work load into manageable parts."[40]

Almost by definition, professionalized legislatures are unlikely environments for certain aspects of integrative leadership. Professional legislatures are less likely to strive for inclusiveness or to value collaborative or accommodative behaviors. After all, a professional is an expert who does not need others to be successful. In fact because the costs of obtaining office and the financial benefits of serving are both higher than for citizen assemblies, committee chairs in professional legislatures are likely to be more entrepreneurial and competitive in pursuing credit for legislative goals. On at least one characteristic, however, professionalization and integrative leadership converge: Both emphasize a policy orientation.

Professional legislatures may also be unlikely venues for integrative leadership because, like other public bureaucracies, they embody culturally male characteristics that pose a dilemma for women in leadership roles. Stivers argues that masculine biases are implicit in bureaucratic structures, in the traditional view of the administrative state, and in leadership images.[41] Authoritative expertise, rational policymaking, and professional autonomy are culturally male and at odds with more feminine qualities of responsiveness, caring, and service.[42] Institutional norms and cultural norms thus may pose a problem for women leaders who face a dissonance between their personal understandings of femininity and society's traditional expectations about leadership.[43]

Empirical evidence suggests women in leadership roles resolve this dilemma by trying to "look like a woman yet act like a man"[44] or by overcoming the double bind of femininity and competence.[45] Recent studies of state administrators confirm evidence of masculine bias in bureaucracies.[46] Women cope by acceding to male norms as they move up the ladder[47] or by trying to avoid female stereotypes and embrace "antistereotypes."[48] The authors of *Breaking the Glass Ceiling* argue that organizations constrain women's behaviors within a "narrow band of acceptability," a veritable tightrope of behaviors that can be neither too masculine nor too feminine.[49] Thus, in professional legislatures, women chairs are hypothesized to adopt culturally male behaviors, such as competition, and to eschew the more culturally feminine manifestations of integrative leadership, such as collaboration, accommodation, inclusiveness, and people-oriented motivation.

## Knowing the Political Territory

Culture influences Representative Evans and Senator Watson's actions. An extensive literature documents the importance of political culture, party, and societal influences in organizational life. Indeed, the essence of contextualist theory, as posed by political scientists Joseph Cooper and David W. Brady, is that congressional party leadership behavior is a dependent variable shaped by societal values, situational variables, and political demands within the system.[50] What then might be the impact of political culture and party influences on committee leadership styles?

The most well-known theoretical work on state political culture is that of political scientist Daniel Elazar, whose categories of moralism, individualism, and traditionalism differentiate political behavior as a distinctive cultural phenomenon.[51] Most consistent with the integrative model of leadership is Elazar's moralistic subculture which emphasizes community, sees government as a positive force for the common good, and values broad-based participation in political activities.[52] By contrast, the individualistic subculture doubts the existence of common public interests and sees the marketplace as the best arbiter of interests. In an individualistic culture, participation is valued only in the sense that citizens and groups inevitably compete for government benefits. The traditionalistic subculture, dominant through much of the South, operates on an elite paternalism and does not value broad-based participation.

Elazar's three cultures also have strong associations with other cultural variables that may shape behavior. For example, traditionalistic cultures are associated with conservative Protestant religions,[53] traditional roles for women, lower levels of representation for women,[54] and resistance to egalitarian public policies.[55]

State-level cultural factors have been found relevant to the election of women as legislators; therefore, such factors might also influence leadership style.[56] Indeed, contextual variables rather than sex may be driving certain dimensions of leadership. Certainly, it is reasonable to expect committee chairs will share the values of a particular political culture and the beliefs of their constituents. For example, Elazar's moralistic political culture with its emphasis on community and broad-based participation would likely be fertile ground for inclusive, participatory behaviors and would reinforce motivations to involve people in the legislative process. Similarly, a moralistic political culture would be an apt environment in which to expect strong public policy motivations, as opposed to utilitarian or anti-government outlooks associated with individualistic and traditionalistic cultures, respectively. Thus, controlling for these influences is warranted. In sum, a moralistic culture should be positively associated with integrative styles of leadership, whereas a traditionalistic culture is most culturally male and thus least likely to be favorable to integrative approaches.

## Analyzing the Effects of Context

In this chapter, I narrow my analysis to those variables most associated with integrative leadership: specifically, a motivation toward policy and people in the legislative process, a collaborative style of dealing with conflict, an emphasis on accommodating the desires and views of others, and inclusive committee behaviors. Integrative leadership is noncompetitive; therefore, I also include in this analysis the conflict resolution style of competing and expect it to show a negative association.[57]

Multivariate regression analysis is the appropriate strategy for unraveling the survey data because it becomes possible to isolate the effects of sex and context while controlling for other possible influences, such as personality, career differences, and the like. Multivariate analysis also provides an opportunity to test for interaction effects, which refer to the possibility that certain variables may have one effect on women and a different or opposite effect on men. For simplicity, a synopsis of the data is presented in tables 5.1 and 5.2. The full analysis is presented in appendix tables 4 to 9.

Included in the analysis are the following variables: a measure of legislative professionalization, the percentage of women in the legislature, the percentage of chairs and leadership positions held by women in a state legislature, and a variable for political culture where a higher value represents Elazar's moralistic culture and a low value represents a traditionalistic culture.[58] Age, years of service in the legislature, party, and personality variables are used as control variables.[59] Party represents an important control variable. Because the Republican Party has traditionally been more oriented toward markets and business, GOP chairs might be expected to be more competitive and dominant in their leadership behaviors than their Democratic counterparts. Also based on party ideology, Democratic committee chairs might be expected to take a more activist policy orientation than Republican chairs.

Briefly summarizing the key findings from the survey data, the analysis shows the following:

- Women chairs are statistically more likely to be associated with a collaborative style and with policy and people motivations even when controlling for context and personality variables.
- More feminine and masculine personality traits—for example, nurturing and dominating, respectively—are strongly associated with aspects of integrative leadership.
- Professionalized legislatures are significantly and positively associated with competitive styles of conflict resolution and a strong policy motivation on the part of committee chairs; the same legislatures are negatively associated with other-directed leadership behaviors such as inclusiveness, accommodation, and a strong people motivation.
- Men and women chairs' other-directed behaviors (i.e., inclusiveness, collaboration, and accommodation) are affected in different ways by the presence of more women in the legislature and the power held by women in an institution. Men's scores decline as the share of women's power increases, while women's scores increase as female power increases.

In all, contextual, personality, sex, and individual variables explain a modest amount of the behavioral differences. Knowing the contextual, personality, and career variables, therefore, explains anywhere from 12 percent to 42 percent of the variance in chairs' scores on most aspects of integrative leadership.

Importantly, age and length of legislative service are also significant predictors of some aspects of integrative leadership even when controlling for personality and contextual variables. Specifically, legislators who are older tend to be significantly less collaborative and competitive and more motivated by policy goals. The collaborative and competitive styles share an emphasis on satisfying one's own goals; thus, older age may presage a less self-centered approach to conflict resolution. Length of legislative tenure is positively and significantly associated with an accommodative style and inclusive strategies. Taken together, age and experience seem to indicate a maturation of styles. In other words, older and more experienced committee chairs are more attentive to satisfying the interests of others and including others in the process. These results may represent life-cycle differences between younger, entrepreneurial, and ambitious committee chairs in contrast to older chairs who may be less concerned with building or advancing personal careers and reputations.

## The Effects of Sex and Gender

The sex of a committee chair remains an important predictor of leadership style when controlling for contextual, personality, and legislative career variables. Just as important, however, are personality factors that may reflect social manifestations of gender. Traditionally feminine and masculine personality traits are strongly and significantly associated with different aspects of leadership style. (See appendix tables 4 to 9, regression models for all chairs.)

The association between the sex of the respondent and leadership style is statistically significant only on the collaborative behaviors of conflict resolution. Although the magnitude of the difference is not great (recall from chapter 4, in this volume, that the average woman scored higher than 66 out of 100 male committee chairs, the sixty-seven percentile), the difference is statistically and substantively significant. The positive association between women chairs and the collaborative style has a probability of occurring by chance less than one time in twenty. Collaborative approaches to conflict resolution emphasize direct discussion of differences and shared problem solving and are a central element of integrative leadership. Thus, the significant association between the sex of the respondent and collaboration is a key finding.

The associations between leadership styles and feminine personality traits are stronger and more often statistically significant than those between styles and sex. In particular, nurturing personality traits are positively associated with integrative motivations and behaviors. The statistical relationships linking inclusive, accommodative, and collaborative behaviors with a nurturing personality would occur by chance less than one time in twenty. The positive association between a nurturing personality and integrative motives focused on policy and people would occur by chance less than 1 time in 1,000. As expected, masculine personality traits such as dominating are negatively associated with inclusive behaviors and positively associated with competing behaviors; both relationships have a probability of occurring by chance less than 1 time in 1,000.

The effects of the variable sex and various personality traits combine in a fairly convincing way to show that integrative leadership is gendered in distinctly female terms. These data illustrate the distinction between sex and gender, the socially constructed understandings of sex, as explanatory variables.[60] Both men and women committee chairs who tend to be more integrative (i.e., score higher on the various measures of integrative leadership) describe their personalities in the more feminine terms of nurturing, preferring to share power, and less dominating.

## The Effect of Professionalization

Certain contextual factors are also significant predictors of integrative leadership, most notably the extent of legislative professionalization. As expected, more professionalized legislatures are associated with more competitive styles of conflict resolution, stronger policy motivation, and less inclusive, accommodative, and collaborative behaviors. Table 5.1 reports the percentage of male and female committee chairs who scored above the mean on various dimensions of integrative leadership by three categories of legislatures.[61] The influence of the type of legislature is clear, more professionalized legislatures are not associated with more integrative behavior.

Table 5.1 also illustrates differences between women and men in different legislatures. In citizen and somewhat professionalized legislatures, women

Table 5.1. Integrative Motivations and Behavior in Three Types of Legislatures

| | % of Chairs Scoring above the Sample Mean | | | | | |
| | Citizen Legislatures | | Hybrid Legislatures | | Professional Legislatures | |
| | Women (N = 46) | Men (N = 56) | Women (N = 64) | Men (N = 58) | Women (N = 25) | Men (N = 40) |
|---|---|---|---|---|---|---|
| **Policy motivation** | 48.9% | 29.1%** | 59.7% | 44.8%* | 55.6% | 60.0% |
| **People motivation** | 66.7 | 45.5** | 59.7 | 37.9*** | 51.9 | 47.5 |
| **Inclusive behavior** | 78.6 | 63.0* | 59.6 | 38.2** | 25.0 | 42.5 |
| **Competitive style** | 40.0 | 48.1 | 54.1 | 44.8 | 50.0 | 66.7 |
| Collaborative style | 60.0 | 40.7 | 50.0 | 29.8** | 48.1 | 35.9 |
| Accommodative style | 55.8 | 57.4 | 46.8 | 50.9 | 42.3 | 43.6 |

Note. $*p < .10$, $**p < .05$, $***p < .01$, $****p < .001$, based on percentage of men and women higher than the mean in each category. The items marked in **boldface** had significant weighted linear trends in analysis of variance using mean scale scores.

chairs hold significantly stronger policy and people motivations and are distinctly more inclusive than men chairs; however, these differences disappear in professional legislatures. Both men and women chairs adopt more competitive styles, eschew collaborative and accommodative styles, and embrace strong policy goals in more professionalized legislatures.

## The Effect of Political Culture

The results of the multivariate analysis show little effect due to political culture. Moralistic cultures are associated with higher levels of women's representation, and thus most of the effects of culture may be evident in the influence of women and women's power on integrative leadership style. One aspect of the analysis, however, is worthy of comment. There is a positive association between a moralistic culture and more accommodating and more competitive leadership behaviors on the part of women only. The pattern for accommodating behavior is as hypothesized but the influence on competitive behavior is not. At a minimum, these contradictory results suggest a greater influence of culture on women's behavior than on men's. (See appendix table 3, regression models for men only and women only.)

## The Effect of Women and Women's Power

The percentage of women legislators and their share of institutional power affect men's and women's leadership styles in different ways. As table 5.2 illustrates, there is no clear pattern of effects.[62] The only simple conclusion to be

Table 5.2. Integrative Motivations and Behavior by Legislatures of Differing Sex Composition

| | % of Chairs Scoring above the Sample Mean In Legislatures with Membership | | | | | |
|---|---|---|---|---|---|---|
| | <18% Female | | 18 to 28% Female | | >28% Female | |
| | Women (N = 24) | Men (N = 53) | Women (N = 64) | Men (N =73) | Women (N = 44) | Men (N = 27) |
| Policy motivation | 33.3% | 44.4% | 56.1% | 44.4% | 65.9% | 37.0%** |
| People motivation | 50.0 | 31.5* | 63.6 | 48.6* | 61.4 | 51.9 |
| Inclusive behavior | 68.4 | 39.6** | 49.2 | 50.7 | 71.1 | 59.3 * |
| Competitive style | 41.7 | 59.3 | 50.0 | 52.9 | 50.0 | 33.3 |
| Collaborative style | 41.7 | 38.9 | 51.5 | 37.7** | 61.4 | 22.2*** |
| Accommodative style | 45.8 | 63.0 | 50.0 | 43.5 | 48.8 | 48.1 |

*Note.* *$p < .10$, **$p < .05$, ***$p < .01$, ****$p < .001$, based on percentage of men and women higher than the mean in each category.

drawn is that the percentage of women matters in important but complex ways.

There is a small positive and statistically significant association between the percentage of women legislators and the two measures of policy and people motivations. In legislatures with a higher percentage of women legislators, male chairs express stronger motivation to include people in the legislative process. Female chairs on average score higher than the men in terms of people motivations, so the overall effect of more women legislators is to decrease the difference between men and women chairs on this measure. (See also appendix tables 5 and 6.)

As Kanter would predict, a greater percentage of women serving in a legislature is positively associated with stronger policy motivations on the part of female chairs. Tilted groups offer more opportunities for coalition building and collective action that turn policy hopes and goals into policy realities.

The presence of more women in state legislatures also seems to be a slight positive influence encouraging male chairs to be more inclusive in managing their committees. Since women chairs on average are more inclusive and participatory than men, the overall impact of more women legislators is to narrow the difference a bit between men and women chairs on this measure. (See also table 4 in the appendix.)

Controlling for women's power in an institution (i.e., the percentage of female chairs and leaders) further complicates the analysis and reveals more pronounced effects. In general, women's power shows a positive and significant influence on the integrative behaviors of women chairs but a negative and significant influence on the integrative behaviors of male committee chairs. An analysis with interaction terms provides three distinct pieces of information: (1) the coefficient reported for female sex indicates whether women and men's average scores differ on the specific leadership variable when women's power equals zero, (2) the coefficient for female power indicates the association between women's power and leadership behavior for men, and (3) the interaction term (sex×female power) indicates whether the association between power and leadership behaviors differs significantly between men and women. (See the interaction models reported in appendix tables 4, 7, and 9.)

The pattern of relationships is most easily understood when portrayed graphically in figure 5.1, which illustrates the contradictory influences of proportion of women and women's power on integrative leadership. To interpret the figures the following guidance may be helpful. For those graphs involving women's power, the coefficient for female sex conveys the difference between women's and men's scores at the point where the regression lines on the figures intersect the y-axis, that is, where women's power equals zero. The coefficients for power convey the slope of the regression lines for men. The coefficient for the interaction term (sex × power) convey the difference in slope between the lines for women and men. The slopes of the women's regression lines can be derived by adding together the coefficients for power and sex × power.

On the three leadership measures of inclusive, collaborative, and accommodative behaviors, women on average score significantly higher than do male chairs. Men's scores on the three measures show a significant negative association with women's institutional power, whereas women's scores on the three measures of integrative behavior reveal a significantly different and positive trend. In other words, as women's share of institutional power increases, male committee chairs become less inclined toward such integrative behaviors of leadership as collaboration, inclusiveness, and accommodation, whereas women committee chairs become more likely to embrace these integrative strategies.

These results suggest that the dynamics identified by Kanter and Yoder both operate at some level on leadership styles of committee chairs. Clearly, Kanter is correct in positing that more balanced proportions provide opportunities for collective and coalitional strategies. But Yoder also seems on point when she identifies the potential threat posed by intruders and the subsequent reaction of the majority culture. In sum, women's power seems to offer women the opportunity for greater collaboration while at the same time prompting men to be less integrative.

The focus group discussions and other data also confirm both points. Even beyond the "care" issues, women from very diverse states—Arizona, Delaware, Wisconsin, Missouri, Kansas, North Carolina, California, Virginia—cited examples where, by virtue of sheer numbers of female colleagues, they have found policy success attainable. Indeed, the strength of numbers earned a moderate group of Arizona female lawmakers the appellation "Sue Nation," which described their pivotal bloc of moderate votes on major legislation in the 1994 session.[63] Similarly, a Virginia woman identified the importance of a formal women's legislative caucus in securing a seat for a woman on the pow-

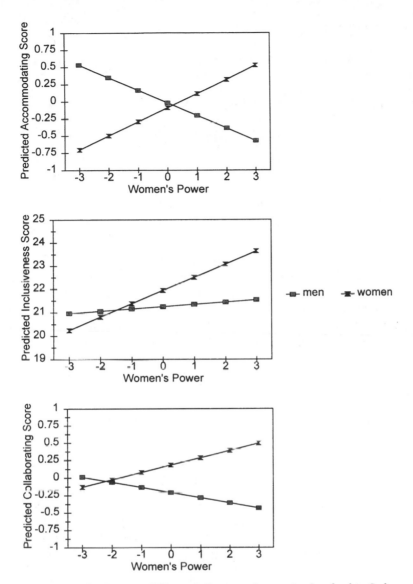

Figure 5.1. The Impact of Women's Power on Integrative Leadership Styles

*Note:* The above figures reflect the regression of the women's power variable, sex and the interaction term on the dependent variables. Other variables in Appendix tables 4, 7, and 9 were not included and thus are not controlled for in the figures. Nonetheless, the pattern and magnitude of results shown in figure 5.1 are substantially the same for the accommodating and collaborating scales. For the inclusiveness scale, the results shown in Appendix table 4 and in the figure reflect how men's and women's scores differ significantly; however when other variables are included, men's scores on the inclusiveness scale actually decline and women's scores increase significantly as women's power increases. In other words, the results in the more elaborated model reveal a greater effect of women's power on men's and women's scores than presented in the figure. Since women's power is calculated as a z-score, the "0" on the x-axis can be interpreted as being the mean of women's power (i.e., women's share of committee chairs plus their share of leadership positions) in the respondents' states. A "–2" on the x-axis represents two standard deviations below the mean of women's power in the sample.

erful Rules Committee.[64] Identifying both the individual-level and group effects of increasing numbers, a Texas chairwoman noted:

> "We're at the point where we have enough women in leadership, a critical mass, that we try to caucus and inform one another about our bills. We meet across party lines, rural, urban, black, white, brown; every constituency has women representing it in Texas now. That was not the case for many years when there were just a few of us. And I don't see anymore the situation where when a woman gets up and blows it, that she's treated as a woman who blew it as opposed to a legislator who blew it. . . . We also have a women's conference committee, it's not for real, we only do it to irritate the men. We just go back in a room by ourselves and talk about something . . . and then they're dying to know what we're doing."[65]

As the last comment suggests, the perception of increased women's power may also be directly threatening to the dominant group. In Minnesota, where women hold more power as chairs and leaders than in most states (see table 1.1), that threat took the form of a head-on challenge to the norms of aggregative leadership in 1996. Two female House members published an unprecedented public critique of then-Speaker Irv Anderson, and a third woman called for his ouster as chair of the House Campaign Committee.[66]

Representatives Mindy Greiling and Alice Hausman described Anderson as "an old-style leader who is a master of reward and retribution" and criticized his emphasis on parochial issues and neglect of bigger policy priorities. Although they did not use the labels of aggregative and integrative leadership, their language was quite clear:

> Under the leadership of Speaker Anderson, legislators have been so busy fighting with each other and inflicting wounds that truly important issues have been ignored. . . . The two unwritten rules have become, "Whoever yells the loudest wins," and "If you're not with me, you're against me." Anderson protects his inner circle at all cost, at times even to the detriment of the majority of the caucus. He enables his "in-group" members to dominate and excludes full caucus participation so that the ideas and energy of many are wasted. A good leader recognizes the strength of a team and produces more than the sum of everyone's resources.[67]

Greiling and Hausman also hinted at the gender link with integrative leadership when they described their caucus's reaction to the ouster move. In response to the challenge, "good old boys of both genders" went "ballistic" in support of the Speaker and "intimidated" backers of a change in leadership philosophy into silence.[68]

As these examples suggest, women's power can be perceived as and treated as a real threat to institutional norms and provoke resistance of a dominant culture to female intruders. Most important, Yoder's dynamics of intrusiveness occur not simply as a result of more women but rather when women hold more power. In a focus group of all male chairs, gender differences were perceived sympathetically or with skepticism depending in part on the number and power held by the women. This exchange between several of the male chairs from various states illustrates this point:

"In our New Hampshire House, we have 100 women, one third of the house, and I've seen women who are every bit if not better at compromising, at fighting over issues, at knowing when to give up, at knowing what can and can't be done. I don't see this gender thing at all."

"But don't you think that explains part of it? I think where there's a very small minority, they're more defensive. I think they're scared of looking weak . . .in Mississippi we have very few [women]."

"Well we do [have women in top leadership in Connecticut]. The majority leader in the House is female, the president pro tem in the Senate is a woman. I'm not saying they shouldn't be in those positions. I just think they tend to hold on to what they feel is so. It's got to be their way. I don't know if it's because of what [Senator . . .] said that they [women] have to appear stronger or better or tougher. I don't know what their motive is. But I know at least three or four of the Senate chairs who are women who are very difficult to deal with. And it's not just my opinion, that's generally their reputation."[69]

Such comments do not necessarily provide conclusive proof of resistence to power. It is noteworthy, however, to consider the institutional contexts from which each chair comes. The previous comments range from acceptance in New Hampshire, where women number one-third but still hold less than proportionate power, to tolerance in Mississippi, where women are part of a very small minority, to considerable tension in Connecticut, where the number of women and their share of power are comparatively higher (see table 1.1). What cannot be discerned from the multivariate analysis is at what point female power no longer provokes a negative reaction from men but possibly becomes a positive force for change. Such questions await future scholars who attempt to unravel organizational leadership and gender.

## Differential Effects of Context

In addition to the interaction effects noted previously, one other observation about contextual influences is clear from these data. By analyzing the influence of context separately for women and men, it becomes clear that context contributes to greater variability of women's leadership styles than of men's. (See appendix tables 4 through 9, regression models for men only and women only.) On the various components of integrative leadership, the personality and contextual variables explain 12 percent to 23 percent of the variance in men's scores. By comparison, the same models explain 21 percent to 43 percent of the variance in women's scores.

Why might women's leadership behavior be more sensitive to contextual influences? Depending on whether one focuses on women chairs, men chairs, or the organization of legislatures, three possible explanations might be offered. First, if leadership norms are essentially norms defined by a predominantly male culture or by historically male institutions, these data may be explained as Stivers suggests: Women face more pressure than men to adapt, modify, or conform their styles to the dominant norms. Because institutional conditions of professionalism and the presence or absence of women and women's power vary, women respond to more complex and conflicting pressures, which in turn leads to greater variability of leadership styles.

By focusing on the smaller variability in men's scores, a second explanation might be offered: Perhaps institutional and cultural norms provide more constraints on men's leadership behavior than on women's behaviors. In an institution or organizational role that is historically male, it might be the case that organizational conformity exerts greater pressure on men. To be sure, women face the same institutional norms, but perhaps because they are pioneers in a sense, they are in effect freer to set their own course. Contrary to the findings of the authors of *Breaking the Glass Ceiling*, it may be the men in legislatures, rather than the women, who must conform to a narrow band of acceptable leadership behaviors.[70]

A third explanation might be that legislatures are different from other organizations and thus findings from other organizations are not always applicable. Leadership in public organizations tends to flow to those who embody the norms and values of the organization. Legislatures differ from other organizations in terms of the higher turnover of members and a less hierarchical structure that recognizes the presumptive equality of each member. Instability and greater equality might negate the powerful socializing norms evident in other organizations. Because legislatures have less stable organizational norms, different styles of leadership brought by women may offer new possibilities for influence and change.

## Conclusion

This analysis underscores the centrality of gender as a defining element of leadership style. Gender shows its impact in three ways. First, sex is a significant predictor of aspects of integrative leadership behavior even when controlling for different situational variables. The differences are not biological but presumably result from different life experiences and socialization. Second, and just as important, gender manifests itself in feminine and masculine personality traits and, therefore, demonstrates a significant influence on leadership styles. Third, gender shows its influence as an organizational phenomenon when we specify the effects of more women in a legislature or more power held by women in a legislature.

Integrative leadership behaviors and motivations are also quite variable given the demands of place, institution, and time. Contextual circumstances matter. Although aggregate-level analysis cannot begin to reveal or fully explain the myriad different pressures and constraints impinging upon an individual legislator, the analysis can begin to paint a broad canvas of how certain factors shape leadership behavior. The results, however, underscore not only the diversity of contextual variables but also the complexity of their interplay.

Of particular import is the connection between legislative professionalization and leadership styles. More than any other single variable, legislative professionalization is negatively associated with the integrative model of leadership. Increased professionalization discourages accommodative and inclusive behavior and encourages aggregative behavior based on dominance and competition. Because legislatures are professionalizing, integrative leadership may be imperiled.

I have argued that the very model of a professional, modern legislature embraces images of masculinity. In such legislatures, the more male traits of dominance and competitive decision making are reinforced. By contrast, the more feminine images of routine care and service, interconnectedness, and mutual dependence, which are manifest in a concern for people and in participatory or inclusive behaviors, are less likely in a professional legislature.[71]

Political culture plays a weak though expected influence in shaping leadership styles. The impact of culture is felt most decisively in its association with greater levels of women's representation in legislatures. The relatively weak results also may be attributed to the inability of empirical analysis to adequately capture the complexities of different states and districts. As the experiences of Representative Evans and Senator Watson suggest, political history, state and district demographics, religious traditions, and temporal circumstances cannot be ignored.

Finally, the potential of women's power to transform leadership behavior is most intriguing. The number and power of women in a legislature seem to have important effects on both men's and women's leadership styles. When serving with more female colleagues, female chairs are increasingly motivated toward policy, use inclusive or participatory behaviors more often, and are more likely to adopt collaborative or self-sacrificing styles of conflict resolution.

The analysis suggests that the presence of more women in the legislature has a modest, positive effect on the integrative leadership behavior of men, but more power held by women has a substantial and negative effect on the behavior of male chairs. As the case studies show, Kanter's description of the "token" experiences of women has considerable merit when trying to understand women's leadership experience. But Yoder's intrusiveness hypothesis is also quite relevant: Men may resist organizational change when women acquire greater power.

The optimism of some scholars and feminists who predict that women's ways will transform institutions may have to be tempered with the realism that institutional masculinism is alive and well in the modern legislature of the twenty-first century. Ellen Goodman, the syndicated columnist, may be nearer the mark when she writes, "It is easier to dress for success than to change the meaning of success."[72]

# 6

## *Oklahoma: Leadership in No-Woman's Land*

Created from tracts of Indian land and the panhandle strip once known as "No-Man's Land," Oklahoma has been described as a "state of competing images" that reflect contradictory but defining trends of traditionalism and transition.[1] In gender politics, the conflict between traditionalism and transition also seems apt: Women are more prominent today in state politics than in days past, yet the state's long heritage of social conservatism remains an impediment. In contemporary politics, leadership in the Oklahoma Legislature is "no-woman's land."

In the 1990s, women have run successfully as statewide candidates, but at the state legislative level, progress has been slow. Oklahoma ranks forty-eighth among the states in terms of percentage of women lawmakers. Legislating has been traditionally and historically men's work.

Looking out over the Oklahoma House of Representatives from the visitor's gallery, one is struck by the absence of women. A few female clerks sit on the raised dais where the Speaker grips the gavel. Fresh-faced teenage girls serving as pages wait attentively at the front desk to be called for some errand. But in the 101 seats on the floor of the House only nine women are seen among the suits and cowboy boots. In the House committee rooms in 1997, only six of the twenty-seven committees have more than two women members, and eight committees have no female members. Only two standing committees are chaired by women, and two other women chair the standing subcommittees of the Education Committee. Only three women sit on the forty-member Appropriations and Budget Committee.

The Senate is not very much different. Six of the forty-eight members' desks are occupied by women, and on the nineteen standing committees there are typically seven men to every woman. Nine committees have only one or no female senators at the table. Women chair only one of the eight subcommittees of the Appropriations Committee and just three of nineteen standing committees.

In a traditionalistic state with few women lawmakers, masculinity dominates the legislature and its norms of leadership. The Oklahoma case clearly illustrates three points[2]:

- Oklahoma's political culture continues to shape legislative politics and behavior, to favor men in key leadership roles, and to contribute to the paucity of women legislators. Gender power is essentially male power.
- Because of their limited number, women chairs experience the performance pressures of tokenism. Their behavior and styles are often defined or interpreted in gender stereotypes, and they are subject to heightened scrutiny and visibility.
- Institutional factors favor an aggregative style of leadership. The legislature's operation and procedures are competitive and interest driven. Pressures due to legislative deadlines and volumes of bills necessitate a committee system not amenable to more deliberative, integrative processes.

As Oklahoma nears the turn of the twenty-first century, students of the Sooner State see a traditional culture attempting a sometimes difficult transition in politics, the economy, and the institutions of government. The transition is to a competitive two-party state, a modern technology-based economy, and a more open society. But even as signs of transition are evident, the Sooner State's political culture remains rooted in a traditionalistic past.

## Women in Oklahoma Politics

Oklahoma's political culture generally has produced a masculine politics, but the state's history contains several success stories that reflect its populist bent. For example, Kate Barnard was the first woman ever elected to a statewide office in the United States, winning election in 1907, ten years before women were allowed to vote in Oklahoma.[3] In 1921, Alice Mary Robertson (R-Muskogee), Oklahoma's sole congresswoman, became only the second female U.S. representative elected.[4]

Oklahoma was among the thirty states that granted women the right to vote prior to ratification of the Nineteenth Amendment. State voters amended the state constitution to provide for women's suffrage in 1918 after two previous unsuccessful attempts—one at the 1907 Constitutional Convention and in 1910, State Question 8. In 1920, Oklahoma became the thirty-third state to ratify the Nineteenth Amendment to the U.S. Constitution.[5] Women first joined the ranks of lawmakers in the state House and Senate in 1921. Until 1942, however, Oklahoma's constitution specified that only men were eligible to be gov-

ernor or to serve in certain executive offices.[6] An exception to the constitutional ban was the Commissioner of Charities and Corrections, an office sought
and held by two pioneering Sooner female politicians, Kate Barnard (1907–
1915) and Mabel Bassett (1923–1947).[7]

Not until the 1990s did women capture major statewide offices, but recently several have been successful: Lieutenant Governor Mary Fallin, State
Treasurer Claudette Henry, Labor Commissioner Brenda Reneau, and State
School Superintendent Sandy Garrett. The 1994 elections featured several
electoral firsts—two women in the general election for lieutenant governor
and a competitive female candidacy in the Democratic primary for governor.

The historic firsts of women in Oklahoma politics demonstrate the state's
populist impulses, but electoral success generally reveals the impediments of
Sooner traditionalism. Like other border and Deep South states, women have
been elected to office in much lower numbers than in other states. For an
eleven-year period during the Great Depression (1930–1941), no women served
in the Oklahoma Legislature.[8] After the 1996 election, women comprised a
fraction more than 10 percent of the legislative membership.[9]

Different reasons have been cited for Oklahoma's low level of female
representation. A traditionalistic southern culture not only reinforces a male
hierarchy but also encourages all but a few (historically a white male elite) to
eschew politics. Scott argues that in southern politics, women were historically socialized into obedient and submissive roles, deferring to men.[10] As recently as 1984, such attitudes seemed to endure among legislators in the eleven
Deep South and five border states.[11] Looking specifically at Oklahoma legislative elections between 1968 and 1982, political scientist Robert Darcy and colleagues ruled out structural barriers, voter bias, and party hostility to female
legislative candidates as causes of women's lower representation. Rather, they
concluded fewer women are elected because women tend to run disproportionately as Republicans in an essentially Democratic state, and women (like
men) are reluctant to challenge incumbents[12]:

> The Oklahoma political system with its high valuation for incumbency and
> its stress on waiting one's electoral turn, not challenging elections, is very
> sluggish in responding to changing situations. Women in Oklahoma are
> like men in Oklahoma. They are reluctant to challenge, preferring to wait
> their turn for political openings.[13]

Darcy and colleagues dismissed the importance of political culture, yet deference to incumbency seems quite consistent with a traditionalistic society. Also,
cultural factors may work in other ways. For example, one cannot rule out the
possibility that Oklahoma women do not offer themselves as candidates because they do not see themselves in political roles or because they see other
aspects of their lives (e.g., religion) in conflict with politics.

The absence of women legislators has endured into the mid-1990s, but
more important, women have lacked power in the legislature. No woman has
ever held a top leadership post—presiding officer or majority or minority leader.

Women have not been elected from rural districts that continue to wield a disproportionate share of legislative power. Women legislators tend to represent districts based in the two major metropolitan areas and the university communities of Norman and Stillwater. Only four of the fifteen current female legislators represent predominantly rural constituencies.

Once elected, female legislators complain that the issues they champion are resisted and often not taken seriously in the legislature. During a 1997 debate on child-support enforcement, conservative male senators opposed revocation of fishing and hunting licenses for parents who are in arrears on their child-support payments and argued that such a policy was nothing short of a threat to American values.[14] In 1994, a proposal to hang plaques for a women's hall of fame in a state building prompted backlash proposals for a men's hall of fame and a state license tag motto: "In Honor of Men."[15] For most of her ten-year legislative career, Representative Linda Larason tried to bring attention to the problems of juvenile justice and the need for a separate state agency. Finally, in 1994, the House leadership took an interest in the issue and muscled through a reorganization bill while Representative Larason, though chair of the Children and Family Services Committee, was relegated to a minor role. Also in 1994, when a breast cancer bill sponsored by Representative Betty Boyd was up for debate, one conservative Republican lawmaker asserted that women were causing their own cancer by delaying pregnancies, bottle feeding their babies, and having abortions. When they present their bills for floor debate, female lawmakers complain "an automatic radar goes up" among the male members.[16] One lobbyist recalled a male member saying about a female colleague's legislation: "She shouldn't sponsor so much of that women's stuff and stick to looking out for her district."[17]

Moreover, the few women who have held real power in the legislature have encountered difficulties of the kind that Yoder describes as dominants' resistance to intruders. Take, for example, the experience of Cleta Deatherage. Elected from a Norman district that has elected female legislators continuously since 1974, Representative Deatherage came to the legislature in 1976.[18] In 1979, as a protégé of Speaker Dan Draper, she was appointed vice chair of the Appropriations Committee where she earned a reputation for hard work, a quick wit, and a sharp tongue. She became one of the most powerful women in state government when she was appointed to chair the committee from 1981 through 1983.[19] During that period Representative Deatherage, with Speaker Draper's support, set out to centralize budget-making power in the committee. Not only did the changes go against the legislature's populist and parochial traditions but also her style grated on many of the rural legislators. When Draper was forced to step down because of a conviction on vote tampering (a charge that was eventually overturned by a federal judge), Representative Deatherage's removal as appropriations chair became a major issue in the speakership race. She resigned as chair rather than face what some political observers felt would be her inevitable removal.[20] She took a backseat in the House during her last two sessions.

By the end of the 1980s, Oklahoma women legislators began to emerge as legislative players. They became recognized as policy leaders in certain areas, particularly education,[21] as key figures in a successful coup to oust Speaker Jim Barker in 1989,[22] and as part of the extended leadership teams of former Speaker Glen Johnson or current President Pro Tem Stratton Taylor.[23] Some earned political leverage the old-fashioned way—by being effective fund raisers and assisting colleagues. But even to the most sympathetic observers, their influence was largely behind the scenes, a "quiet revolution" in style if not in real power.[24]

Women, therefore, remain numerically underrepresented in the Oklahoma Legislature, and the influences of a conservative political culture seem evident. Even when positioned as major players, they have encountered resistance and a barely veiled hostility that is consistent with Yoder's intrusiveness theory.

## The Context of Legislative Leadership

Scholars see the Sooner State making a transition from the traditionalism that has dominated political culture and state politics. Factors in the legislative institution, however, tend to reinforce the long-standing inclination toward an aggregative style of legislative leadership that thrives on a politics of log rolling and distributing district goodies.

### Culture and Politics in the Sooner State

As a border state, Oklahoma shares strains of two political cultures: the traditionalism of its sister states to the south and a less dominant, but nonetheless distinct, form of individualistic culture typical of the middle and mountain western states.[25] Elazar describes politics in a traditionalistic culture as usually dominated by a single party but characterized more by highly personal and factional politics than by party unity and cohesion. The orientation of political leaders is conservative, with a posture toward maintaining existing social and economic hierarchies. Broad-based political participation is weak and generally not encouraged, and antigovernment attitudes often prevail.

The individualistic culture contributes a different set of attributes to Oklahoma politics, including an emphasis on parochialism, competition by interest groups for a share of public goods, and public tolerance of a fair amount of political corruption. In Oklahoma, governments, particularly local units, often perform caretaker roles, and historically, party unity has been less important to legislators than taking care of the needs of constituents back home.[26] As a result, public institutions—whether prisons or colleges—are as regionally dispersed as almost any state in the nation.

A religiously conservative and homogeneous population, relatively low levels of educational attainment, a lack of urbanization and industrialization, and low personal wealth tend to reinforce the legacy of traditionalism. Though the state is home to the second largest number of Native Americans, Oklahoma's population is remarkably homogeneous in terms of race and ethnicity.[27] Less than 15 percent of the population is nonwhite. The state's population is socially conservative with one of the highest percentages (44.1 percent, ninth among the states) of Protestant fundamentalists.[28] According to the 1990 U.S. Census, Oklahoma ranks thirty-eighth in the percentage of high school graduates and thirty-fourth in college-educated citizens.

Although becoming more diverse, the state's economic base is still rooted in agriculture and the extraction industries of oil and gas. When the state's economy collapsed with sinking oil prices in 1982 and 1986, state policy emphasized economic diversification. By the close of the decade, however, progress was mixed.[29] Although the boom-and-bust cycles of the energy industry created many wealthy individuals over the years, median household income remains low, forty-second among the states according to the 1990 census. Like other traditionalistic states, personal income is maldistributed.[30]

Typical of traditionalistic cultures, one political party dominated until the 1990s. Democrats have controlled the statehouse for most of the state's history but not always with cohesion.[31] Legislative voting studies in the 1970s revealed the Democrat label to be a poor guide to understanding legislative performance.[32] Localism and factionalism have set Democrat against Democrat when issues involve urban versus rural interests, Oklahoma City versus Tulsa, labor versus management, or public sector versus private. The Republican Party, although solidly conservative, also has embraced a range of perspectives from the pragmatism of the state's first-ever Republican Governor Henry Bellmon (later U.S. senator) to the sometimes strident conservatism of the state's largest daily newspaper, *Daily Oklahoman*.

The state's geographic and economic quadrants reflect diverse political factions. In the southeast, "Little Dixie" enthusiastically embraces populism, patronage, and pork-barrel politics in the finest southern courthouse tradition. In the southwest, conservative Democrats predominate in the agricultural areas. The sparsely populated northwestern corner and the panhandle are solidly Republican areas, dependent on the oil and gas industry. The northeast around Tulsa, Bartlesville, and Claremore has been home to major corporate oil and gas companies. Although inclined toward Republicanism, the more prosperous and culturally upscale Tulsa has cultivated a civic-minded business community prominent in working to modernize state government, diversify the state's economic base, and invest in public education. A small contingent of relatively liberal Democrats hails from the university communities of Norman and Stillwater and the black inner-city neighborhoods of Tulsa and Oklahoma City. Finally, a very conservative brand of Republicanism emanates from Oklahoma City where the *Daily Oklahoman* cranks out antigovernment, antitax, and anti Democrat editorials.

In terms of policy, the electorate also demonstrates its historic social and fiscal conservatism. Only Mississippi was still legally "dry" when Oklahomans formally repealed Prohibition in 1959. Not until 1984 did state voters give localities the option of allowing liquor by the drink. In 1994, Oklahoma became the first state to turn down a citizen referendum for a proposed lottery. In 1993, voters approved a constitutional amendment requiring all revenue-raising measures to be approved by a supermajority in the legislature or a vote of the people. A property-tax rollback placed on the ballot by antitax groups was defeated decisively in 1996 but encouraged lawmakers to write their own property tax reform measures that were passed by voters in November 1996. In spite of significant tax increases in the 1980s, the state's tax effort remains below the national average.[33]

Culture is not immutable, and signs of change are evident. Economic development and diversification have been policy priorities of every governor, legislative leaders and a chorus of civic and business leaders over the past fifteen years, and the economy is growing.[34]

Since the 1960s, the Republican Party has enjoyed growing success, particularly in federal and statewide races. GOP victories have been harder to secure in the legislature, but in 1994 the party won a sufficient number of legislative seats to sustain vetoes for newly elected Republican Governor Frank Keating and to block enactment of emergency clauses. In 1994, the GOP won a remarkable reversal of the partisan makeup of the congressional delegation in part on the activism of voters who identified with the Christian Right.[35] Republican strategists hoped for statehouse control in 1996, but they had to settle for two state Senate seats and the last Democrat-held seats in Congress. Republican success is rooted in a growing suburban electorate and a declining rural Democratic constituency,[36] fading habits of partisan predictability and loyalties,[37] and a Democratic Party unable to marshall stronger voter allegiance.[38]

In sum, Oklahoma has shed the confines of one-party politics, but traditionalism and factionalism remain. The state lacks the kind of communitarian heritage that might demand integrative leadership and has perfected a parochial distributive politics.

## Institutional Factors

The legislature has undergone dramatic changes in the past three decades, but an aggregative style of legislative behavior has endured. In the 1960s, annual legislative sessions were approved, constitutional restrictions on legislative salaries were eliminated, and a streamlined committee system was established.[39] Court-ordered reapportionment in the 1960s and 1970s carved out new legislative seats in the state's urban and suburban areas and helped the Republicans steadily erode Democratic hegemony.[40] In addition to more GOP members, reapportionment brought younger, better educated lawmakers to the Oklahoma capitol.[41] In 1971, these changes resulted in the Citizens Conference on State Legislatures, ranking Oklahoma fourteenth in terms of legislative capacity, higher than all of its southern neighbors except Florida.[42]

Structural modifications and an influx of new members, however, did not transform the institution as much as might be expected. The influence of political culture and pork-barrel politics endured. Kirkpatrick noted that in spite of greater representation, metropolitan-area legislators actually lost influence to rural forces between 1963 and 1970 as measured by their share of legislative leadership and committee positions.[43] Moreover, even as salaries increased, most lawmakers continued to see themselves as part-time, citizen legislators whose primary concern is "bringing home the bacon" to their districts.[44]

In addition, leadership dominates the legislative system. Based on ratings by legislators of the importance of committees in legislative decision making, legislative scholar Wayne Francis categorizes the Oklahoma Senate as one of the most centralized, with decision making dominated by the leadership; the Oklahoma House is somewhat less so.[45] Traditionally, leaders have accumulated power through small political favors and populist policies. The leaders embrace a populist orientation and divvy up state resources to line up difficult votes. For example, when the legislature was forced to raise taxes in 1987, reluctant Chickasha legislators supported Speaker Barker's position only after a not-too-veiled threat to close the town's struggling University of Science and Arts of Oklahoma.[46]

Appropriations bills probably best illustrate leadership strength and populist policy fragmentation. Under the Oklahoma constitution, all legislation without an emergency clause must be delayed for ninety days to allow voters the opportunity to circulate a petition forcing a popular vote on the law. To skirt this requirement and to enact budget legislation for the fiscal year that starts July 1, the legislature must routinely attach an emergency clause which requires two-thirds support or sixty-eight votes in the 101–member House. Faced with the emergency-clause requirement, the Democratic leadership in the mid-1980s used "pork barrelling" as the primary method of coalition building on budget and revenue measures.[47]

Today, a strong but parochially motivated legislature vies with a relatively weak governor presiding over a balkanized bureaucracy of thirty-one constitutionally created agencies, 230 separate boards and commissions, and ten administrative officials elected separately from the governor.[48] Whether Republican or Democrat, recent governors have run headlong into the legislature's individualistic and distributive tendencies. The legislature in the 1980s refined its tradition of pork-barrel politics with the practice of inserting "special projects" into the appropriations bills in an effort to secure votes.[49] Some of the promised expenditures were hidden in the budget and agencies received a phone call, letter, or other covert instructions on how the money was to be spent.[50] In an attack on the practice, Governor Bellmon issued Executive Order 8816 in 1988, forbidding state agencies to expend funds for purposes not detailed in law. During the Walters administration, the antipathy between legislative leaders and the governor amounted to open warfare. More recently, in 1995, Governor Keating ran afoul of senatorial prerogatives over executive appointments. By tradition, a prospective appointee must be nominated by his or her home senator before confirmation can proceed. Keating's nominees declared alternative residences when several senators refused to offer up the governor's candidates.[51]

Public unhappiness with the legislature came to a head in the late 1980s, fueled by a series of tax increases and a legislative pay raise to $32,000 a year, higher than any other state with a part-time citizen legislature. Through most of the 1988 campaign season, the *Daily Oklahoman* called for removal of Speaker Jim Barker and criticized his leadership team for its heavy-handed tactics and pork-barrel politics.[52] Although the voters failed to turn out the leadership team, a group of dissident moderates (the "T-Bar Twelve") and disaffected freshmen Democrats joined forces in an unprecedented ouster of Speaker Barker three weeks prior to the close of the 1989 session.[53]

But the damage to the institution in terms of public disregard had already been done. In 1989, voters approved a constitutional amendment to shorten annual sessions, and in 1990 Oklahoma became the first state to limit the terms of lawmakers, who can now serve no more than a total of twelve years in the House, the Senate, or a combination of both.[54] Less than a year later, State Question 640 effectively prohibited any future state tax increases without a vote of the people.

The session limit has complicated the Oklahoma Legislature's functioning as a modern policymaking assembly. The state constitution and more recent voter-imposed constraints impose deadline and workload pressures readily apparent at the committee level. As a result, legislative leaders have a tendency to fall back on traditional policymaking approaches.

## The Practice of Committee Leadership in Oklahoma

Three themes emerge from a study of committee leadership within the Oklahoma Legislature. First, the scarcity of women committee chairs makes them "tokens." Tokenism is a system construct, defining the individual and casting tokens in roles that are interpreted in highly stereotypical terms.[55] Second, the legislature reflects institutional values and operating procedures that favor a classically aggregative style of leadership. Third, women chairs generally conform to aggregative behaviors but show some tendency to be more collaborative by emphasizing listening and educating as leadership. The combination of organizational norms and token numbers means that Oklahoma women have limited ability to move toward a more integrative model of leadership behavior as seems to be the case in Ohio and Colorado.

### Understanding the Committee System

The *Legislative Manual* asserts that committees are the legislature's "primary tools for initiating inquiry, ascertaining the facts regarding legislation, and performing many of the oversight tasks."[56] In committee, the *Manual* continues, "bills are reviewed, amendments offered, policies explored, citizens lobbyists and agencies heard, disagreements explored, and solutions offered."[57] The description is accurate but overstated because a lack of time, an unwieldly workload, and other factors undermine the deliberative aspects of committee work.[58] Committees winnow through some 2,500 introduced measures and the legislature ultimately enacts approximately 800 laws and joint resolutions each biennium.[59]

The change in the session length in 1989, coupled with self-imposed deadlines for legislative action, compresses committee deliberations into a narrow time frame. Each legislative session convenes on the first Monday in February and continues through the last Friday in May. Deadlines further constrain committee action. In the 1995 legislative session, for example, committees had at most three opportunities to meet and act on bills before the deadline for committee action in the house of origin. Several legislators and staff recalled one session in which the House Education Committee considered eighty-eight bills over twelve hours of meetings.[60] In contrast with the manual's description, the typical committee review of a bill consists of a brief presentation by the sponsor and sometimes one or two questions from the members. Public testimony generally is not taken, and lobbyists are present but do not participate unless called on. As a practical matter in developing agendas and deciding what bills to consider, committee chairs may be able to allocate no more than five or six minutes per bill.[61]

In addition, "shell" bills are an important feature of the truncated session.[62] Though only the Senate has tracked the number in recent sessions, there is a consensus in both chambers that "shell" bills have become more common since the short session was imposed. In 1995, almost 20 percent (137 of 699) of the bills introduced in the Senate were "shells." "Shell" bills may be introduced because the drafting staff has not had enough time to flesh out the details and complexities of a legislator's proposal. But, in many instances, "shell" bills are complex, and the sponsor or the interest requesting the legislation hopes to avoid a time consuming markup and potentially fatal logjam in committee. In presenting the bill, a sponsor promises "to work with the committee," but a conference committee[63] usually determines substantive details. "Shell" bills have the effect of enhancing the power of party leaders at the expense of committee chairs. Although concerns about potential committee logjams may be real, "shell" bills can be manipulated by the sponsors, lobbyists, and others who wait until closed-door conference committees to make the substantive decisions.

Reliance on conference committees is far more common in Oklahoma than in other states and also tends to undermine the committees' policy role. In the 1995 legislative session, 346 bills were assigned to conference committees. Of that number, sixty bills, the majority of which are appropriations bills, were assigned to the General Conference Committee on Appropriations (GCCA). The GCCA in 1995 included sixty House members and every member of the Senate. The conference committees are technically limited to resolving differences between House and Senate versions, but in practice they are free to consider any issue that would be broadly germane to the bill's subject matter. Typically, the bill sponsor and two others, not necessarily from the appropriate committee, serve on the conference. In one hearing, a House chair openly complained about this practice and reported he had asked the leadership to make it a policy to appoint a committee representative to conference deliberations.

A great deal of substantive legislation also gets referred to the two appropriations committees rather than to standing committees. In part this is the result of the later deadlines to which the Appropriations and Budget Committees are subject. In the Forty-fourth Legislature (1993–1994), the House Appropriations and Budget Committee was referred 462 bills and joint resolutions, more than fourteen House committees combined and two and a half times more than the next busiest committee.[64] As the committees most closely aligned with the leadership, the appropriations committees provide a venue for centralizing control over the policy process.

Time constraints, shell bills, the conference committee process, and the centrality of the appropriations committees tend to reinforce the central role of the leadership in the Oklahoma Legislature. To the extent that a committee chair is part of the "inner circle," his or her influence may be great or relatively modest. Under House Speaker Glen Johnson, the leadership team was more diffuse and a collective decision-making process prevailed. But inclusion on the House leadership team remains a key determinant of a committee chair's power. Those women chairs who have exercised influence in the past have usually done so by qualifying as "team players." Though the smaller Senate operates with a high degree of collegiality, the leadership is more tightly centralized with the president pro tem and his two or three closest lieutenants. Members expect the leadership to set the direction or to take strong positions. Senate chairs have their particular domain of power, but that influence is enhanced by a close relationship with the pro tem.

In sum, the practices and procedural changes of the late 1980s have created a committee system relatively weak in terms of deliberative policymaking. The formal procedures frustrate both public and legislative participation beyond a small circle of legislators on any given bill. These processes prevent more integrative norms of committee leadership from developing.

## Tokenism in Oklahoma

The number and experiences of female legislators in Oklahoma conform with what Kanter calls "tokenism." Three conditions of tokenism have an impact on behavior within an organization: (1) tokens' higher visibility and associated pressures on their performance, (2) the tendency to exaggerate differences between tokens and the dominant group, and (3) the consequent efforts at assimilation by taking on stereotypical gender roles.[65] The examples, which

Kanter uses from the corporate world to elaborate on these conditions, might have been drawn as easily from the committee hearings and personal experiences of Oklahoma committee chairs.

Visibility imposes an extraordinary responsibility to perform faultlessly and introduces symbolic expectations that the token woman represents the category of all women. State Senator Bernice Shedrick's recollections of her first term in 1981 as the lone female senator reflect this burden of public symbol. She told a reporter:

> I felt a challenge because I knew I was quite visible. If I made a mistake, there was no hiding behind any other female. I was challenged to do my very best and to make certain I studied the issues very carefully, read every bill and tried to be as well-informed as I possibly could.[66]

Not only does the token experience accrue to women, but it is experienced by any person whose status is unique within a particular institution. When asked about the different experiences that men and women bring to their roles as legislative committee chairs, Senator Kelly Haney, the Senate Appropriations Committee chair and a Native American, gave this answer:

> We never really know if we experience the same things. . . . I don't know [about gender differences]. But as the first and only full-blood Indian in the Legislature, I've thought about it a lot . . . it's almost like you have something to prove. If I do a bad job, it doesn't only affect me; it reflects on my people.[67]

These pressures are not only self-imposed but also generated by others. After expressing frustration about the performance of a newly elected lawmaker, a veteran female staff member added this comment: "When there are so few women, you really want them to be good."[68]

These comments reflect the "double-edged sword of publicity."[69] By being visible, the token may reap notoriety whereas most dominants escape critical judgment. Because of their visibility, female Oklahoma legislators are often the first to be mentioned in interviews. The woman who violates the legislative norm of collegiality is variously described as a "loose cannon," "not a team player," and "flaky and unpredictable." The female who sponsors a wide variety of bills and speaks often on the floor violates the norm of specialization and is described as a "loudmouth" and "know-it-all." A promising and capable new chairwoman attracts more than her share of heavy assignments and then is judged harshly if she "can't handle it." Although men might be similarly described, they avoid the glare of the limelight that comes with token visibility.

In response to visibility, Kanter argues that tokens have three alternatives. They can carefully construct a self-conscious public persona that minimizes organizational and peer concerns, can accept public notoriety and turn it to advantage, or can seek social invisibility.[70]

The first alternative encourages tokens to "work twice as hard to prove their competence."[71] Recognized expertise is the goal articulated by Oklahoma women chairs:

"I have tried to establish my reputation as being very knowledgeable. I sometimes have to give members the nod, and I need to know the issues. I read
more than most members. I find myself in the staff mode, reading, studying, developing my knowledge and expertise as opposed to being a member
who is dependent upon staff."[72]

Similarly, another woman chair focused on the need to present her knowledge in an unthreatening way:

"I believe I have earned the respect of the members in [my subject area] . . .
by doing my homework. I've learned to temper my own ideas and opinions
and to be more open to the ideas of others. Sometimes if you take a step
back, you can work toward a reasonable, realistic, well-researched solution.
I've also learned that I can have influence by setting an example. If they
[the men] do not feel threatened, they are more amenable. . . . That's an
especially difficult hurdle for a woman. You don't want to be thought of as
a know-it-all."[73]

As the last comment suggests, the token who pursues the "superwoman"
strategy also faces certain risks. On the one hand, expertise and hard work can
be parlayed into real power and influence, but powerful women also may be
resisted and risk being labeled as overly aggressive. That is the lesson of Cleta
Deatherage's experience, described earlier. Other Oklahoma women lawmakers have earned positions of power or exercised considerable policy influence
by dint of sheer effort and hard work. For example, the landmark education
reform legislation, H.B. 1017, in 1989 proved the mettle of three women: State
Superintendent Sandy Garrett, House Education Chair Carolyn Thompson,
and Senate Education Chair Bernice Shedrick. Through persistence and expertise but not without personal criticism, the three carved out a previously
nonexistent role for women in the all-male world that dominated the appro-
priation of education funding.[74]

The second strategy of accepting and playing off one's notoriety as a token
is also evident in Oklahoma. In an article entitled "Those Wondrous Women,"
Frosty Troy, editor of The *Oklahoma Observer* and a self-styled liberal/populist
alternative to The *Daily Oklahoman*, described one woman chair as "the Sooner
Ralph Nader" indicating both her notoriety and her success in generating media
attention: "Rep. Peltier is a lightning rod for male criticism, probably because
her passion for frugality and fairness are a reproach to the go-along-to-get-
along crowd."[75]

Again, the strategy comes with costs. Notoriety can marginalize the token
as undependable or quirky. The "Sooner Ralph Nader" did not earn an appointment to chair a committee until 1995 even though she was one of the
most senior woman in the legislature.

The second condition Kanter emphasizes is the exaggeration of differences between the dominants and the tokens. Kanter identifies exaggerated
"displays of aggression and potency: instances of sexual innuendos, aggressive
sexual teasing and prowess-oriented 'war stories'" and sports laurels.[76] Such

displays subconsciously underscore the social camaraderie of men and the exclusion of women. Again, women committee chairs in Oklahoma encounter such experiences. On being appointed to chair her committee in 1995 and forewarned of its tough issues, one woman was told by her presiding officer that "this is the committee where you have to have really big balls."[77]

In committee meetings, the exaggeration of difference takes several forms. Chairman O, who heads an all-male business-oriented committee, peppers his opening statement with a litany of sports metaphors that bespeak a coach's locker-room pep talk.[78] Chairman P dutifully addresses the male witnesses as "Dr." and then calls on a woman of comparable administrative status by her first name.[79] In another committee in which a bill on prostitution is being considered, the men joke, exchange knowing looks, and watch for a reaction from the female chair when one of their colleagues comments: "I don't think anybody at this table is in favor of prostitution."[80] Finally, there are literally war stories drawn from an era when women did not serve in combat or near-combat duty.[81] In every instance, as Kanter notes, the token "functions as audience for dominant cultural expressions."[82]

Female committee chairs generally choose to ignore such comments or provide only tacit acknowledgement. As one chair commented, "I don't feel picked on or put down, but we still have some members with red rings around the collar."[83] Another women added, "Sometimes you just have to let the sexist remarks roll off you."[84] This may or may not be possible depending on the chair's relationship with the committee. One chairwoman described her method of coping with the social dynamic on her committee:

> "Most of my personal legislative agenda—children's issues, minority business concerns—doesn't come through the committee so I don't have anything I want from them. My goals tend to focus on meeting deadlines and getting the work done. Maybe I'm oblivious. . . . They [male colleagues] will gig me a lot, calling me 'queen bee.' I am very formal, a hard charger, but you have to be with that crowd . . . it's a survival mechanism."[85]

Either way, the result is, according to Kanter, "boundary heightening," the increased contrast of differences and a separation between tokens and dominants.[86] It does not matter that such social behavior is practiced by a limited segment of the dominant group. What is critical is the social distance perceived by the token.

The final condition of tokenism is assimilation, the process of taking on stereotypical characteristics that fit preexisting generalizations about the token group. In effect, stereotypes define comfortable but very limited roles that allow the tokens and the dominants to fall back on familiar expectations and modes of action. Assimilation minimizes the discomfort of differences.

Assimilation is clearly a condition in the Oklahoma Legislature. In interviews and published reports, the female committee chairs frequently adopt gender archetypes to self-describe their leadership styles. For example, one member adopts a "grandmotherly" role of warmth, geniality, a touch of absent-

mindedness, and a disarming approach in dealing with other members.[87] Another described her initial legislative style as the "bratty kid sister" (better than
"playing the dumb blond") who asks too many questions and tends to push
issues people do not want to hear.[88] A third woman found success by being
what Kanter calls the "Iron Maiden"[89]—a style emphasizing dominance over
issues, an aggressive presentation of her position, and a tough approach to
engaging other members on issues.[90] Acting the role of "flirt" also can be used
to advantage:

> "I have been pinched more at the Capitol than anywhere else. . . . I judged
> Representative Q very critically for putting up with the sexism. I didn't like
> seeing it with her. But I have learned not to put up a fuss and to go along
> with the kidding. I've even used it on occasion to sidle up to one of the guys
> to ask him if he's going to vote for my bill. I don't get offended when they
> ask what I'll do for them in return."[91]

Alternatively, one chairwoman told a reporter that women legislators find
it helpful to "play the wife"—"You make them think it's their idea" to win
support on an issue.[92] A senior staff person also recalled two former committee chairwomen "playing the feminine card." One, who was an acknowledged
and unabashed feminist, invited committee members to dinner and assumed
the role of "Miss Hostess," using the wife-homemaker archetype to put the
members at ease. The other woman was effective at building alliances with
other members by deliberately cultivating friendships with their wives.[93]

The combined effect of token visibility, exaggerated differences, and assimilation is to distort behavior and thus make it difficult to assess organizational behavior and in this case leadership style.[94] The ambiguities of inter-
preting the behavior of a token are evident in the following comment from a
woman whose dominant style was described by others as "more male than the
males":

> (*Laughs*) "That's probably true. I think that refers to the fact that I have
> courage of steel and I will speak very directly and honestly about an issue
> even when others will not. . . . Often times I have been mistaken for being
> mean, but I'm really being thorough."[95]

The same lawmaker added that her experiences as a teacher and a parent taught
her how to use questions as a method of instruction; that same strategy, however, was described as prosecutorial by her colleagues. For the individual
token, behavioral style is inherently ambiguous because of ambivalence about
one's role, repression of self or conformance to a constructed public persona,
and the stress of life in the spotlight. Even when presenting one's "true self,"
others can easily misconstrue behavior.

Given the conditions of tokenism, not surprisingly, women express some
role frustration. One chairwoman, when asked to select an analogy that is
descriptive of her committee leadership, compared herself to a babysitter—a
person with parental responsibilities but lacking authority to effect the course

of events—or more like a "custodian than a leader."[96] Another woman commented:

> "I want the committee to feel supported by me. I think that's what they would define as good leadership. In the past I think I've been seen as loud-mouthed, an upstart, even adversarial. It's important that they see me philosophically as someone who's not a lone voice."[97]

Concerns about establishing authority and developing effective working relationships with their colleagues, therefore, are typical frustrations of the token experience.

## Aggregative Influences on Committee Leadership

Women's experiences are shaped not only by the fact of tokenism but also by a system operating with aggregative norms of committee leadership. Clearly, through the roots of its political culture and the more recent practices of legislative politics, the Oklahoma Legislature has adopted the logic of consequentiality—the reciprocity of the pork barrel.[98] In addition, the procedures and practices of the Oklahoma Legislature tend to limit opportunities for policy collaboration and participative decision making. Competition among the members is encouraged. The press of time increases the importance of procedural control. In short, the environment seems friendlier to aggregative rather than integrative styles of committee leadership.

Almost without exception, procedural control is the primary concern of Oklahoma committee chairs. When asked to articulate goals for the committee, most begin with the concern of being able to process the bills in the time allowed. As head of one of the busiest committees, Chairman M emphasizes: "My goal is to hit all the deadlines."[99] Similarly, another says, "I would like to have all the major bills heard and none held in abeyance. I hope not to be stalemated."[100] That can be no small task when time is precious and bills are numerous. In those circumstances, Chairman N recesses rather than adjourns his committee from meeting to meeting so that he always has an official quorum to take action.[101] He warns the new members:

> "Don't hang out somewhere thinking you don't need to be here. I don't like to waste time, at least not in my committee. I don't mind if other committees waste time, but I can't afford to."[102]

Several of the committee chairs illustrated their concern over procedural control by mentally calculating the number of minutes to be allocated for each bill.

Oklahoma chairs have autonomy to decide what bills will be heard. With the busiest committees, which are also usually the most influential, gatekeeping involves considerable power. According to one committee chair, who identified Harry Truman as "one of my heroes":

"Not everyone is going to agree with my cuts, but that's my job and I'm comfortable with it. . . . When you are the one in charge, you take charge and do what you think needs to be done. If people don't like that, they can put someone else in charge."[103]

Agenda control is not exercised capriciously, but the decision rules tend to be fairly vague—"I'm trying to weed out the weak legislation," or "at the head of the list, I try to get the ones that are legally sound, are timely, and have not been debated before."

Fairness is another critical standard, as these comments illustrate:

"I try to be open-minded to the legislation that is proposed. That doesn't mean I'm for everything, and I try to give everybody the opportunity to scrutinize a bill within certain time limits, but you've got to have limits. Once when I was the vice chairman, we heard 49 bills in four hours. That's one bill every six minutes. I don't know that that was a good way of conduct-ing business. I'm not a strong-arm chairman . . . but I hope I maintain con-trol without being controlling."[104]

Veteran staff and other nonlegislators use the terms "command" and "control" to describe one style of committee leadership, a style associated with a number of former or still active military personnel serving as members.

Even the physical environment in which Oklahoma committees operate underscores the hierarchical or closed aspects of an aggregative style of leader-ship. The typical Oklahoma committee room is dominated by a huge table at which only legislators and staff sit. Chairs for lobbyists and the public are available around the perimeter, but by sheer proportions the centrality of the committee is emphasized and others are mere observers. The House Educa-tion and Appropriations and Budget committees, which are traditionally the most publicly scrutinized committees, meet in a room dominated by a raised dais and three large tables reserved for the members.

In addition, Oklahoma committees do not usually have public hearings; instead, meetings are essentially work sessions on bills involving only the mem-bers. In contrast with Colorado, where average citizens and a host of interest groups frequently engage in committee discussions, Oklahoma committee hearings convey little sense of collective purpose and open deliberation. Col-laboration and consultation, if they go on at all, take place in other venues that are generally inaccessible except to those who are party to the brokering. Oklahoma's committee sessions are more like those in Ohio, in the sense that they communicate a stark separation between the technical functions of law-making, which require aggregative skills, and the affective goal of defining values and shared purpose, which would benefit from integrative skills.

In contrast with the concern for procedure, few of the committee chairs emphasized policy goals as integral to their committee leadership responsibili-ties. Several articulated amorphous and global policy goals (e.g., "improving the business climate" or "restoring confidence in public education"), and when pressed for details, chairs identify specific bills expected to generate controversy.[105] By and large, however, policy leadership is viewed as something rather distinct from a chair's committee responsibilities, which focus instead on scheduling and processing. To be sure, committee chairs often are appointed for their expertise in the subject or close ties with important interest groups, and therefore they sponsor the major bills that come before their committee. But because of shell bills, a heavy reliance on conference committees, and the increased involvement of the appropriations committees in substantive policy, the opportunities for policy leadership have been shifted from the standing committees to more restricted venues. One chair commented that he saw the committee hearings primarily as a preview of potential floor debate that could help a sponsor develop amendments.[106]

In formal meetings, committees deal with policy content in a fairly cursory manner. Sponsors briefly summarize their proposals, and a few general factual questions are posed. Committee substitutes are introduced with little comment and reflect changes agreed on between a sponsor and interested parties. Of fourteen committee meetings observed, only three provided members with multiple perspectives or detailed interpretive testimony and engaged members in open discussion of policy trade-offs and possible alternatives. Two of the three meetings were chaired by female senators.

Quite at odds with the procedural emphasis articulated by most of the chairs, one of the two chairwomen outlined an extensive personal policy agenda for her committee. In the committee meeting, she actively invited other members to state their policy positions and asked them for substantive input. In committee, the second woman not only dominated the procedures but also acted as the source of most of the policy questioning, interpretation, input, and clarification. Her vision of committee leadership was to exercise not only procedural but also substantive control—"That's the only way you get good policy."[107] The third meeting, chaired by a man, was somewhat unique because it was not concerned with specific legislation but rather was a select study committee. Because of session time constraints in Oklahoma, interim task forces and select committees are increasingly a vehicle for policy deliberations.

The factors discouraging or frustrating policy leadership also reinforce competition rather than collaboration. At least half the committee chairs saw conflict resolution as simply a matter of votes taken (up or down) rather than differences to be mediated or brought together in a collaborative way. When asked how they resolve conflicts or disagreements, these chairs said in effect: "Count noses and take a vote."[108]

A second manifestation of a competitive norm is the tendency for members to work alone as sponsors of bills. As a time management strategy, committee chairs sometimes threaten not to hear legislation unless sponsors get together to combine similar bills. The strategy is not always successful, however. Sponsors can always appeal to the leadership for a referral to a friendlier committee chair. Because the principal sponsor is generally appointed to chair a conference committee if one is necessary,[109] collaboration may result in losing one's place in the critical negotiations. Cosponsors typically sign onto a bill later in the process after it has cleared committee.

Further, separate bills on the same or closely related topics often appear in one or more committees simultaneously. For example, in the 1995 legislature, eighteen bills were introduced on the topic of child-support enforcement. These went to six different House committees (Human Services; Judiciary; Children, Youth and Family Services; Public Safety; Commerce, Industry and Labor; and Appropriations and Budget) and two Senate committees (Judiciary and Human Resources). Three of the bills ultimately passed.

Competing bills may reflect a variety of factors: an incrementalism favoring small changes in policy, a lack of consensus around a given issue, the natural percolation of ideas in the policy process, or fundamental philosophical differences. As a practical matter, however, sponsors have few incentives to collaborate, and the rewards of being able to claim credit for an incremental legislative change may be more enticing than cosponsorship of a more sweeping bill.[110] If an issue rises to a critical point or leadership deems the topic a priority, a special interim task force may be appointed to serve as the forum for developing a comprehensive policy.[111]

In sum, the Oklahoma committee process tends to value aggregative rather than integrative skills. Because of the shortened legislative session, public participation and even broad-based legislative participation are viewed as hazards that could delay a bill's progress. The committee chair's greatest leadership role is as gatekeeper, a role requiring strict control over the agenda and what bills will be heard. The use of shell bills, the fragmented pattern of bill referrals, and reliance on conference committees have transformed the policy process into one that rewards individualism, encourages competition, and leaves little room for collaboration and consensus building.

## Women and Integrative Leadership

Because of the effects of tokenism and the norms of the Oklahoma legislature, it should come as no surprise that differences between male and female committee leaders are relatively few. Clearly, Oklahoma women lack Colorado's advantages of numbers, long-term involvement, and an environment more amenable to integrative leadership. Oklahoma women also lack the power and influence of Ohio's Speaker Jo Ann Davidson. But is there evidence that Oklahoma women inch toward the integrative mode? Insofar as they emphasize listening and collaboration and see education as the purpose of leadership, the answer is "yes."

Several staff and lobbyists, for instance, emphasize listening as a skill Oklahoma chairwomen bring to their leadership roles. As one staffer noted:

> "The women are listeners. That is sometimes viewed as a weakness around here, but from what I've observed the women listen more. Senator [. . . .] will make sure that everyone who has something to say has an opportunity."[112]

Another senior staffer commented, "Senator [. . . .] wants to hear every side of an issue. She meets and meets and meets."[113]

All the female committee chairs identified the importance of listening as a leadership skill. In contrast, only one man emphasized listening skills. As a means of managing conflict, one chairwoman noted, "The technique I use is to let people be heard."[114] Another woman noted that her particular committee dealt with appropriations and thus factual data drove most discussions, nonetheless she commented: "I like folk to talk and say what they believe to be so. . . . Then I try to look for common ground, build from there, and to ask what are the common denominators."[115]

Contrast those methods of resolving conflict with the comments of a senior House chairman: "Conflicts are not going to be resolved. The chairman just has to decide whether to hear the bill and how to vote in case of a tie."[116]

Another integrative quality attributed to the women chairs involved their view of leadership as educating their colleagues. In part, this view may reflect the backgrounds of women serving in the Oklahoma Legislature.[117] A significant proportion of past and current women lawmakers were teachers. Several chairwomen employed classroom terminology to describe their committee experiences. One compared her committee style to that of a college instructor leading a graduate seminar.[118] Another explained that she asks a lot of questions in committee because "I teach by asking questions. Even with my grandchild that's the method I use. By my questions I try to cause people to think."[119]

Seeing education as an aspect of leadership may be primarily a function of background and socialization, but it also carries a different emphasis. Whereas many of Oklahoma's male legislators honed their leadership skills in a military environment emphasizing command, control, loyalty, and discipline, educators have been instilled with other values including nurturing, guiding discovery, and encouraging self-expression. Summing up the difference, one woman said, "I believe educators should be facilitators, not dictators."[120]

## Conclusion

The Oklahoma Legislature is not the friendliest environment for women as committee leaders. It has proven a hard club for women to join, and when they acquire power, they are treated as "intruders."[121] Their status as tokens makes them lightning rods for attention and defines them with stereotypes.

Furthermore, the Oklahoma Legislature's procedures are at odds with the "female" styles of consensus building, collaboration, and noncompetitive decision making. The demands of being a committee chair place a premium on parliamentary control, autonomous decision making, and an almost mechanistic approach to scheduling and workload management. The physical setting similarly reflects an environment in which aggregative leadership is more at home. Quieter, more deliberative forms of leadership take time, a commodity in short supply in the Oklahoma Legislature.

The policy environment for all members is limited by a lack of time, a lack of public resources for new or expanded programs, and a citizen distrust of governmental interventions and grand plans. What remains are narrow, particularistic, and incremental opportunities for policy changes that individual members can pursue and then take credit for when seeking reelection.

For all leaders, adaptation to organizational processes and culture can be a challenge, but that may be doubly so for women in the Oklahoma Legislature. A substantial impact on institutional behavior and the practice of committee leadership will have to await both the advent of more women in the Legislature and a fundamental change in state politics and institutional processes.

# 7

## Ohio: Gender Power in a Time of Leadership Transition

On February 22, 1995, Senator Merle Kearns was presiding over one of her first meetings as chair of the Human Services and Aging Committee. A standing-room-only crowd was on hand to hear a bill dealing with child custody and parental responsibilities in cases of divorce. As Senator Grace Drake began a line of questioning with the sponsor, she abruptly stopped to ask Senator Kearns what title she preferred in her new role. "Do you want to be called 'Madame Chairwoman,' 'Madame Chairman' or what?" Senator Drake, who up until then had been the only woman chairing a Senate committee, added: "Personally, I have always preferred 'Madame Chairman.'" Senator Kearns responded, "Whatever works." An almost identical question was posed by a male lawmaker a day earlier to Representative Cheryl Winkler, the new chair of the House Family Services Committee. Her preferred title is "Madame Chairperson."[1]

The two events are not merely incidents of self-conscious "political correctness." They reflect the transitional stage at which female committee chairs in Ohio find themselves. Unlike the few women chairs in Oklahoma, who are largely defined *by* their token status, institutional practices, and political culture, Ohio women are defining roles for themselves during a period of institutional change and leadership transition. Because Ohio women are still relatively few in number and new to leadership positions, however, their long-term imprint on leadership practices seems less certain than that of women chairs in other states. But their impact has thus far been considerable because of real power rather than numbers.

The story of leadership in Ohio in 1995 is one of transition. As the Ohio General Assembly's 120th session came to a close in late December 1994, the state's major newspapers announced the end of an era and heralded the coming of "the new guard."[2] Republicans had taken the majority in the House of Representatives for the first time in twenty-two years, and with legislative control, they dominated both the legislative and executive branches for the first time since the 1960s. The Speaker's gavel was soon to pass from "the definitive House speaker," Democrat Vernal G. Riffe, to the first woman speaker in state history, Republican Jo Ann Davidson.[3] That transfer would mark a dramatic change in leadership styles from the firm-handed (some say dictatorial) Riffe to the open and explicitly consensual style of Davidson. Speaker Davidson held center stage, but in both houses and on both sides of the aisle, the thirty-one women legislators were ready to make their presence felt. Complicating the situation was a "restlessness" felt among all legislators uncertain about their future because of term limits, according to then-Senate President Stanley Aronoff.[4]

The full bloom and implications of the changes in Ohio legislative politics are yet to unfold, but the key elements are these:

- Women have moved beyond token status and are demonstrating a more integrative style of leadership. More important, Speaker Davidson's prominent example has the potential to transform legislative leadership norms, thus implicating the significance of power, more than numbers, to organizational change. As the intrusiveness hypothesis suggests, however, her power has not gone unchallenged.
- Aspects of integrative and aggregative styles of leadership coexist in Ohio's professional legislature. The luxury of time and staff resources gives chairs an opportunity to exert formative and collaborative policy leadership, but formalized procedures, hierarchy, and a chair's autonomy tend to discourage inclusive or participatory decision making.
- Ohio's history and politics do not suggest a clear preference for one style of leadership or another. Regions compete for public resources and benefits in a manner consistent with aggregative politics, but decentralized power also necessitates moderation and cooperation that warrants more integrative approaches.
- Followership is on the wane due to declining party cohesion and legislative term limits. Therefore, the seeds of integrative leadership may not germinate even though Ohio women have the power and potential to nurture its development.

This chapter begins with the question of women's roles in Ohio politics and then turns to political and institutional factors that have pushed legislative leaders toward integrative or aggregative styles.[5] The chapter closes with a look to the future.

## Women in Ohio Politics

The first women were elected to the Ohio General Assembly in 1922, two years after the Nineteenth Amendment to the U.S. Constitution was ratified. Six women served in the Eighty-fifth General Assembly (1923–1924), all Republicans, taking four seats in the House and two in the Senate. For the next sixty years the number of women serving in the General Assembly never exceeded ten and fell at one point (1939–1940) to only two.[6]

In the Eighty-fifth General Assembly, Nettie Loughead and Maude Waitt chaired committees dealing with Soldiers' and Sailors' Orphans' Homes, Benevolent Institutions and Libraries. Their leadership of committees was less remarkable than it seems. In earlier legislatures, the number of committees was much greater and virtually all majority lawmakers earned committee assignments.[7]

From 1985 to 1993, the number of women in the legislature increased steadily with each election cycle to a high of thirty-one (23.5 percent) of the ninety-nine representatives and thirty-three senators. The 1994 election saw no increase, and in 1996, the number of women lawmakers declined to twenty-nine (22). The changing numbers have a partisan subtext. For most of the 1980s, Democrat women outnumbered Republican women almost two to one. In 1992, with the Republicans' campaign effort led by Jo Ann Davidson, GOP women doubled in number from seven to fourteen. In 1994, Republican women again increased their number while the Democrat women lost seats for an overall GOP edge of eighteen to thirteen.[8] The number of Democratic women continued to drop with the 1996 elections and now totals only ten. While Democrat women were frustrated in their efforts to win party support in 1994 statewide races, the Republicans made history by electing Ohio's first statewide female officeholder—in fact, two: Attorney General Betty Montgomery and Lieutenant Governor Nancy P. Hollister.

Although women are more visible in the General Assembly, their committee assignments are not much different from those of their predecessors of the 1920s. Female committee chairs in Ohio still tend to be found predominantly heading human services, family, and health committees, which also are composed in substantial proportion by other women. In fact, one chairwoman complained that the membership of her committee—almost exclusively female and black—was "very patronizing."[9]

The increase in numbers has transformed women's presence in the General Assembly in a fashion that resembles Kanter's shift away from "token" status to a "tilted" subgroup.[10] In days past, for example, one veteran House member described feeling personally isolated during her first term and often left behind when social events took place. "I was always real busy and the men were always very nice. But they usually hung out together as a group. . . . I often ate supper alone."[11] Another woman felt immediately accepted after she was appointed to her late husband's legislative seat but acknowledged that she was already comfortable in legislative social circles because she had attended sessions with her husband.

One woman reported the classic form of gender stereotyping that takes place in token situations: A longtime woman legislator in the early 1980s was dubbed the "den mother" by her male colleagues, who used the nickname to characterize (and dismiss) her "take-charge and march" style.[12] Kanter predicts that an increase in the proportion of women begins to drive out stereotypes such as these. When tokens become more numerous, they are treated less as symbols of the category and are freer to be individuals.

On an organizational level, the women in the Ohio legislature show the impact of moving from token to tilted group proportions and gaining gender power. Women's share of the legislative membership passed Kanter's 15 percent mark in 1989 in the House and 1993 in the Senate. Evidence of women legislators working collectively on issues became more evident in the 1980s, and family issues in particular were the common cause.[13] By 1989, a bipartisan group of six women sat on the powerful House Finance Committee and, once there, achieved a separate line item for day care, increased funding for housing for the homeless, and lobbied for more money for family services. Veteran Democratic Senator Linda Furney has continued to provide leadership on these issues through the Women's and Children's Budget Coalition.[14] Leadership on welfare reform legislation and health care issues in 1995 came almost exclusively from women legislators on both sides of the aisle. In 1995, the women added to their efforts at coalition building and collective action by taking aim at acquiring greater political power.

Within the Democratic Party, the push for greater power and visibility resulted from frustration among female officeholders. Two women running in the 1994 Democratic primaries for the U.S. Senate and governorship failed to garner enthusiasm or support from the party hierarchy, and one party official admitted that top party leaders have traditionally viewed women candidates as long shots.[15]

As a result, in March 1995, women organized the first statewide conference of Women Elected Democrat Officials of Ohio (WEDO). At the conference, they criticized the party's male leadership as unresponsive and set out to develop an alternative network for women in the face of a resistant party hierarchy. One purpose of WEDO is to develop a "farm team" of female candidates to run for the statehouse, according to Jane Campbell, formerly assistant Democratic floor leader in the House, a WEDO founder, and now local government officeholder. Campbell's own failed bid for the gubernatorial nomination was blamed on the party's "plain old-fashioned" male leadership.[16]

In the Republican Party caucus in the Senate, women are also flexing their collective organizational muscle. In an unprecedented, albeit informal, caucus prior to the 1995 session, female GOP senators met to discuss the possibility of supporting female candidates for the four Senate leadership posts and increasing their political clout. Although representing one-fourth of the GOP caucus, the women held none of the four top leadership jobs and chaired only one of the Senate's thirteen standing committees. None of the women who ultimately ran for leadership was successful, but a new standing committee was created and Senator Kearns became the second female Senate chair. Senator Drake, the most senior woman in the majority caucus, also became the first GOP woman named to serve on the Finance Committee and on the powerful Controlling Board that oversees the approval of state contracts and expenditures. In the process, Senator Aronoff offered to create a fifth leadership position, but the women rejected the post because it might become labeled the "women's slot." Whether as a direct consequence of this organizing or of other factors, in 1997, when a vacancy occurred in the Senate leadership lineup, Senator Nancy Chiles Dix won the slot of majority whip and Senator Karen Gillmor became the third woman committee chair.

Whether the collective strategy on the part of the female senators will continue as a formal organization is unclear. Some of the women involved professed qualms about meeting as a separate caucus and expressed the belief that GOP women were not inclined by ideological temperament to create a women's caucus. Moreover, one senior Republican senator suggested that the impetus for the leadership challenge was not a feminist or women's agenda but rather the pressures of term limits and the ambition of individuals who hope to make their mark before time runs out. "What surprised me was the competition among the women," he added. "They didn't act like a caucus making demands for the group. To the contrary, their attitude [as individuals] was: 'If it's not me [who gets a leadership post], I don't care.'"[17]

The increase in the number of women legislators has taken years and has stalled somewhat in recent legislative elections. Nevertheless, in 1994, women in Ohio took some of the state's most powerful political offices—speaker, attorney general, lieutenant governor, and key committee chairs. The transition from token status seems to be more a result of visibility and power than of numbers alone. Women are organizing coalitions and alliances to improve their political power. The increasingly favorable power base of Ohio Republican women seems to confirm Kanter's predictions about the advantages of numbers. The lack of enthusiasm for women candidates in the Democratic Party, however, may also testify to Yoder's thesis of instrusiveness, the resistance of the dominant powers that be to new and different actors.

## The Context of Legislative Leadership

Rooted in an individualistic political culture, Ohio has a history of distributive or aggregative politics and a preference for conservative but centrist policies. As one of the handful of full-time, well-staffed and professionalized state legislatures, Ohio's General Assembly, however, values the kind of policy leadership associated with integrative leadership.

### Political Culture and Party Politics

Buckeye State politics represents anomalies and paradoxes that are fertile territory to a classically distributive or bargaining style of leadership. An industrialized state, Ohio's economic base, however, remains in agriculture. Although largely urban, Ohio does not have a single, dominant metropolitan area, as for example, does Michigan with Detroit or Illinois with Chicago. City rivals (e.g., Republican Cincinnati and Columbus vs. Democratic strongholds in Cleveland, Toledo, and Akron) often compete and cancel each other. As a result, for example, the state's urban redevelopment efforts languished from the mid-1940s through the mid-1970s because the "Cornstalk Brigade" (conservative, rural Republicans) dominated state and local government while city representatives competed with one another rather than cooperated.[18] Though populated by many union members, Catholics, and European ethnics, the state has not been unfriendly to the Republican Party, nor has it embraced a liberal Democratic agenda.

These partisan and economic paradoxes are the product of Ohio's political history and demographics[19] but continue to play a moderating and conservative influence on public policy. Political scientist Alexander Lamis argues that the state's anomalies "temper ideological extremes, and the resulting compromises favor conservative postures."[20]

The Ohio GOP grew from roots in Civil War Republicanism and turn-of-the-century Progressivism and did not wither during the New Deal era. The party flourished in rural areas among Anglo-Saxon Protestants, small-town businessmen, and farmers. The economies of Columbus (mostly white-collar government, education, and commercial workers) and Cincinnati (a manufacturing center for household necessities, processed food, and clothing) were less susceptible to the vagaries of the Great Depression and, therefore, not as enamored of New Deal policies. Moreover, the party drew a substantial population of ethnic Germans who objected to the New Deal farm and spending policies, the war efforts, and Catholic candidates associated with the Democratic Party.[21]

The Ohio GOP has a tradition of organizational strength dating from the turn-of-the-century machines of Mark Hanna in the north and George "Boss" Cox in the south. Under Ray Bliss, the state party chairman from 1949 to 1965, the party flourished in spite of its smaller voter base. The legislature provides a measure of Bliss's success: Between 1941 and 1970, the Republican Party's control of the Ohio General Assembly was interrupted only twice.[22]

Ohio Democrats in contrast have a history of division, in part because the pattern of urban development fragmented Ohio's urban working class among competing regions and economic interests. Because of the absence of a single dominant large city, relatively weak labor unions, and an isolated working class, the New Deal Democratic realignment that took place in other northern and midwestern states passed by Ohio. The Democrats also suffered from internal urban-rural and ideological divisions.[23]

From the turn of the century to 1945, Ohio's partisan politics have been highly cyclical—the two parties taking four-year stints in the statehouse and the voters turning out the rascals with regularity.[24] The post-World War II era has been described as "issueless" with Ohio voters generally uninterested in state politics.[25] Campaigns were principally contests of personalities in which

Democratic disorganization encountered Bliss's prescription for Republican success: "Keep issues out of campaigns."[26] John Fenton, author of *Midwest Politics*, concluded that Ohioans simply did not see "any visible association" between the problems of everyday life and their votes.[27] While noting that the label of "issueless" might be overstated, scholars Lawrence Baum and Samuel C. Patterson write:

> Division within the Democratic party and the absence of a labor movement with a broad policy agenda limited the Democrats' issue orientation, and the Republican party deliberately avoided issues to help maintain its electoral advantage.[28]

Partisan lines continue to be relatively stable, but there is some evidence of increasing activity by single-issue groups and ideological activists that may force more divisive issues to the fore.[29]

Elazar describes Ohio and its neighbor states as predominantly "individualistic," an orientation that is suspicious of governmental intervention, prefers the individualism of the marketplace, and sees political participation as a means to individual goals rather than a quest for common good.[30] Unlike the "moralistic" states of Michigan, Minnesota, and Wisconsin, where a concern for public policy drives politics, Fenton argues that a desire for jobs and contracts motivates participation in Ohio politics.[31] In recent years, Riffe developed his own version of individualistic politics with a "pay-to-play" system of campaign fund raising. Special-interest lobbyists were expected to give generously to Riffe's campaign committee, which in turn rewarded House members for their loyalty and acquiescence to the speaker's rule. For their role in supporting the Democratic majority, interest groups got favorable treatment.[32]

Individualistic politics spawned a centrist, fiscal conservatism and relatively low funding of public services. Not until 1971, for example, did the state adopt a personal income tax. But, from 1945 to the present, "boom and bust" economic cycles sorely tested the state's low-tax, low-service posture. During periods of relative prosperity, state political leaders balked at increasing funding for public services, and as population growth ceased and its industrial base declined, Ohio faced a series of state financial crises during the down cycles.[33]

The cycles of financial crises and divided party control of the statehouse have forced Ohio's political leaders in recent years to follow a model of cross-party accommodation and pragmatism. The Democrats briefly controlled the governor's seat and both houses of the General Assembly in 1983–1984, but one must go back to Republican Governor James Rhodes's first eight-year stint as governor (1963–1971) to find a chief executive who enjoyed loyal legislative majorities in both houses for an extended period of time. Bipartisan cooperation thus has been necessary to win approval of tax increases and to impose budget slashing. Between 1985 and 1994, the General Assembly's two principal leaders—Democrat Speaker Vern Riffe and Republican Senate President Stanley Aronoff—maintained a cooperative personal relationship built over thirty years of serving together in the legislature and tempered by their institutional and personal ideological pragmatism.[34] Through the 1980s, Ohio politics spawned a conservative temperament, moderated extremism, and encouraged compromise and accommodation.

Ideological fissures, however, are appearing. Based on a 1988 survey, Patterson noted that GOP legislators are "quite homogeneous ideologically" in contrast with the more divided Democrats.[35] But the GOP now has more social conservatives who "seem bent on needling their more moderate leaders—the governor, House Speaker Jo Ann Davidson of Reynoldsburg and Senate President Stanley J. Aronoff of Cincinnati."[36] Governor George Voinovich's 72 percent share of the 1994 vote led a GOP sweep of all the top statewide offices and control of the General Assembly, but half of the fifty-six House Republicans were first- or second-termers and many came with staunchly conservative agendas.[37] One House Democratic leader predicted that Republican division will provide the Democratic minority with their best opportunity to influence public policy.[38]

On the Democratic side, signs of division continue. The party emerged from the 1994 election debacle more divided than ever with much criticism and blame for its poor showing heaped on organized labor. Moreover, the party faces discontent among its female officeholders, who have been unhappy about the party's lack of enthusiasm or support for women candidates. WEDO was created as an alternative party network in the face of resistance from party stalwarts.

## Institutional Factors and the Committee Process

During Speaker Riffe's tenure (1975–1994), the Ohio General Assembly was transformed from "a part-time amateur debating society that generally rubber-stamped administration proposals" into a full partner in state policymaking.[39] Modernization began under the progressive Republican Speaker Charles Kurfess, who preceded Riffe, but Riffe made legislative improvement a priority when he first accepted the gavel.

Over the next two decades, the change was remarkable. Today, the institution has more staff, lawmakers are better paid, the legislature maintains a year-round schedule of committee and floor work, and modern office space and advances in computer technology allow for a professional and businesslike process.[40] In addition, the historic State House has been restored, while Senate members are officed in a beautifully renovated State House Annex. House members and staff are comfortably quartered in a thirty-two-story modern skyscraper that also houses the governor's office and several state agencies. The building is complete with theaters, art galleries, and restaurants. The former speaker presided over construction of the building that now bears his name, the Vernal G. Riffe Center for Government and the Arts.

Today, Ohio is considered among the nine most professional state legislatures.[41] Lawmakers are paid $42,467 but receive no per diem living expenses while in Columbus.[42] Ohio's legislative budget still reflects the state's fiscal conservatism as Ohio lawmakers receive the leanest package of benefits of the nine full-time legislatures; typical perquisites may include salary, per diem, personal staff, and district office allowances. Although Ohio spends less per capita on its legislative branch of state government than any other state, by comparison with more part-time legislatures, the Ohio staff and pay are relatively generous.

Not surprisingly, the modernized Ohio legislature began to attract a "new breed" of legislator for whom politics and legislative service are a vocation rather than an avocation. As for Riffe and Aronoff, legislative careers of more than thirty years became thinkable. In stark contrast with legislators in the 1950s, Patterson notes that in 1988, two-thirds considered themselves full-time legislators, three out of four came from some prior elective or party office, and most aspired to run for another political office if the opportunity arose.[43] As a practical matter, the stability and length of service of the House and Senate's elected leadership gave few members the chance to move up in the legislative ranks, but committee chairs could have a substantial hand in making policy within the limits set by Riffe in the House or by majority caucus in the Senate.

Ohio's committee system grants chairs and ranking minority members additional pay and several powers. Prior to changes in House rules in 1995, chairs in both chambers had the power to decide when, if at all, a bill was taken up. Chairs also control the hearing process that traditionally extends over at least three days to hear separately from the sponsor, proponents, and opponents.[44] Chairs can direct the testimony by seeking out witnesses and orchestrating the proceedings. Moreover, a chair can become the policy leader if he or she chooses to dominate the process of shaping bills and negotiating with interested parties.

In the Ohio General Assembly, committee chairs play a central part in the system of power. In prior years, former Speaker Riffe demanded loyalty first and foremost from his chairs and did not hesitate to remove them if they violated a leadership directive. Stories of those chairs who encountered the Speaker's discipline are legend.[45] But in exchange for loyalty on demand, committee chairs were allowed free rein in running their committees and deciding the fate of most bills. As Riffe commented:

> I told them they could run their own committee and that I wouldn't dictate. Ninety-five percent of the time they ran their own show; they were on their own. But when I made a point, I wanted them to be there when I needed them—no buts, no back-talk. . . .[46]

Riffe reinforced committee work by running a tightly controlled floor process that allowed few amendments and often little debate.

In the smaller and more collegial Senate, the members see decision-making power as far more dispersed.[47] To be sure, a committee chair's power still depends in large part on a successful relationship with the Senate president, but the Senate leader has less absolute control over the fate of a bill and policy positions are developed in the majority caucus. In interviews in 1988, senators were far more likely to accord a variety of players—the governor, the speaker, the Senate president, the caucus, committees—with a significant share of decisional influence than did House members.[48]

But change is coming to the Ohio General Assembly under the aegis of Speaker Davidson and specifically to the old House system of mutually rein-forcing interests of leadership and committee chairs. The new Republican House majority approved legislative rules changes in January 1995 that have the potential to pull at the Speaker's centralized power. Among the most sig-nificant rules changes are provisions that all bills referred to a standing com-mittee shall be scheduled for a minimum of one public hearing (Rule 34)and that "all amendments submitted on the floor of the House . . . shall be con-sidered" (Rule 66).[49] During the Riffe years, minority party amendments were subjected to minimal floor debate and then routinely tabled.[50]

The effect of the changes is to eliminate a chair's power to sit on a bill and to curtail the speaker's power to protect legislation from partisan ambush and embarrassment on the floor. Speaker Davidson also introduced a collegial process of discussion and debate into decisions of the Rules and Reference Committee, which refers bills to committee and sets the floor calendar. Whereas Riffe directed and controlled the Rules Committee through a loyal lieutenant serving as chair, now Speaker Davidson chairs the committee and leads by consensus. Speaker Davidson sees the changes as consistent with her commit-ment to openness and fairness. While conceding that the earlier practice of limiting floor amendments reinforced committee work and may be more effi-cient in a ninety-nine–member House, she argues, "I've had my mind swayed during floor debate."[51]

Even more than the legislative rules changes, the most fundamental change in the General Assembly is the advent of term limits. Under a term limit refer-endum passed in 1992, legislators may serve no more than eight consecutive years, and by the year 2000 many current members will see their legislative service ended. The old system demanded and rewarded patience: Members earned the opportunity to chair committees after several years of loyal work in the trenches. Deference was granted to more senior members and committee chairs while less experienced lawmakers learned the issues and the ropes and waited their turn. Representative Robert Netzley, the General Assembly's most senior member, noted the change in the new members, "They're feisty. . . . These folks aren't intimidated. They know they have to make a difference soon 'cause they'll be gone soon."[52] Other legislators echo the sentiment best sum-marized by a female senator:

> "When I was first elected, you moved up the ladder if you lasted, if you were successful in being reelected. That's all changed. . . . You can't wait. You have eight years. All of the older rules no longer hold."[53]

Legislative careers of thirty or more years, like those of Vern Riffe, Senate President Aronoff, or Representative Netzley, will be eliminated. There is, however, an important gender dimension to truncated legislative careers: Given that Ohio women have tended to run for the legislature at an older age, lengthy seniority has been principally a feature of men's legislative careers, not women's. As one woman legislator quipped, "Guess who runs the show in a seniority-based system?"[54] Theoretically, therefore, a more open system of leadership development may emerge, assuming that other factors such as opportunity, ambition, and talent have no other hidden bias against women in leadership.

## The Practice of Leadership in Ohio

It is tempting to characterize the practices of Ohio leadership by looking no further than the contrast between Vern Riffe and Jo Ann Davidson. The high profile of the speakership naturally attracts immediate attention, and the transition from Riffe's "hardball," top-down and sometimes autocratic rule to Davidson's newly energized legislative democracy is striking.[55] Evidence of gender differences, however, can also be seen among committee chairs. In part, the coexistence of different styles is possible because the political and legislative environments have factors that are supportive of both integrative and aggregative styles.

### A Woman in Power: Jo Ann Davidson

In late April 1995, the extent of the change in Ohio legislative leadership was starkly clear to all who observed the machinations in the state capital. In one dramatic event, which dominated much of the 1995 legislative session, Speaker Davidson's actions defined the differences between her integrative leadership approach and that of former Speaker Riffe. The incident also represented a direct challenge to her power and philosophy of leadership. An intricate parliamentary wrangle to discharge a controversial abortion bill from the House Judiciary and Criminal Justice Committee juxtaposed the contrasting eras.

The bill, which would outlaw an abortion procedure known as dilation and extraction used in late-term abortions in which the mother's life is endangered, drew fifty-eight cosponsors from both sides of the aisle. In an effort to head off a potentially divisive philosophical rift among the majority Republicans, however, the bill was not on the list of legislative priorities endorsed by Governor George V. Voinovich and Republican legislative leaders.[56] Assigned to the Judiciary and Criminal Justice Committee, the bill was the subject of two hearings at which pro-life advocates presented graphic and emotional testimony. Deviating from legislative tradition[57] and declaring further hearings a waste of time, Judiciary Chair Edward Kasputis abruptly cancelled hearings at which medical experts and other opponents of the measure were scheduled to speak.[58] Apparently the bill, as written, lacked sufficient committee votes and thus could only be moved to floor consideration by the discharge strategy.

Kasputis himself provided the required fiftieth signature to the petition to circumvent Judiciary Committee action.

But when Kasputis recessed his committee rather than adjourning, three women (two Republicans and one Democrat) assembled a bipartisan rump group of eight abortion rights supporters on the committee, researched the rules, and quietly mobilized their forces. They convened a special meeting without Kasputis, elected a temporary chair, and voted to postpone the bill indefinitely, thus rendering the discharge effort moot because such petitions apply only to bills a committee has not acted on.[59] In all, five female committee members, two Republicans and three Democrats, spearheaded the committee rebellion, leading one legislator to characterize the fight as "the boys against the girls."[60]

The struggle cast a long shadow over other aspects of the session. The discharge petition coincided with House consideration of Governor Voinovich's budget, on which every Republican vote was essential. With Speaker Pro Tem William Batchelder as a key supporter of the discharge petition, the precarious peace crafted by Speaker Davidson within her ideologically-divided Republican caucus was endangered from the top down.[61] Speaker Davidson was also caught in a personal dilemma: whether to retreat from her consensus leadership style and commitment to openness or to use the power of the speakership on behalf of the pro-choice agenda she supports.[62] Likewise, there were other seemingly no-win political considerations: She could uphold the actions of the bipartisan committee faction and risk rebellion within her restive Republican caucus. Or, alternatively, she could support a key committee chair whose actions violated the procedural openness to which she was publicly committed.

Statehouse observers mused that the divisive drama would never have occurred "under the heavy gavel" of former Speaker Riffe.[63] And Riffe himself, while full of praise for his successor and loathe to criticize her, admits he would have stepped in and immediately stopped the discharge effort at the first rumors of the petition.[64]

Faced with seemingly unreconcilable personal and political choices, Speaker Davidson used her personal leadership skills and intervention to try to find a collaborative solution. Rather than rule on either the discharge petition or the postponing actions of the rump committee, Speaker Davidson spearheaded closed-door negotiations between pro-life and pro-choice legislators in an effort to find middle ground on an issue that defies compromise.[65] The negotiations continued for almost a month, while in floor sessions Speaker Davidson declined to take up the discharge petition from the House calendar. Democrats, lobby groups, and the media were excluded from the closed-door meetings. The ultimate objective was to find a policy compromise that would render the procedural battle moot but not create any winners or losers in the Republican caucus.[66]

In the end, Speaker Davidson's efforts led to a revised bill sent back to the House judiciary committee for action and then on to the House floor where it passed 82–15.[67] Remarkably, the bill contained provisions that both abortion-rights advocates and foes could embrace.[68] The sponsor, Representative Jerome Luebbers, proclaimed Ohio a leader in banning late-term and postviability abortions, and Representative Ann Womer Benjamin, one of the Republican women who led the committee rebellion, stated, "It is not strictly a pro-choice bill. It is not strictly a pro-life bill. It is a realistic compromise which tries to balance the rights of the mother with the rights of the unborn."[69] For Speaker Davidson, the compromise avoided the potential political costs of the discharge petition fight and provided a vehicle for maintaining party unity.[70] The House compromise sailed unchanged through the Senate on a 28–4 vote and was signed by the governor.[71]

Is Davidson's style distinctly female or contextually driven? In interviews, several Ohio chairmen speculated that Davidson's style is little more than the appropriate fit of personality and context, an astute politician responding to the political needs of her caucus, or "the right person at the right time." Among the women interviewed, the more typical answer was: both. One female House Democrat focused specifically on Davidson's "power through" rather than "power over" others:

> "She is incredibly patient with her caucus. She lets them talk and argue endlessly. She gives up on stuff that she really cares about, but that she concludes is not in the best interests of her caucus. The men think it is weakness, but not in any way is that weakness. Before [Davidson became leader of the caucus] all they could ever do was fight. On our side of the aisle, we loved it! She was able to bring them together, but she gave up a tremendous amount of personal power along the way."[72]

As the last point suggests, resistance to Davidson's leadership has extracted a cost.

Speaker Davidson herself sees her style as the product of circumstances and gender.[73] Is she the right person at the right time? "Definitely!" She sees her style not only as responsive to the immediate concerns and requirements of her fragmented caucus but also as shaped by a changing world:

> "Consensus is what is needed in today's world. It relates a lot to the changes in demographics, the sheer diversity of our society, the change in the job mix to more teamwork. The times require a different kind of leadership."[74]

Is her style in some way gender based? "Definitely!"

> "A male style is more top down. Women (most of us) learned our leadership style working in volunteer organizations, school groups, PTAs, scouts, church groups. We've done those things, and if you have the skills, eventually you get the opportunity to lead. You learn that it's important to give people a reason to participate, a reason to be there."[75]

These quotes clearly reveal a distinctive self-perception of leadership style, but actions, more than words, provide powerful confirmation. Davidson publicly emphasizes the importance of moderation and advises new legislators to "stay in the middle, in the mainstream. Don't let yourself get categorized by one extreme or the other."[76] In addition to the abortion controversy, Speaker Davidson's consensus leadership was key to achieving compromises on the governor's 1995 budget and on a controversial bill reauthorizing parts of Ohio's certificate of need law.[77] Moreover, in the years prior to assuming the speakership, she was cited frequently in media ratings of legislators for her effectiveness in working across party lines to achieve policy solutions.[78]

## Leadership in Committees

Jo Ann Davidson's style stands out in large part because it is cast in bold relief against the Riffe era, yet other women also identify gendered experiences as leaders and an integrative emphasis. Among the women committee chairs interviewed, all agreed that they brought to their legislative duties either a unique set of formative experiences or a fundamentally different and more integrative style. Only two of the five chairmen interviewed in-depth thought their leadership style or committee experiences were any different from that of the women. One chairman noted that women are much more likely to have encountered sexual harassment. Two men felt they did not have enough experience serving under female committee chairs to reach any conclusions about leadership style.[79]

On the surface, of course, the average woman chair has had quite different experiences from her male colleague in Ohio. For example, the type of committee and the male-female composition of its membership are distinct and frequently sex segregated. Women tend to chair human services, education, and health committees, where other females and minorities are disproportionately represented. By contrast, men chair a wider range of committees that often have only token proportions of women and minority legislators. Besides being younger, on average, when they initiate their legislative careers, the men rarely, if ever, come from nonpaid backgrounds in the community or volunteer sectors. Three-fourths of the women, by contrast, pointed to a personal history in volunteer organizations, local government, or the League of Women Voters.

Another gendered dimension of committee life involves deference or, specifically, the lack of deference given to women. Three observers, again all female, cited instances in which male committee chairs walked out of hearings when women were testifying or when "women's issues" were being discussed. One such incident occurred during a hearing on the 1995 abortion bill and involved a female legislator who gave poignant personal testimony of having to consider with her husband the dilemma of a late-term abortion due to complications endangering her own health.[80]

The Ohio women also saw a variety of differences in committee leadership style, ranging from an inclination toward inclusiveness, a less territorial view of their power base, a desire to find a win-win solution, a willingness to use nontraditional decision-making strategies such as facilitator-mediated dispute resolution, to a highly personal and invitational approach to committee proceedings. The totality of these behaviors more than any one single aspect looks to be distinctly integrative. The differences are admittedly quite subtle, but to a one, the women see, feel, and sense that palpable differences exist between their committee leadership styles and that of the men. In the words of one:

> "I think that women understand that other people's time is important. They are not the person whose time is the most important. The men may be more efficient in terms of time, while the women are much more invitational. There is an effort to make the witnesses feel comfortable. These are generalities of course, and I'm certainly not describing every man or every woman. But with the more typical male, his power precedes him into the room. He is much more likely to cut off the witnesses and get on with the next presentation. It's never spoken aloud, but he communicates that: 'you're on my turf and you'll do it my way.'"[81]

The differing committee leadership philosophies can be seen in the policy strategies employed by two veteran Senate chairs, both considered highly effective by their peers and others. One prefers to "develop my own solution to a problem, have it drafted, drop it in the hopper and watch everyone scream."[82] His strategy is intended to get the attention of all interested parties, force the opposition to prepare and raise their strongest arguments, and then hammer out a compromise. By contrast, the other chair has on more than one occasion called in a trained facilitator to mediate policy disagreements between contending interest groups and to draft consensus legislation on complex issues.[83] Her approach is to start a process rather than prescribe a solution.

What one observes in formal committee hearings is highly formalized and structured, but there are hints of the underlying gender associations with integrative and aggregative styles. The practice of dividing the hearing process into separate hearings for sponsors, opponents, and proponents minimizes confrontation and controversy and provides procedural formality from one committee to the next. But within the boundaries of formal procedure, contrasting personal styles emerge. A few examples are instructive.

When an outburst of audience protest is heard in the packed House hearing room, Chairman A responds almost instantaneously, gavels for order and silence, and threatens to clear the room at the next outburst.[84] In an interview, he explains his action in terms of a desire to avoid an emotional head-to-head conflict—"That's not the best way to do public policy"—and a commitment to running a very business-like committee that balances efficiency with openness.[85] Indeed, he finds little to criticize in the firm-handed committee process under former Speaker Riffe, and there is a hint of doubt when he comments: "For better or worse we [Republicans] have hooked our star on more openness." Acknowledging that his committee deals with issues on which there are sharp partisan differences, Chairman A prefers to assign controversial bills to a small subcommittee to work out compromises whenever possible and then let the majority of the committee decide the bill's fate. His vision of committee leadership emphasizes substantive fairness through procedural order; the indicator of success is a technically well-drafted bill that a majority of the committee supports. It is a classic aggregative vision of leadership as a process of putting together the necessary votes (50 percent plus 1).

By contrast, Chairwoman B shepherds a complex 900–page reform bill through her committee. Her hearings seem to proceed in haphazard fashion: Witnesses are addressed on a first-name basis, interruptions are frequent, and topics seems to follow no particular order. Committee members raise questions at will and make statements on a variety of concerns at the expense of the hearing's substantive coherence and procedural clarity. The chair frequently asks (almost rhetorically or to no one in particular) who is going to follow-up on a particular issue and get additional information.[86] Explaining her approach, Chairwoman B says she wants the committee to at least touch on the myriad issues in the bill even if in-depth review within the time allowed is impossible. A longtime League of Women Voters activist, she emphasizes a desire for members of the committee to take personal responsibility to gather information and resolve issues within the bill. She says that her goal is to produce a consensus substitute bill: "I don't want anything in the bill that doesn't have consensus, unless it's clear that it is a Republican initiative."[87]

Chairwoman B's vision of committee leadership is not procedural order or control—"I try to be organized and prepared, but I don't always succeed." (*Laughs*) Rather the purpose of leadership is to educate others and thereby facilitate completing the task:

> "I'm one of the few people who understands these issues. I have to be very careful to bring people along in my caucus. But I have to be careful not to mislead them because they'll believe me! They trust me because I have the knowledge."[88]

Although her hearings suffer from a lack of direction, Chairwoman B's perspective is distinctively integrative—a faith in consensus and mutuality and a desire to educate.

In another committee hearing, Chairwoman C is displeased by spontaneous audience applause and troubled by a new member's lack of discipline in following strict parliamentary procedure in gaining permission from the chair before speaking. Rather than issue a public rebuke, however, she resolves to meet privately with the new member to go over committee procedure. Chairwoman C cites both incidents while stating the goal: "I want to work toward a more business-like approach. . . . It's an interesting ritual to address your questions through the chair, but it's an important way to control the flow of the meeting."[89]

Unlike Chairman A, procedural control is not a primary goal for her but, rather, a means to her other committee objectives: "I would like to do more educational work for the members and with the press."[90] Her measure of the committee's success will not be in votes on bills but, rather, on whether she has used the committee effectively as a forum to raise and explore issues. Although clearly differing in their attentiveness to an orderly process, both Chairwoman B and Chairwoman C share a vision of leadership as educational and consensual. Chairwoman C describes her leadership style as including integrative traits such as good listening and facilitation skills and a desire to be inclusive and make others a part of the process.[91]

Chairman D, however, leaves little doubt as to who is in charge of his committee. Unlike the other three, he asserts definite personal control, not just procedurally but substantively. At a hearing, he postpones one scheduled bill with the announcement he is meeting with the sponsor because he is not convinced of the need for the bill. A second bill, his own, is presented with the joking comment—"I'm already convinced of the need for it." In consideration of a third, which garners considerable opposition testimony, Chairman D engages in active questioning and at one point dismisses a statement by a witness with the comment: "Your argument just ain't so." As the meeting approaches the noon hour, Chairman D reminds the witnesses not to be repetitive and to keep testimony brief and on point.[92]

His actions reflect his self-perception that his leadership style grows first and foremost out of knowledge and expertise:

> "You not only have to have a grasp of subject matter but you need to be able to communicate it succinctly while not making the other members feel that you are lording over them. That's why the social side of this business is so important. That is where you talk about baseball, your kids in college, whatever to take the edge off."[93]

In the past, his substantive expertise, persistence, and willingness to take on complex issues have been attributes that placed Chairman D's name on media rankings of the best legislators.[94] At the same time, Chairman D prides himself in being "firm and fair" in managing the committee process and keeping order and focus during testimony and the amendment process.

Chairman D sees committee leadership as aggregative—a competition of ideas, an opportunity to demonstrate his political savvy and intellectual prowess, and a contest of legislative skill. The process and the issues are mastered by sheer force of personality, intellect, and a facile blend of humor and interpersonal skills. Attention to interpersonal relationships serves an instrumental purpose, a means to an end, smoothing over hurt feelings that may result from achieving his policy goals. Collaboration is not his concern. Indeed, he notes with a smile, "My biggest problem now is a Republican administration. When it was Democrat, I didn't have to worry about them."[95] The political reality of Republican control of the legislature and the governorship in fact imposes upon him a mandate of cooperation rather than an invitation to competition.

In Ohio, the most apparent public differences from committee to committee are confounded by yet another factor—experience. Among the most experienced committee chairs, for example, there is greater substantive control over the proceedings (i.e., providing information and using orienting and summarizing messages). These chairs exhibit greater certainty in the use of parliamentary procedure, handling the necessary formalities and official actions. The contrast in experience is starkest between the House, where the GOP is a new majority, and the Senate, where the GOP has enjoyed extended control. Though the turnover in party control in the Ohio House affected men and women simultaneously, experience may be an important consideration in other states particularly because women on average have fewer years in committee leadership (see chapter 3, this volume).

## Integrative and Aggregative Influences

The foregoing examples suggest that both integrative and aggregative styles are possible within the Ohio General Assembly. Certainly there are contextual factors described earlier in this chapter from which both styles can draw and which explain the dramatic transition from master deal maker Riffe to consensus builder Davidson.

Transactional distributive politics give rise to a centrist impulse. Ohio's "issueless" and "jobs-oriented" politics revolve around the competition for jobs, contracts, and material benefits. The regional fragmentation of interests and power necessitate moderation and cooperation, and regional competition for a share of the pie can be settled by classically aggregative leadership. Indeed, one of the more prominent movements in contemporary state politics is "the Other Ohio" movement. Representatives from outside Cincinnati, Cleveland, and Columbus feel they have gotten a less than satisfactory share of public investment and economic development effort. In a campaign for greater recognition, leaders of the Other Ohio effort are attempting to work together to alter the distribution of resources.

The same centrist impulse, however, might benefit from integrative leadership styles that similarly value moderation. Ohio's history of tempering ideological extremes and fostering bipartisan cooperation provides an important legacy. Because power is fragmented among various regions of the state, cooperation becomes necessary and essential. In the past, legislative leaders practiced a brand of ideological pragmatism and pursued fiscal policies that were conservative though centrist. An integrative leader like Davidson might achieve the same end but use more inclusive means than Riffe employed through special interest fund raising and campaign finance loyalty.

Within the General Assembly, legislative procedure similarly gives rise to both aggregative and integrative styles. Integrative leadership requires time for listening, educating, and participating. To a much greater extent than in less professionalized legislatures, Ohio committees have the luxury of time because of the longer legislative session spread over a year-round schedule. The full-time professional legislature can be more deliberative and thoughtful, and public input can be easily accommodated. The Ohio General Assembly, for example, considers 1,600 bills each biennium compared with Oklahoma's 2,500 bills and Colorado's 1,100.

But in Ohio's committee rooms, another manifestation of legislative professionalization reinforces an aggregative approach in the sense of emphasizing expertise, autonomous judgment, and separation through hierarchy. Ohio's hearing process has become a highly formalized ritual. Committees literally sit in courtroom-like surroundings, and members array themselves in a line across a dais and peer down on lobbyists and interest groups that come as supplicants. Hearing testimony over a series of separate hearings, legislative committees take on the unmistakable ambiance of a courtroom. It is a highly open process but not a collective one. Give-and-take over issues takes place elsewhere. There is none of the public intimacy of Colorado's hearing rooms, or even the interaction among committee members as you might see around an Oklahoma committee table. In short, the facilities convey a clear hierarchy and separation, a sense of the politician as "professional." The formal procedures communicate order, autonomy, rationality, and a top-down orientation to policy.

Finally, party divisions in Ohio have given rise to both integrative and aggregative styles. Speaker Davidson uses listening, patience, and education to bring together her ideologically divided and fractious Republican caucus. As one of few rural, smalltown legislators within a largely-urban and regionally divided Democratic Party, former Speaker Riffe built a system of power based on reciprocity—"you support me, and I'll support you." That is not to imply the Republican Party is more amenable to integrative leadership and the Democratic Party to more classically aggregative leadership. Rather, the Ohio context suggests that an absence of party cohesion does not dictate one leadership approach or another. Both styles have the capacity to be attentive to individual members, to deal with more diffuse interests, and to respond to the demands of a "therapeutic" culture.[96]

## Conclusion

Ohio's history, political background, and legislative institution do not dictate a clear preference for any one style of leadership; indeed, its history cites examples of both integrative and aggregative styles. The serendipitous intersection of place, time, and person, however, bode well for the integrative styles characterized by the current group of women chairs. But in a future of term limits, no one can expect to hold power for long.

In 1995, the evidence of transition around the state house was everywhere. Someone added a handwritten amendment to a sign hanging in the construction area of the capitol restoration project: Caution **Women &** Men Working Above. One of the first floor amendments that Speaker Davidson allowed from the minority party added gender-neutral language to existing statutes about the governor.[97] And even the female reporters of the Ohio Legislative Correspondents Association have organized their own group.[98] Gender power is no longer exclusively male power.

Resistance to women's power was muted but nonetheless detectable in 1995. The Democratic Party had neglected its female candidates for statewide office, and the number of Democratic women state legislators had fallen. Speaker Davidson's authority had been challenged on the 1995 abortion bill in ways that would have been unthinkable during the Riffe regime.

At this time, female committee chairs are relatively inexperienced and still too few to predict a shift to a more integrative leadership style. The growing number of GOP female legislators, however, along with well-placed statewide female officeholders, will likely bring greater visibility and power for Republican women as long as the party retains its majority. Thus far, they seem to reflect a more integrative style of committee leadership styles. Moreover, Ohio's politics and history provide a climate in which both aggregative and integrative leadership styles might be supported. Whether female leaders will push norms toward a more integrative approach is unclear. To be sure, Speaker Jo Ann Davidson and other prominent Ohio women legislators provide high-profile examples. Yet, already, there are rumors that Davidson may be a two-term speaker and thus may have less time to mentor others in her integrative approach.

Although the impact of women on committee leadership styles is hard to predict, there is remarkable consensus on the impact of term limits. The members of the Ohio legislature are aware that the clock is ticking, and they are restless, feisty, impatient, and ready to make their mark. In spite of term limits, the attractions of a professional legislature should continue to draw legislators with ambition and a desire to make politics something of a career. Considering the makeup of the legislative membership and greater ideological division within the parties, term limits are likely to continue the erosion of cohesion and followership.

Term limits will, almost by definition, prevent the kind of leadership symbolized by Speaker Riffe. No leader will stay as long or have similar opportunities to develop and maintain power based on loyalty, reciprocity, and the potential threat of rewards and punishment. At the same time, integrative styles may be at risk. The words of one veteran female lawmaker provide an apt summary:

> "Term limits will have a negative impact on women. The way that women got established in the legislature over the years was through hard work, building a reputation, doing their homework. That opportunity is truncated now. The successful women are women who are willing to listen and bring their colleagues together. It's hard to get people to invest that kind of energy and time under term limits."[99]

# Colorado: Defining the
# Standards of Leadership

In the Colorado Senate chambers, seven stained glass windows hold the faces of the state's leaders from days gone by. From five of the windows, the images of mustachioed men peer somberly down: John Routt, the last territorial governor and the first state governor; two U.S. senators, Charles Hughes and Edward Wolcott; and two men of industry, David Moffat, whose famed railroad tunnel provided transportation and water to the Queen City of the plains, and Samuel Nicholson, whose mining technology revolutionized gold and silver exploration in the Rocky Mountains.

The other two windows are of women. One window contains the picture of Virginia Neal Blue, state treasurer from 1966 to 1970 and the first woman elected to a statewide office. The most recent addition to this pantheon of notables is Ruth Stockton, who served twenty-three years (1961–1984) in the General Assembly and became one of the most powerful women in the state as the first female chair of the Joint Budget Committee (JBC) (1975–1980) and the first female Senate President Pro Tem (1979–1980). Senator Stockton's window speaks volumes about what distinguishes the Colorado General Assembly from other state legislatures. While other states struggle to elect women legislators and every woman is in some way a first, Colorado women have established themselves not only as powerful players but as part of the basic furnishings of the legislature.

Indeed, the activities going on below Senator Stockton's window on the last day of January in 1995 are testimony to the presence of women throughout the legislature. Republican Senator Elsie Lacy, current chair of the powerful JBC, holds forth at the floor podium, providing her colleagues with a budget briefing. Down the hall in the House chambers, Republican Representative

Norma Anderson, then chair of the House Education Committee, is presenting a bill on higher education curriculum standards. Representative Anderson has earned bipartisan praise for carrying and passing more "impact" bills
in a single legislative session than most lawmakers do in a career.[1] Leading the
questioning and debate against the bill are two members of the Democratic
leadership team: Representative Dianne DeGette, then assistant minority leader
and now a U.S. congresswoman, and Representative Peggy Reeves, the caucus
chair. In the *Rocky Mountain News*, a preview of the session identifies three
women among seven legislators who will be "key players."[2]

In 1995, exactly 100 years after the first women served in the Colorado
General Assembly (or for that matter in any state legislature), women's contributions are becoming remarkably unremarkable. In fact, women are setting
the standards of leadership, an indication of what happens when gender equality
in numerical representation (or the closest thing to it) is reached.[3]

In Colorado, integrative styles of leadership are also more a part of the
legislative norm than in most other states.[4] No single reason explains the difference in style, but three factors have had a positive impact:

- The state's egalitarian history, a political culture that is "populist cum
  moralistic,"[5] and an in-migration of activist residents fuel expectations
  about public participation in policymaking. These expectations are not
  so much about who gets what but about who gets involved.
- The legislative institution values its public policy role, and the committee system is organized to enhance that role. The General Assembly
  attends to the collective enterprise of making policy more than it practices individualistic, pork-barrel politics.
- Women chairs bring a more integrative approach to committee leadership with a particular emphasis on listening, education, and moderation. Colorado comes closest to what Kanter calls balanced groups when
  stereotypes recede and the institutional culture begins to reflect attributes of the different subgroups.[6]

This analysis cannot determine definitively that Colorado is a venue for
integrative leadership because of the presence of more women. It could be,
conversely, that the political values of a particular institution attract more integrative leaders, many of whom are women. None of the three factors is
dispositive, certainly not gender alone. Culture, however, undoubtedly inter-
acts with gender and organizational practices to shape leadership.

## Women in Colorado Politics

In 1894, Colorado became the first state to elect women to serve in the state
legislature, a full twenty-six years before Oklahoma's first female lawmaker
and twenty-eight years before that milestone occurred in Ohio.[7] The first legislators came after a twenty-five-year struggle for equal political rights for women.

In 1870, the territorial governor proposed that Colorado follow the lead of Wyoming Territory and grant women the right to vote. The proposal was rejected by the territorial legislature, but popular pressure for women's suffrage was mounting when the 1875–1876 constitutional convention for statehood was convened. The convention turned down suffrage by a vote of twenty-four to eight, but a compromise was fashioned, granting women the right to vote in school board elections and calling for a referendum on full suffrage.[8] In 1877, one year after statehood, male voters defeated the measure by a margin of two to one.

It would take another sixteen years and active support of the Colorado Populist Party to arrange another vote. In 1892, the Populist Party made women's suffrage a part of its platform. The party enjoyed considerable popularity due to its leadership in the struggle to retain silver coinage and held the governorship and a substantial number of legislative seats. With their political clout, the populists were able to force a new, and this time successful, referendum on the suffrage issue. Though the second state to grant women the vote, Colorado became the first to provide for suffrage by a separate vote of an all-male electorate.[9]

The first three women elected to the state legislature in 1894 were all Republicans.[10] Frances Klock and Clara Cressingham, both of Denver, were recruited by the party that was eager to win the loyalty of the new voters. The third woman, Carrie Clyde Holly of Pueblo, had been active in the suffrage movement and sought office. Their first legislative session drew packed galleries of women from Denver, nationwide attention from suffragettes, and a curious press. Representative Klock became the first woman ever to chair a state legislative committee. Representative Holly caused the greatest sensation with legislation to grant mothers the same rights to their children as fathers, a bill to raise the "age of consent" for girls from sixteen to eighteen, and a proposal for an early version of the Equal Rights Amendment. The first two bills passed. If Representative Holly was an outspoken advocate for women, Representative Cressingham was the model of moderation, sponsoring legislation to encourage the infant sugar beet industry. She told a *New York World* reporter, "We are all aware that the suffrage movement may be injured by indiscreet actions on our part, and we have to be very careful."[11]

More recently, Colorado has continued to lead the nation in progress toward gender equity. In 1975, the General Assembly had twice the national percentage of female state lawmakers.[12] The current percentage of women state legislators nationally (21 percent) was reached in Colorado sixteen years ago.[13] Since the mid-1980s, women's share of legislative seats has hovered around one-third of the General Assembly's 100 members. In 1987, the Colorado House had a higher percentage of women lawmakers (38.5 percent) than any other legislative chamber in the country, and women made up 45 percent of the House Republican majority caucus.[14] In 1997, the General Assembly had a record thirty-five female members, who held half of the committee chairs (including the JBC) and a third of the top leadership posts.

In congressional and statewide races, women have also been competitive vote-getters. Denver voters elected U.S. Congresswoman Patricia Schroeder twelve times, making her the longest serving female member of Congress. In 1992, Democrat Gail Schoettler served as state treasurer, while Republicans Natalie Meyer and Gale Norton were elected secretary of state and attorney general, respectively.[15] Several other women have been competitive, although as yet unsuccessful, candidates for the U.S. Senate.

Though numerous in the legislature, Republican women did not crack the top ranks of leadership until 1997 when Norma Anderson became the first female majority leader. No woman has ever been elected speaker or Senate president. Senator Dottie Wham came closest in 1992 when she narrowly lost to Senator Norton in the GOP caucus vote for Senate president.[16] Some political observers thought sexism was a factor in the race, but Senator Wham felt that her moderate politics were simply unacceptable to the conservative wing of the caucus. The GOP women generally are seen as more moderate in their philosophy, quietly feminist in the legislation they sponsor, and by and large pro-choice.[17] If such positions have blocked their ascendance to leadership, they have not prevented the GOP women from exercising considerable influence as committee chairs and sponsors of major legislation.[18]

On the Democratic side of the aisle, women have served in the top legislative leadership roles since the 1950s. In 1995, women comprised the entire House Democratic leadership. The slate of female candidates emerged somewhat unexpectedly and wholly unplanned. Some of the male members of the caucus expressed concern over the possibility of an all-female leadership team, but those concerns were not expressed until late in the process when the individual candidates already had their votes committed. As one senior Democratic legislator commented, "This was no grand design. It just happened. But it reflects years and years of work and progress before."[19]

Colorado women appear to have shattered the "glass ceiling" of leadership positions, but there is some evidence that they have been considered intruders into a dominant culture. When the 1996 race for a new majority leader began as a two-woman contest between Representative Anderson and Representative Jeanne Adkins, some men in the House GOP caucus balked at the prospect of a female leader and tried unsuccessfully to recruit a male candidate.[20] Despite rare bipartisan praise for her navigation of the House "through rough waters, long calendars, and controversial bills," Majority Leader Anderson has nonetheless been unable to escape gendered stereotypes.[21] She has been called the "Dragon Lady" for her no-nonsense, tough-minded approach.[22] Assessments of the abilities of Senator Dottie Wham, a highly influential and effective Denver legislator, are frequently laced with gendered references— "one shrewd grandmother," or "She'll make you feel guilty as sin . . . just like your mom does."[23] Moreover, the Democrats' inability to win control of the legislature is presumed to discourage some men from competing for leadership positions. Some feel that despite their numbers GOP women were held back from top legislative leadership roles due to the party's conservative philosophy, a reliance on tradition, and some vestiges of sexism.[24]

In sum, Colorado has a long history of women in politics and today they are major actors in state and legislative politics. In both parties, women exercise considerable influence by virtue of their number, committee and leadership positions, and a commitment to full-time service.

## The Context of Legislative Leadership

Colorado embodies many aspects of frontier politics. The frontier represents a newness, transience, and population turnover that bring not only opportunity but also the political challenge of growth and change. According to Elazar, each new frontier is to some extent at odds with the old.[25] Colorado's relatively short history encompasses four frontiers: (1) the taming of land for farms, ranches, mines, and towns; (2) the creation of new industrial urban centers; (3) the forces of suburbanization and technology; and (4) a rurban-cybernetic future that places high value on the state's abundant, but environmentally fragile, resources.

The frontier experience produced the distinctive forces shaping Colorado state politics. To understand the Colorado context of committee leadership, it is necessary to know something about the state's political geography and culture and its legislative institution. The state has contrasting political cultures, diverse regional interests, competitive partisan politics, and a policy process that is open, porous, and with "no epicenter" of governmental power.[26] In such a system, leadership by consensus and compromise is highly valued.

### Culture and Politics

Historians suggest that contemporary Colorado is not one but rather "five States," specifically Metro Denver, the Eastern Plains, the Front Range, the Western Slope, and Southern Colorado.[27] Metro Denver includes the city of Denver and its suburbs, where most of the state's wealth, 60 percent of the population, the major universities, businesses, and government institutions are located. Politically, Metro Denver comprises the partisan strongholds of each party—the Democrats of central Denver and working-class Adams County and the affluent, conservative Republican suburbs of Jefferson and Arapahoe counties.

The Front Range includes all the larger cities, except Denver, that form a metropolitan necklace stringing from Greeley to the north to Pueblo in the south. These cities developed along the foothills of the Rocky Mountains and around military installations, universities, and industries such as manufacturing, technology, and tourism. The region's main public policy problems involve growth. Fort Collins and Colorado Springs, for example, have ranked among the nation's fastest growing communities.

Rolling prairies, dry-grass farms, and ranches make up the Eastern Plains which extend from the Nebraska and Kansas borders to the easternmost suburban edge of Metro Denver and the Front Range. One of the first areas to be settled, the Eastern Plains suffer from cyclical agricultural economics, a continuing concern over water, and declining population. With the exodus of population has come a loss of political clout. The Eastern Plains constitute 40 percent of the state's land but less than 10 percent of its population.

Southern Colorado is the sparsely populated home to a large Spanish-speaking population, Native Americans, and Anglo-Americans. The San Luis Valley, bounded to the east and west by spectacular peaks, lies at the heart of this agricultural region. Water rights have been a dominant political concern but dwindling population (now less than 5 percent of the state's residents) has dealt the region an ever weaker hand. Southern Colorado's Hispanics tend to vote Democratic in presidential elections.

The Western Slope is defined by the Continental Divide west to the Utah border. The region has the most of what the rest of the state needs—water. The Western Slope is rich in resources of all kinds—minerals, oil and gas reserves, and spectacular scenery for tourism and recreation. The dominant concerns are how to prevent exploitation of its vast resources and to fend off Front Range water boards, developers, and political leaders. Voters in Grand Junction and surrounding areas are dependable GOP partisans in presidential elections.

Today, the population and political center of the state resides in the suburbs.[28] Denver's share of the state electorate, for example, declined from 28 percent in 1966 to 15.6 percent in 1988, and city voters make up less than one-third of the metropolitan area electorate.[29] The vast in-migration of the past decade settled in the suburbs,[30] and many of the new legislative districts elected moderate Republican women.[31] Although the newcomers generally embrace the state's right-of-center politics, they also are drawn by the state's famed natural and recreational amenities and thus are pragmatic about the trade-offs between economic growth and environmental protection.

Colorado's partisan politics have undergone "a slow drift toward the GOP over the past thirty years."[32] Nonetheless, each party can claim dominance of one branch of government. The Republicans have controlled both houses of the state legislature for forty-two of the past sixty-six years (1928–1994) whereas Democrats have won seven of the ten gubernatorial contests from 1958 to 1994.[33] Democrats have also been successful in congressional races. Party switching is something of a pattern,[34] with U.S. Senator Ben Nighthorse Campbell's conversion to the GOP as the latest example.

This pattern of divided control and party competition reflects in part the "continuing struggle" between the impulses of moralistic and individualistic political cultures.[35] The two competing visions captured the cultural divide:

the "Old West" of rugged individualism and "leave me alone" independence and the "New West" of environmental protection and balanced growth, a "green" style of moralism.[36] The Republican Party in the General Assembly reflects the individualists' embrace of unfettered economic markets, opposition to taxes, and aversion to intrusive, big government. Moderates of both parties embody the moralistic vision of government as an instrument to promote the general welfare and public good and politics as an arena for activism and participation in community life. Colorado's moralistic impulses were evident during the nineteenth century and, of more recent vintage, fueled the anti-Olympics campaign of 1972, the state's "sagebrush rebellion" of the 1980s, and a host of ballot initiatives in the 1990s seeking government reform and openness. Open meetings laws and sunset reviews of the bureaucracy are among the moralistic reforms that Colorado pioneered.

During the years of divided legislative and gubernatorial control, the clash of cultures has sometimes been waged as institutional warfare. The Republican Party has used its institutional control of the legislature to enact individualistic policies, whereas the Democrats have taken advantage of voters' independent streak to impose moralistic governmental reforms on the GOP. Conservatives won tax cuts and expenditure restraints during Governor Lamm's twelve-year tenure. Unhappy with GOP legislative hegemony, particularly in the budget process, Democrats in 1988 drafted and voters approved a constitutional amendment reforming legislative practices and limiting majority power in the General Assembly. The GAVEL amendment (Give a Vote to Every Legislator) eliminated the power of chairs to "pocket-veto" bills, killed the House Rules Committee's control over the floor calendar, and forbade the practice of "binding caucus" votes that effectively locked Democrats out of the key budget process.[37]

These contrasting political cultures, diverse regional interests, and competitive partisan politics created a policy process that is open and porous and benefits from integrative leadership:

> Critics might justifiably call it a "nobody's-in-charge" system. In reality, Colorado has a system of multiple vetoes and a system that forces alliance building and the forging of coalitions across party, ideological, and regional lines. In a state that has distinctive regional barriers and competing political cultures, it is accurate to say leadership in Colorado is dispersed and decentralized.[38]

In 1992, the policy process became even more decentralized when voters approved Amendment 1, a constitutional amendment that requires the state and localities to get voter approval for new taxes, tax rate increases, tax extensions, new bonds, government-backed debt, and license, permit, or fee-based services.[39] Limited revenue growth is allowed for inflation and local growth in the property tax base. As a result, no single office, party, interest group, or leader dominates Colorado politics and policymaking.

## Institutional Factors

In many ways, an Oklahoma legislator would recognize attributes of the Colorado General Assembly—its conservative political outlook, its part-time schedule, its institutional prerogatives and powers when compared with the executive, and split-party control of state government. But, in the details, the differences are quite significant, with Colorado having a more decentralized and collegial system.

In Colorado, the 1962 U.S. Supreme Court ruling in *Reynolds v. Sims* had the immediate effect of shifting political power in the legislature from rural to urban hands.[40] Before that time, the legislature had been "pure and simple, a cowboys' club,"[41] or "an outstate men's club."[42] When not voting on bills at the state capital, the small rural elite mulled legislative decisions "at night over drinks at a few downtown hotels and bars."[43] Their common bond was not partisan politics (both Democrats and Republicans were part of the rural clique) but rather their smalltown values and agricultural interests.[44]

With the loss of rural seats, power shifted briefly to the urban areas and environmentalists in the early 1970s. Helped along by Governor Richard Lamm's successful anti-Olympics campaign in 1972 and the Watergate scandals, Democrats briefly ruled the House of Representatives in 1974–1975. In the latter half of the 1970s, however, a rightwing band of Republican ideologues came to power, their campaigns bankrolled by the likes of business interests such as the Coors brewing family.[45] Comprising "educated, articulate professional people who saw Colorado . . . as a refuge from the big-government decadence of the East,"[46] the conservatives, known as the "Crazies," unseated moderate Republican Speaker Ron Strahle and installed one of their own, Bob Burford.[47]

Ideological cousins of Ronald Reagan, the "Crazies" brought to the General Assembly an agenda of tax cutting, social conservatism, and antigovernment libertarianism. They succeeded in reducing income taxes across the board, indexing tax rates, and capping the growth of state spending. But the movement may have been a victim of its own success as some of the key leaders left the legislature feeling their agenda was complete.[48] Others, including Speaker Burford and Representatives Anne Gorsuch and Steve Durham, served as administrators in the Reagan Revolution.

The Colorado General Assembly is a part-time legislature limited to meeting in formal session for 120 calendar days from January to May. Prior to the 1988 constitutional amendment that imposed the 120-day limit, some legislative sessions extended for seven months.[49] But even with the shortened session, many legislators, not just the JBC members, find that legislative work can extend past the January–May period with special sessions and interim committees. For their efforts, Colorado legislators are paid $17,500 a year, much less than the Oklahoma legislators at $32,000 and Ohio's lawmakers at $42,427.[50]

Ehrenhalt cites the Colorado legislative pay as a major factor in paving the way for more women to serve in the General Assembly. He argues that legislative service in Colorado has become the preserve of those who can afford the time at a relatively low rate of pay; as a consequence, members are more likely to be retirees, independently wealthy, or women whose income is not the primary support of the household.[51] Indeed, a Colorado Legislative Council study in 1988 revealed that 12 of the 100 members considered themselves full-time legislators and 11 of the 12 were women, comprising 44 percent of all female lawmakers.[52] As one female legislator noted, "If we had a seventy-thousand-dollar-a-year legislature, I don't think the numbers would be the same."[53]

Institutionally, much of the legislature's power centers on the JBC.[54] With three members (two majority party, one minority) from each house, the JBC has had a four-two Republican-Democrat composition since the mid-1970s. The party makeup of the legislature and the structure of the process have combined to vest the "power of the purse" firmly in the majority party's hands.[55] GAVEL reduced the GOP caucus's influence over the budget by banning binding caucus votes and thus further concentrating budget power in the tight-knit and collegial JBC.

Working virtually year-round, with extensive hearings and its own independent staff, the JBC produces the "long bill," a legislative budget for state government. The majority caucuses review the long bill and line up the necessary votes for passage.[56] Floor action becomes a formality, ratifying the majority party's budget blueprint. The JBC members have the final word, however, because the JBC becomes the conference committee to resolve House and Senate differences after floor consideration.

Like the collective power arrangement within the JBC, legislative power elsewhere in the General Assembly is shared with the majority party caucus, the leadership, and standing committees all playing a role.[57] Colorado committees give careful scrutiny to the details and advisability of bills, and their work is accorded considerable deference on the floor where the committee version is often accepted with little debate and without substantial revision.[58] On average, Colorado has fifty to sixty conference committees each session (about one-fifth the number in Oklahoma but still twice as many as in a typical session in Ohio). Colorado conference committees are limited to considering only the specific issues on which the House and Senate disagree.[59]

Although obviously lacking the more leisurely pace of Ohio's year-round session, Colorado's schedule is not as truncated as in Oklahoma, and committees can be more deliberative. There are fewer committees (only ten in each house), and they have more time to meet each week and before their first reporting deadline. Furthermore, a limit on the number of bills a Colorado lawmaker can introduce alleviates the assembly-line pressures experienced in Oklahoma and other states. A five-bill limit encourages cosponsorship and cooperation and discourages piecemeal, multiple introductions.[60] Colorado legislators consider 1,100 bills in a typical biennium compared with Oklahoma's 2,500 and Ohio's 1,200–1,300. All three states pass some 300 to 350 bills each year.[61]

Finally, like both Oklahoma and Ohio, the Colorado legislature has seen the passing of an era of strong-arm, more traditional legislative leadership. From 1981 to 1991, Speaker Carl "Bev" Bledsoe ruled the House with a tight rein and highly partisan outlook. Speaker Bledsoe, the longest serving speaker in Colorado history, is a rancher from Hugo on the Eastern Plains who kept alive the traditions of the old "cowboy caucus."[62] Though their ability to exercise raw power certainly varied, Bledsoe along with Jim Barker in Oklahoma and Ohio's Vern Riffe served at a time when speakers were expected to be strong and even heavy-handed when necessary. Bledsoe used the powers of the speakership to their fullest extent, particularly to advance conservative rural policies and Republican priorities.[63] One veteran reporter described Bledsoe as "the Republican boss" who believes:

> His position gives him absolute power over the activities of the House. He demands that his opinions dictate the outcome of legislation, even when they are in conflict with the vast majority of his colleagues.[64]

Bledsoe's successor, Speaker Chuck Berry, is considered less partisan and more open to including House Democrats, who now feel "set free from years in solitary confinement."[65] A spirit of bipartisanship flourished during the first two years of Speaker Berry's tenure, as moderate Republicans and Democrats constituted the controlling middle ground on House votes. But in 1995, after the GOP picked up additional legislative seats (many on the conservative side), the minority Democrats complained of a "chill" in bipartisanship.[66]

With its numerically smaller and more experienced membership, the Senate operates in a more intimate and collegial manner. The Senate president is less powerful than the speaker,[67] but the leadership difference between the two houses is also a matter of temperament. Since 1981, Senate leaders have been considered more moderate. Former Senate President Ted Strickland provided Democrats with opportunities to participate in the process,[68] and the current Senate President Tom Norton has carried on that tradition. Norton has been described as more objective when it comes to bill assignments to committee, where Speaker Berry has acceded to pressure from social conservatives for favorable committee referrals.[69] Jeff Wells, who served as Senate majority leader under both Strickland and Norton, is considered a master at compromise "who works effectively behind the scenes, often one-on-one, to bring lawmakers together on tough issues."[70] In the 1980s, Wells's Democratic counterpart, Senator Ruth Wright, was similarly considered "softer in [her] approach."[71]

In sum, the Colorado General Assembly has the attributes of a more integrative institution. The legislature features a decentralized policy process in which committees play an important role. Bill limits encourage cooperative and collective policy efforts. Rules and procedures discourage the kind of individualism evident in Oklahoma and reinforce a deliberative committee role. An era of strong, autocratic leadership has given way to a more moderate style of legislative leadership.

## The Practice of Committee Leadership in Colorado

Committee leadership follows a more integrative model, and the legislative institution is approaching a point of gender power and parity that is far more balanced than in other states. The long-term presence of women in the legislature, the state's egalitarian history, a decentralized and open policy process, a strong moralistic tradition, and the necessity of geographic and political alliances provide the impetus for a collaborative style of committee leadership.

Having approximated "balanced" subgroups of men and women for almost a decade, the General Assembly is closer than other legislatures to allowing women to operate free of stereotypes. That is not to say that Colorado has reached some epiphany of gender neutrality. Rather, Colorado female chairs, as much as the men, are setting the standards of committee leadership and not merely trying to accommodate themselves to an existing, predominantly "male" norm.

### *Understanding the Committee Process*

The physical setting in the gold-domed state capital building communicates a sense that the public's business is being conducted in plain view. A typical hearing room is fairly intimate: The members face one another around a conference table or in a U-shaped panel. Witnesses sit at the committee table or at a separate table immediately in front. Lobbyists, staff officials, and members of the public are seated in chairs around the perimeter or in a theater-style arrangement depending on the shape of the room. Hearings are often convened before standing-room-only crowds, and interested observers frequently outnumber the legislators. Because legislators have no personal staff or private offices, the hallways are beehives of activity—cellular phones, huddles of lobbyists and members conferring, and markups conducted at tiny cafeteria tables.

The "publicness" of the process is evident. Committee meetings are subject to public notice requirements and are not exempt from the state's open meetings law. All meetings are tape-recorded. Parliamentary formalities facilitate the tape recording but also provide the chair with a mechanism for controlling the meeting and recognizing witnesses and members of the committee to speak.

In spite of the veneer of formality, behavior in committees can be quite informal. More important, there is a certain public intimacy to Colorado committee hearings that is not evident in Oklahoma and Ohio. Testimony and questioning between members and witnesses can be lively and extended. It is not unusual in a Colorado hearing room for witnesses to engage in give-and-take exchanges with committee members and others. A sizable "citizens' lobby" is present along side the usual contingent of business, industry, and professional associations.[72] Frequently, average citizens attend and express their opinion on issues, and public participation is treated with deference: "We might get tough on a 'pro' lobbyist but we make citizens from Limon feel comfortable," said one committee chairman.[73]

By contrast, in Oklahoma only lawmakers participate in the proceedings, and those on hand are an extension of the business—lobbyists, the press, and agency personnel. Oklahoma committees are driven by the imperatives to act; thus, nonlegislators are seen but not heard. In Ohio, the process is highly formalized and almost distant, with the lineup of witnesses scheduled well in advance and often orchestrated by the chair. Witnesses deliver prepared statements and expert testimony in a courtroom-like setting.

Colorado does not have a committee system based on seniority that would tend to reinforce stability of the membership.[74] Thus, even before the full effects of term limits, there is very substantial turnover in the membership of committees. In 1995, of the eight committees observed, almost 40 percent of the members were new to their assignments. Five of the eight chairs who were interviewed expressed concern about the "newness" of their committees. In particular, one chairwoman worried about the ability of new members to participate in a process of collective decision making: "I'm not sure how the committee will work until people get comfortable with each other. . . . I don't know for sure how it will go. It takes a little time for any group to jell. I like my groups to jell."[75] Noting that four of his seven-member committee were new, a senior Senate chairman said, "It means I must make absolutely sure that the committee has no hidden agendas."[76]

In committee and on the floor, the Colorado legislative process looks very different from the more leadership-dominated operations in Oklahoma and Ohio. Legislative scholar Wayne Francis found that Colorado lawmakers see most policy decisions as the domain of standing committees.[77] That responsibility is enhanced with the demise of the House Rules Committee and the prohibition on binding caucus votes after the passage of GAVEL.

Chairs control the scheduling of bills for hearings. GAVEL, however, requires committees to hold a hearing on all bills and has stripped committee chairs of the pocket veto.[78] Before GAVEL, a chair could simply refuse to bring up a bill for committee consideration, though, as a practical matter, Senate chairs almost always scheduled all bills. GAVEL democratized committee action by providing that a motion to report a bill is always in order.

A chair also can decide to entertain a motion to refer a bill to another committee where its fate can be decided. In particular, the State Affairs committees have earned reputations as the graveyard committees. At one time the chair of state affairs was known as "Dr. Death."[79] Committee chairs unilaterally can remove a bill from the table after a hearing and thus have more control over timing of committee action. The chair can also limit testimony or recognize those members who will offer the motions to ensure the outcome he or she desires.

## Leadership in Committees

Where procedural efficiency dominates the concerns of Oklahoma committee chairs, policy leadership and procedural fairness are the principal goals identified by Colorado committee chairs. These are traits one might expect given Colorado's moralistic traditions.

The committee chairs tend to think in terms of broad policy initiatives rather than incrementally. For example, when asked about their expectations for the session, the chairs identified major policy issues such as maintaining the integrity of the state's water laws, restructuring the state's higher education system, reforming welfare, constructing prisons in the face of limited budgets, providing primary health care to underserved communities, and establishing a consistent philosophy with regard to business regulation. To be sure, not every bill is a sweeping policy change. One chair articulated a classic incrementalist perspective when she noted that her committee had already done a lot ("I think I've shot my wad.") and that much of her emphasis would be on cleaning up major legislation passed the year before.[80]

With only nine substantive committees in each chamber, the jurisdictions are broad and no committee lacks for issues to tackle. The Appropriations committees usually only receive bills with a fiscal impact after a standing committee of reference has reviewed the proposal. That is not to say committees do not deal with narrow, parochial, or relatively simple issues, but none of the committees can escape being thrust into the middle of major policy questions. Nor can any of the committees be solely oriented toward a single constituency or be the captive of a particular agency or department.[81] For example, no committee is devoted solely to insurance but, rather, the Business Affairs and Labor Committee serves as the "referee for fights between the trial lawyers and insurance companies."[82] The Judiciary committees are not dominated by the legal community; in fact, neither of the two chairs nor the majority of committee members are attorneys. The Education committees preside over a divisive community of interest groups:

> "You have your boards, you have your executives, you have your teachers in unions and your teachers not in unions, you have your PTAs and you have parents and you have a business community. So there you are with a half-dozen or more different groups, and they don't coordinate their efforts."[83]

Not every committee is so divided, but most have their share of contending interest groups.

In such an environment, the committee chairs emphasize policy leadership as an essential part of their role and even see themselves presiding over fundamental philosophical discussions of societal values. For example, one chair framed the dominant issues of his business and labor committee in terms of defining the boundaries between public and private and balancing freedom of opportunity versus protection against risk.[84] The chair of the Agriculture,

Natural Resources, and Energy Committee, still the heart and soul of the old cowboy caucus, described his policy domain as "anything that does something with the earth."[85]

Some of the committee chairs converse adeptly in the language of policy analysis; they do not speak simply in terms of processing bills but rather of formulating policy that will have major implications for years to come. In discussing an issue facing her committee, one woman discussed the legacy of federal court involvement in the state's programs, identified long-term cost considerations, detailed a series of policy and administrative nuances, and worried about the difficulties of siting new facilities. In discussing child support enforcement, another chair framed the issue first as a philosophical question, then raised its practical administrative dimensions, and finally discussed the larger context of federal initiatives and welfare reform. These chairs talk more in terms of broad issues than of specific bills.

Equally important is the desire for procedural fairness, a goal identified in every interview with a Colorado committee chair. For example, fairness is the standard by which one chairwoman evaluates the session:

> "It's a dynamic process; it's not static. How do you measure success? Some will measure success by how many bills we killed. . . . The thing I look for is: Did we satisfy the needs of those who asked us for help? Did they have a fair and adequate hearing?"[86]

Similarly, another chairman commented:

> "You have a lot of votes that are 4 to 3 . . . that's the process. But if the process has been fair and open, that's it. Was everyone heard who wanted to be heard? Was the process fair? Was notice given on markup and voting? I don't want any one to feel abused procedurally."[87]

Procedural fairness is part of the institutional culture, and committee chairs evaluate each other by this norm. Though not asked to judge other chairs, several volunteered their assessments. The primary criteria for identifying a "good" committee leader seemed to be fairness. A pair of *Denver Post* feature articles on the two Education Committee chairs also focused evaluations on their fairness:

> Anderson is praised for keeping issues focused and for her fairness. She is known as one of the best vote-counters in the General Assembly. "She's structured and fair," said House Minority Leader Peggy Kerns, D-Aurora. . . . She doesn't play games, adds Becky Brooks, lobbyist for the Colorado Education Association. "If she can support you, she will tell you that. If she can't support you, she'll tell you that too."[88]

Representative Anderson's Senate counterpart was described similarly: "Friends and foes agree that Meiklejohn wields his power judiciously with an eye toward fairness and compromise."[89]

The norm of fairness is strong but violations do occur. During the 1997 session, Representative Mark Paschall forced a physician who performs abortions to take an oath "to the living God" to tell the truth before being allowed to testify.[90] No other witness was required to take an oath even though testimony was taken from a convicted felon who was escorted to the hearing by the state patrol. The incident provoked an admonition from House Majority Leader Norma Anderson to treat all citizens respectfully and alike. Paschall disobeyed the leadership order less than a week later in a similar situation.[91]

Aside from the emphasis on policy leadership and procedural fairness, the Colorado committees tend to reflect the personalities of their chairs or each committee's special role in the process.[92] For example, because the leadership uses them as "killer committees" to stall unwanted legislation, the State Affairs committees are the "least sensitive to public outcry."[93] There are also House and Senate differences. The smaller Senate committees have seven to nine members compared with the ten- to thirteen-member House committees. As a consequence, the Senate committees offer members more opportunity for input and their review is usually more detailed, collegial, and "hands on." Senate committees also do not require a second for any motion made.

Different personalities are apparent when observing committee meetings. There are those chairs who are extraordinarily patient with witnesses. The Judiciary committees, both chaired by women, often meet well into the evening hours to accommodate individual citizens who come out to testify on emotional issues such as "child custody, adoption, kids on drugs, issues that leave the committee weeping every day."[94] Other chairs are more abrupt: counseling witnesses not to be repetitive, cutting off members when questions and comments wander, and tightly controlling the discussion.

In the observation of twelve committee hearings, the longest hearings were before committees chaired by women. Indeed several of the women chairs have reputations for extraordinary patience in dealing with public input. But the pattern of longer hearings seems to be less related to gender than to the type of issue before the committee, its complexity and the degree of controversy.

In sum, committee leadership in Colorado is conceived as policy leadership conducted with an emphasis on procedural fairness. Within those widely held norms, committee chairs are free to conduct their committees according to personal preference.

## Approaching a Balance of Men and Women

The kind of stereotyping characteristic of "token" groups has virtually disappeared in Colorado. A decade ago, the term for some of Colorado's female legislators was "House Mommas."[95] The label was intended to contrast the tough-minded, no-nonsense image of a father with the nurturing (perhaps meddlesome) and less worldly mother. It was a term not meant to be entirely flattering, but it is also a term that has disappeared, according to longtime legislative observers. During the same period, Anne Gorsuch was remembered as much for her "bitchiness" as for her part in the conservative movement.

Acceptance of women legislators has grown as their number has increased. Though women were largely ignored in the party, former Speaker Bledsoe reportedly came to the conclusion that it was necessary to pay more attention to "his women."[96] By 1992, Bledsoe was gone and the new Speaker Berry painted a very different picture for the press. The women of the Colorado legislature were described as "major players," "power brokers," "excellent legislators," "bright newcomers, and savvy veterans" who were no longer "pigeon-holed in 'women's issues'" but were "key participants on nearly every issue."[97]

In 1995, women were being recognized for their considerable lawmaking skills and the legislation they sponsored. Not shying from controversy or tough issues, the women sponsored bills that "were not easy, dog-and-cat, hometown bills" but the kind of tough issues that could "start a fight in an empty room."[98] In the 1995 session, Senator Dottie Wham earned praise as "the very picture of wisdom" for scuttling House proposals that landed in her Senate Judiciary Committee.[99] Gender and cultural stereotypes defined the most dramatic fight of the session. Senator Wham opposed a concealed-weapons bill backed by the gun lobby:

> It was the unlikeliest of six-gun showdowns: the tall, sinister, long-haired, macho man from Leadville, attired in tight black western clothing and snake-skin boots, against a plump, gray, soft-spoken bespectacled grandmother from Denver. Sort of like Aunt Bea facing down Jack Palance.[100]

Failing to persuade her opponents to accept a limited expansion of permits to carry concealed weapons, "Aunt Bea" outdrew her opponents in a parliamentary fight and then publicly criticized their unwillingness to compromise.[101]

Two factors seem to explain Colorado's relatively "ungendered" environment. First, new and less autocratic leaders are in power, and they are credited with treating women as equal partners in the legislature. Second, there is the matter of sheer numbers. Comprising more than 30 percent of the legislative membership since the mid-1980s, women have changed the legislature in precisely the ways that Kanter (1977) describes as "balanced" subgroups. Unlike token conditions that heighten perceptions about the differentiating characteristics of dominants and tokens, in balanced subgroups the distinguishing factor recedes in importance while individual performance takes center stage. Contrasting a prominent woman lawmaker of the 1970s with recent female legislators, a longtime political reporter exemplifies Kanter's point:

> Dittemore was an exception confirming the rule—a shrewd, tough-minded and gregarious "Good Ole Gal" who played brilliantly at a game designed by Good Ole Boys. In contrast, women played much more varied roles in recent years as they passed the 25–30 percent level. For one thing, women in our legislature have now won the right to screw up without bringing discredit upon anyone but themselves.[102]

In the 1995 legislative session, women were recognized as defining the standards of quality leadership. One veteran statehouse journalist gave an account that marked the transformation from stereotype to standard setter. He singled out Representative Jeanne Adkins as the "outstanding legislator" of the session and noted that the designation "probably should have been made years earlier." The columnist noted that Adkins was once criticized for being "the queen bee" and was "not the most popular legislator" because of her work ethic, strong opinions, and relentless attention to business. Nonetheless, she has developed a solid reputation as a "firm and fair committee chairwoman" who thoroughly understands the legislation she introduces and works hard at the details of the policy process.[103]

Colorado female committee chairs are less constrained than other states' female chairs by gender stereotypes and category expectations. Not one of the Colorado women interviewed felt the need to adopt a gender role to present herself or her legislation in ways designed to be more palatable to male colleagues. In contrast with Ohio and Oklahoma, none of the Colorado chairwomen perceived that their sex uniquely shaped their experiences as committee leaders. According to one female senator:

> "We've had women in the past and that was a big deal with them. . . . It's different now. We're just trying to be people. We want to be judged on our capabilities and don't want to be defined narrowly."[104]

Another chairwoman commented:

> "I don't look for my experiences to be different [from the men] and so they are not. That's partly because I'm older and I don't take any guff from anyone, male or female. It's also because Tom [Norton, Senate President] and his predecessor have not had any difficulty with women in power roles. . . . I realize that's not necessarily typical. Other women have had experiences where they feel they have been treated differently."[105]

## Variations on an Integrative Style

Though Colorado's legislature is less gendered and more amenable to the integrative style, the leadership styles of men and women are not identical. The differences again are subtle, but the women chairs are more likely to emphasize listening, educating others, moderating differences and seeking consensus, and including others. Three-fourths of the women chairs interviewed identified these as personal goals, but none of the men did.

In her analysis of committee speaking behaviors drawn from twelve Colorado House hearings in 1989, Kathlene found marked differences between male and female chairs. Women speak less often, interrupt witnesses and others less frequently, and tend to use their speaking turns for procedural purposes (i.e., to facilitate discussion) rather than for substantive purposes (i.e., to express opinion or direct questions). Kathlene suggests the data reflect a feminized, democratic approach as contrasted with an assertive, autocratic male style. But she also cautions that speaking behaviors may reflect imbalances in gender power.[106] Other factors such as when a woman chairs a committee or when women members sit together contribute to more balanced speaking patterns.[107]

Kathlene's data seem reflective of the aggregative and integrative leadership styles and their association with male and female committee chairs, respectively. The present work provides additional understanding of Kathlene's findings. Several of the people interviewed in 1995 associated skillful listening with women committee chairs. In part, an emphasis on listening may explain the less frequent interruptions of the female chairs in Kathlene's data. It was a trait identified by all the female chairs and by all the legislative staff, lobbyists, and other observers who were interviewed in Colorado. Several women cited "listening" as an essential component of procedural fairness. As one House chairwoman stated:

> "Not everyone is going to be happy with every bill, but I always try to be fair.
> . . . It [fairness] means I've listened. I've heard their objections. I know why
> they are objecting. But if it doesn't facilitate the [committee] process then
> we're going to move on. It's my job to facilitate the process. Fair . . . means
> I've listened and I've explained why."[108]

Echoing that perspective, another woman commented, "It is more important to hear what people have to say. That's more important than whether you agree with what they say."[109]

Majority Leader Norma Anderson illustrates the subtle difference between integrative and aggregative styles. Her reputation as a vote counter, a critical aggregative skill, is widely touted,[110] but when asked about her leadership skills, Anderson focuses on listening. Vote counting and listening are not unrelated, but difference in emphasis matters:

> "You have to listen. I have to listen to all seven constituencies [that divide
> the committee] and be able to mold them together. There's a lot of listen-
> ing. Every member needs to be able to listen, but for a chairman it is abso-
> lutely necessary."[111]

A House Democrat sizing up the skills of the different committee chairs similarly focused on the more integrative abilities of two women:

> "The critical skills of the best chairs are good time management skills. You
> need to allow the public adequate time for testimony while still being able
> to move the agenda along. The other key skill is the ability to pull things
> together. Senator . . . and Senator . . . are able to step outside of the fray, to
> listen to everyone's position and then to get back in and put things together
> in a creative way."[112]

As these comments suggest, listening is not simply passive and empathetic but, rather, active, purposeful, and interpersonal. Through the activity of listening, common ground and purpose are discovered. Whereas vote counting and log rolling are essential to the aggregative style of leadership, listening is fundamental to the integrative style. As the last quote acknowledges, listening engages and brings together others in the process of finding consensus. In pluralistic bargaining, one need not understand (or hear) the concerns or position of the other parties; the leader needs only to assemble bit by bit the necessary majority.

The skill of listening was not exclusively associated with Colorado women, but only one man was singled out in connection with the trait compared with six women. Moreover, the skill was identified by several observers as the distinguishing characteristic of several chairwomen.[113]

Also indicative of the integrative leadership model is the emphasis female chairs place on leadership as education. They do not see their role as simply presiding over committee markups, discussion, and votes, but rather they articulate the goal of developing the committee's knowledge. By contrast, education was not mentioned by any of the male committee chairs, except in a purely instrumental sense of instructing new members in the use of the rules or proper procedure.

One woman chair described the care that she puts into structuring meetings so that members gain a more intimate knowledge of the issues. She instructs the staff to provide background memos to focus the debate on key issues and invites witnesses and resource people who can provide analysis and expertise. When one member expressed frustration about the "seminar" format, she took offense. For her, educating is an essential part of a chair's job.[114]

Another chairwoman emphasized education, particularly with an eye toward impending term limits. Though a sponsor of an extensive agenda of issues, this woman did not specify a particular policy as her primary objective. Rather, she wants her committee to develop a thorough understanding of the agencies under the committee's purview and of the budgeting process:

> "Term limits make you recognize that a committee chair has a different role. You can't let them learn on their own. On-the-job training is a luxury which we no longer have. You have to direct that learning earlier on."[115]

At a subsequent hearing on a technical legal issue, she briefly recessed the committee so that legislative staff could be brought before the committee to explain the legislative history and ramifications behind the bill under consideration. She also planned to schedule budget briefings so that her committee would better understand major capital construction projects and agency operating budgets. With ten of her thirteen committee members in their first or second terms, she feels a responsibility as committee chair to build the level of committee expertise.

Unlike in Oklahoma, where many of the women chairs come from teaching backgrounds, the emphasis on education seems more related to the Colorado women's experiences in community work. All the Colorado chairmen identified legislative or professional experiences as their formative preparation for chairing a committee, but three-fourths of the women identified volunteer, community-based experiences.

The third trait that seems to distinguish the women from the men is an emphasis on inclusiveness and participation that goes beyond the norm already evident in Colorado. For example, even before the GAVEL amendment required hearings on every bill, only two committee chairs—both women—held serious hearings on all bills.[116]

Another chairwoman surveyed all the witnesses who appeared before the committee in an effort to find out their perception of the experience and to solicit suggestions on how to improve committee meetings. Many of her colleagues could not understand why she had gone to such lengths to survey witnesses, but in her mind the reason was quite clear: "I try to make my style emphasize who we serve—the public."[117] Another chairwoman, known for being hard driving and business-like, ticked off a list of committee rules: no beepers or phones in committee, clear absences with the chair, be on time, listen to the testimony and show an interest, always be courteous to the public.[118] For both chairwomen, punctuality, attentiveness in committee, being prepared to conduct hearings in a business-like fashion, and an unwillingness to reschedule bills once they are publicized for a committee meeting are commitments to public participation and sensitivity to the public's time.

The same sensitivity to public involvement leads another woman to adopt a very different approach, an informal, almost folksy style. For example, when she conducts her hearings, witnesses are frequently invited to sit at the committee table and discuss the issues like a family might. In one hearing, she reassured one witness who was clearly nervous and uncomfortable, "That's OK, we get nervous too." Later, she thanked a couple who shared a personal tragedy: "Thanks for lending faces to this."[119]

None of the examples should be taken to suggest that the male committee chairs are insensitive or loutish toward members of the public. Indeed, the commitment to citizen participation is widely held in the General Assembly and should be reiterated. Many of the men voiced a concern for punctuality, courtesy, and comity. The difference cited here is one of degrees, with the women tending more toward the integrative ideal. For example, a slightly different conception of fairness is seen in hearings: For one male chair, the best way to manage testimony is to allot everyone the same amount of time; meanwhile for a female, the best way is to be patient and hear everyone while gently counseling against repetition or "loving a bill to death."

Finally, one aspect of the moderating influence Colorado women seem to bring to the process is the partisan and philosophical middle ground they provide on various issues or in their parties.[120] Several women have earned reputations in recent years as leaders in resolving some of stickiest issues facing the state—school finance, prison construction, health care, juvenile crime, AIDS care, and fiscal issues. Their approach tends to emphasize hours of discussion and meeting with the various stakeholders in an effort to find common ground. Those who are critical of this approach argue that women are "too much driven by compromise."[121] But as Senator Wham's trauma care legislation demonstrated, some issues defy simple, legislatively imposed solutions. After more than eight years of effort and spurred in part by a tragic automobile accident that demonstrated the need for a trauma response network, legislation was finally drafted that was acceptable to the various interest groups. All the parties involved credited Senator Wham's personal efforts in keeping a task force together and working on an acceptable compromise.[122]

Moderating as implied in an integrative style of leadership also means common purpose and mutuality. Mutuality is also at the root of this chairwoman's prescient comment, made more than four months prior to the concealed-weapons showdown described earlier:

> "The men have to have someone else lose to feel that they have won . . . we [the women] look for the win-win situation. They want it all or they are willing to lose the bill. The women compromise . . . compromise in the best sense of the word. They try to talk it out off the floor."[123]

Finally, an interpersonal dimension of mutuality was echoed in the comments of the female committee chairs. All the legislators identified the importance of comity and collegiality. The difference between the men and the women, however, is that male committee chairs tend to describe comity as an instrumental goal, a means to accomplishing other goals, a value that facilitates the committee process. Not surprisingly, some chairmen pursue comity in counterintuitive ways. For example, one chairman described his "greatest trick" for teaching newer members humility: "Everybody on the committee knows the play." The committee "ambushes" the sponsor, promptly and without explanation killing his or her bill only to resurrect it later.[124]

For the women, maintenance of interpersonal relations is not only a procedural value but also a goal in and of itself. One female senator worried about the emotional toll some issues would take on her committee over the course of the legislative session. Asked to describe what would make for a "successful" session, she said:

> "I want us to become a team. That does not necessarily mean we will agree on everything. But success would be that we showed respect for one another, that witnesses never felt mistreated or abused in committee, that we finished our work on time. . . . I want us to do our work thoughtfully."[125]

Among the female committee chairs, relationships developed through team building, educating, and maintaining collegiality are an end goal as well as a modal goal that facilitates the process of decision making.

Burns makes a similar distinction between modal values such as due process and fair play and end values such as equality.[126] Transactional leaders are concerned with and driven by modal values, whereas transformational leaders seek to realize or achieve end values. He writes:

> "The object in these [transactional] cases is not a joint effort for persons with common aims acting for the collective interests of followers but a bargain to aid the individual interests of persons or groups going their separate ways. . . . The premise of [transformational] leadership is that, whatever the separate interests persons might hold, they are presently or potentially united in the pursuit of 'higher' goals, the realization of which is tested by the

achievement of significant change that represents the collective or pooled interests of leaders and followers."[127]

## Conclusion

In 1988, then House Majority Leader Chris Paulson complained that the women of the Colorado legislature had perfected the skills required for campaigns but not for lawmaking:

> "They go home at night and write notes to thank the people that helped them get elected. Those are sure votes. But they don't have the right skills for legislating. They don't have any business experience. They don't have any experience making decisions. They don't understand why everything cannot be done."[128]

Ehrenhalt argues that Paulson's frustrations do not reflect a gender difference but rather characterize a new breed of legislator and the tension between the politics of campaigning and the politics of legislating.[129] Indeed a new breed of legislator may be caught up in campaigning and less concerned with policymaking, but Ehrenhalt is too quick to dismiss the possibility of a gender difference and may have identified the wrong tension.

Paulson's criticism of women in 1988 reflects the assumptions of aggregative leadership—the command-and-control philosophy of the military world and the logic of exchange and reciprocity found in markets and business. The integrative style, which many women embrace, is a fundamentally different way of approaching the legislative institution and the processes of lawmaking. In ways that a former military man like Paulson would appreciate and presumably see in the business world, aggregative leaders are decisive, give orders, understand the logic of the marketplace, and keep situations under control. By contrast, integrative leaders try to educate, to bring people along, to seek seemingly impossible consensus, and to communicate their appreciation for everyone's contribution. The circumstances that provoked Paulson's comment in 1988 are obscure, but his frustration may reflect the clash of these different leadership perspectives. Legislating in the old aggregative style means counting noses and putting together winning coalitions. Integrative leadership values listening and participation, strives for consensus in the face of disagreements, and sees value in thank-you notes.

The environment in Colorado tilts toward the integrative rather than the aggregative model of leadership so clearly dominant in Oklahoma. A collaborative policy process is necessary to bind together the state's diverse interests, a moralistic tendency motivates political leaders, and an open participative process is a tradition of the Colorado legislature. But it also seems to be the case that women in their committee leadership roles are pushing the envelope subtly closer to the integrative ideal.

# 9

# A Vision of Integrative Leadership

There are more people buried in Arlington [National Cemetery] than
you think. On the back of many tombstones—who would look there?—
is another inscription. It says, "His Wife." That's it. His Wife. A few, *very
few*, say something like "Lucy, His Wife." Almost never a date of birth or
death. Buried behind Her Husband, not next to him, no tombstone of
her own.

—Maxine Berman, *The Only Boobs in the House Are Men*

State Representative Maxine Berman describes the anonymity of the un-
known wives of Arlington cemetery to drive home the point that women
remain collectively invisible in American politics. In a bitingly sarcastic, sometimes bawdy portrayal of life in the Michigan State Legislature, Representative Berman laments the absence of women wielding visible political power
and wonders whether politics and legislatures would be different if they did.[1]
The picture of women as committee leaders suggests that when legislatures
reflect the diversity in the general population, they also may "think, feel, reason and act" in a different fashion. Indeed, the perspective from the other side
of the tombstone has the potential to be quite different.

I conclude where I began this inquiry by interrelating gender, leadership,
and legislatures, the institutional context in which committee chairs "do leadership." By studying women in legislative leadership roles, a distinctive pattern
of legislative leadership emerges. Just as Jeane Kirkpatrick proclaimed twenty
years ago "political woman exists,"[2] here too the most important conclusion is
that an integrative style of legislative leadership exists and is more visible in
the committee behavior of women than of men.

## The Promise and Possibility of Integrative Leadership

At the outset, I described two styles of leadership drawing from a variety of
theoretical perspectives. These two types—aggregative leadership and integrative leadership—differ in their underlying logics, their styles of behavior, and
their structure and purpose. (Recall figure 2.1 in chapter 2.) Integrative leader-

ship is transformational, involving a mutually empowering emphasis on shared values. Integrative institutions are concerned with the appropriateness of how decisions are made, and their participants act out of a sense of communal purpose. In contrast, aggregative leadership is explicitly transactional; participants calculate the consequences of different strategies and compete for advantage or a share of a decision; aggregative institutions are judged by their outcomes rather than by their procedures.

Transactional or aggregative leadership is understood to be the norm of legislative leadership; it is, however, a paradigm based on the study of institutions historically populated by men. As this study suggests, integrative leadership (like transactional leadership) also has an empirical reality, a reality made clear by examining institutions in which *both* men and women occupy leadership roles.

In this examination, the pattern of female committee leadership stands closer to the integrative type. Certainly, I make no suggestion that a sex-linked gene predetermines leadership behavior. Quite the contrary, leadership is a complex phenomenon of individual experiences, circumstances, and relationships. Nonetheless, on a wide variety of individual measures of leadership traits, motivation, or behavior, women and men differ in ways that are substantively and statistically significant. Admittedly, the differences are modest, placing the "average" woman at no more than the sixtieth to seventieth percentile of men on any given leadership trait. And, to be sure, aggregative and integrative leadership are best conceptualized as a continuum rather than two distinctly separate forms. Nonetheless, the cumulative weight of the evidence becomes too stubborn to deny: Integrative leadership is a more feminine mode.

The real utility of the aggregative-integrative typology moves theory beyond the distributive paradigm dominating legislative studies, a paradigm perpetuated by the study of mostly male institutions. The alternative vision, although not wholly new, clearly has been underappreciated. Celebrated today as "a prophet of management," Mary Parker Follett voiced this vision in the 1920s. But as management guru Peter Drucker notes, Follett was rejected in the 1930s and 1940s because her views ran contrary to the "men and creed" and "zeitgeist" of leadership as domination, economic self-interest, and competition. Follett wrote:[3]

> The leader guides the group and is at the same time himself guided by the group, is always a part of the group. No one can truly lead except from within . . . the leader must interpret our experience to us, must see all the different points of view which underlie our daily activities and also their connections, must adjust the varying and often conflicting needs, must lead the group to an understanding of its needs and to a unification of its purpose. He must give form to things vague, things latent, to mere tendencies. . . . The power of leadership is the power of integrating which creates community. . . . The person who influences me most is not he who does great deeds but he who makes me feel I can do great deeds.[4]

## When Women Lead

For much of the nation's history, women have been largely invisible as political leaders. Although Abigail Adams offered sage advice to her husband John, as did other presidential helpmates, she participated in politics through "republican motherhood," a distinctly private, vicarious, and feminine understanding of public spiritedness expressed in the familial nurture and support of sons and husbands.[5]

Clearly as more women have entered politics, they have become more visible, yet a certain element of republican motherhood remains. Women even today are more likely to leave the pursuit of political office to men. A recent study by the National Women's Political Caucus concluded that underrepresentation of women in office was not a result of a lack of electoral success but rather a lack of female candidates.[6]

Republican motherhood also brings the formative forge of hearth and home to bear on a feminine understanding of leadership. More often than men, female committee chairs approach politics with an understanding and skills that have been shaped by family, community, volunteerism, and education. They are like their male colleagues in many ways, but important differences exist: Women are older, defer political careers until past their primary years of childrearing and family responsibilities, and hone their leadership ability in the classroom and community center rather than in the boardroom and locker room. Admittedly, some women today run at an earlier age or launch political careers from their professional lives, and men share more in family duties. The fact remains, however, that differences in childhood socialization, sex-segregated work, and specialization in different forms of emotional labor persist prior to legislative service for men and women.

Because of background, female committee chairs bring different motivations to the practice of committee leadership. Though no less driven by a desire for power, status, or good legislative service, female committee chairs articulate a different set of motivations than do their male colleagues. Women tend to be more motivated by policy, to want to champion issues, and to strive to use legislating for creative problem solving. At the same time, these female committee chairs place more emphasis on the goals of involving people in the policy process, building coalitions, empowering others, and forging consensus.

As predicted, background differences also lead to diverse behaviors. Women committee chairs consult more frequently with other members and other committee chairs, they more often share strategic and political information, and they spend more time developing the skills of others. They are task oriented. When resolving conflicts or deciding contentious issues, women committee chairs prefer to tackle issues head on but with a collaborative style that never assumes the primacy of their own position. The women lead by listening. In some contexts, a gendered interpretation portrays this approach as both feminine and implicitly weak—too willing to concede to others. But women tend not to see consensus as concession or to calculate victory by the defeat of others.

Of course, all legislators are not cast from a single mold. Researchers have attached labels to a diversity of types: promoters, pragmatists and accommodators[7]; advertisers, reluctants, spectators, and lawmakers[8]; inventors, brokers, tribunes, ritualists, and opportunists.[9] Nor is there an Everywoman. Women in politics come in a rainbow of representational styles: leaders, personalizers, moralizers, problem solvers;[10] women's rights advocates, benchwarmers, traditional civic workers, and passive women's rights supporters.[11] In spite of this individuality, commonalities or central tendencies in leadership styles distinguish male and female committee chairs.

Cynthia Fuchs Epstein argues that much of social science research emphasizes sex differences and gives too little attention to similarities.[12] To be sure, male and female committee chairs are quite alike on many criteria. They are equally ambitious, highly satisfied with their legislative roles and successes, and from backgrounds that are racially, economically, and religiously comparable. Men and women also are found chairing committees across the gamut of state policy issues. Nonetheless, men and women serve in gendered institutions where their experiences as committee chairs—with social networks, mentoring and overall visibility— differ considerably.

This study demonstrates that sex, the social understandings of gender, and gendered institutions all influence leadership style. As chapter 5 (in this volume) shows, the sex of a committee chair is a significant predictor of committee style, even when controlling for personality, demographic, and organizational variables. Personality variables, however, suggest that the social expressions of femininity and masculinity are also important influences on leadership. Integrative leadership behaviors and motivations are positively associated with personality traits of nurturing but negatively linked to dominance. In other words, chairs who describe themselves as dominant and competitive are least likely to embrace integrative motives and behaviors.

The sex composition of legislatures and the institutional arrangements of gender power are key dimensions of gendered legislatures, and this study ilustrates their significant role in shaping leadership. Most important, the exploratory analysis of interactions between gender and context suggests two important points: (1) the presence of more women and the share of power held by women affect male and female chairs differently, and (2) women's committee behavior varies more with contextual circumstances than does men's. In institutions and political cultures predominantly and traditionally male dominated, women leaders face unique pressures as leaders.

The stories from Colorado, Ohio, and Oklahoma illustrate the centrality of numbers and power. For example, tokenism imposes gendered stereotypes in ways that distort behavior. Individuals may *say and do* one thing while others *hear and perceive* behavior that is highly stereotypical. It is no coincidence that women chairs in states with a history of more substantial numbers of women lawmakers, for example, Idaho, Kansas, or Arizona, see the fewest barriers, feel more accepted, or experience less sexism. In many state legislatures, however, women still find themselves in token circumstances, where they confront stereotyping and are typecast to play gendered roles. The most salient feature of a token female committee chair is her womanhood, her "otherhood."

For men, the presence of more women increases the likelihood of mentorship by or exposure to women in leadership. Men who have female mentors appear to be more accepting of integrative styles. When men have honed their skills under female mentors, they tend to be more participatory, less competitive, and more collaborative.

Notwithstanding the impact of more female colleagues, when women begin to hold real institutional power as leaders and chairs, they sometimes meet resistance. The woman-led confrontation over leadership philosophy in the Minnesota House in 1996, the difficulties accepting powerful women in Oklahoma, and day-to-day encounters with sexism are examples. The interaction analysis in chapter 5 provides additional evidence. The experience in Colorado suggests that when women's voices are well established and placed throughout the legislature, resistance eventually disappears. Given that the Colorado General Assembly has greater experience with women lawmakers than any other state, changing norms of leadership or creating institutions open to integrative leadership requires considerable patience.

I have argued that professional legislatures are least accommodating to integrative styles of leadership. These lawmaking bodies tend to place a higher priority on policy entrepreneurship and competition and to undervalue public participation. Professions by definition tend to distinguish themselves from others by their expertise, autonomy, and self-contained brotherhoods. Not surprisingly then, the female chairs in these institutions also are more likely than chairwomen in "citizen" legislatures to subscribe to traits such as dominance, less inclusive committee management, and competition.

In the end, the integrative aspects of women's committee leadership behavior are all the more striking because they exist and flourish in spite of culturally and institutionally ingrained male leadership images[13] and in spite of a logic of economic rationality and consequentiality that pervades political institutions.[14]

## Gender Equality and Integrative Institutions

I asked at the outset whether more descriptively representative legislatures would act differently, practice politics in different ways, and necessarily embody a different approach to leadership. A clear-cut answer to this query remains illusive. Though it is tempting to immediately say yes, the case studies demonstrate that gender equality (or inequality) does not operate in a vacuum. Institutional procedures and traditions, political culture, social conditions, partisan politics, and individual personalities also are part of the face of a representative institution. Might the Oklahoma Legislature operate differently with more women? Certainly. But bringing more women into the institution probably will not come without other changes in societal or political dynamics. Is the Colorado General Assembly the way it is because of the number of women chairs? Again, the answer is yes. Nonetheless, it is difficult to unravel the causal chain of gender, moralistic culture, political geography, and legislative tradition. Will the Ohio General Assembly be a changed institution under its next speaker? Yes, but it is impossible to predict how enduring an impact Jo Ann Davidson's example will have.

What would it take to create institutions in which integrative leadership takes its place alongside classically distributive strategies? The case studies sketch out the preconditions of such a transformation. Certainly integrative institutions would have a balance of men and women sharing power and responsibilities so that performance pressures of tokenism disappear and women's power is accepted. Integrative institutions would have deliberative procedures and a collective, rather than individualistic, sense of purpose. The larger political culture and social values of the state would be open to, and supportive of, moderation, good followership, and community building. Sociologist Robert N. Bellah and his colleagues, the authors of *Habits of the Heart*, call this conception "the politics of community"[15] and acknowledge that it requires a transformation of our social ecology away from its extreme individualism.[16]

Political scientists Cooper and Brady have proposed a "contextualist" theory of leadership behavior,[17] and Ronald M. Peters Jr. has extended it in his historical examination of the speakership.[18] The gist of Cooper and Brady's argument is that a leader's style adapts to or is shaped by the institutional circumstances in which he or she serves. In turn, the institutional context reflects societal forces and the broader evolution of the political system. In Peters's analysis of the speakership, the key historical determinants of the office are the policy agenda, the party system, the role of the presidency, and the institutionalization of the House. Because of the evidence presented here and women's growing presence in politics, I argue that the list of contextual determinants can no longer neglect gender and the gendered nature of political institutions. By gender, I do not mean the biological fact of sex but, rather, the social, cultural, and political meanings associated with male and female.

Political theorist Mary Hawkesworth proposes that oppression can only be overcome by fundamentally altering the constitutional order and mandating sex parity in public office. In lieu of such a radical constitutional change, it appears that steady movement toward parity in state legislatures (or any public institution) also inches toward a "reconstitution of political life."[19] This movement, however, is likely to be something less than a dramatic conversion of interest-group transactional politics into communitarian-style integrative politics.

Indeed, some problems are best solved by the political logic of economics. As Peter Drucker writes, "Economic interests can be compromised, which is the great strength of basing politics on economic interests. 'Half a loaf is still bread' is a meaningful saying."[20] For similar reasons, Burns asserts that legislative leadership is inherently transactional.[21] Because many legislative issues remain primarily matters of "who gets what, when and how," there will continue to be a place for leaders who are skilled in the arts of bargaining and compromise.

Increasingly, however, legislatures are asked to deal with issues of values around which conflicts seem irreconcilable or for which half a solution is no solution at all. In this environment, leaders are needed who are skilled in the process of listening, educating, and facilitating the definition of shared values. A legislature composed of equal numbers of women and men alters the mix of leadership skills and increases the probability that leaders with integrative skills can move to the fore.

In the end, we are reminded that legislatures serve many functions and thus require different skills, abilities, and types of leaders. Deliberation involves a complex of contrasting elements: analysis and intuition, persuasion and listening, forcefulness and accommodation, decisiveness and patience. Representation entails the often contradictory responsibilities of leading while following, standing for yet acting for, reflecting the interests of different parts and at the same time seeking a common whole. When a legislature comprises only one segment of society or utilizes only a single style of leadership, the institution falls far short of its promise and its possibilities.

In one other respect, a more descriptively representative legislature would be a different kind of institution. Gender is deeply embedded in American culture and is threaded through the images we hold of politics, administration, and leadership.[22] Those images communicate meanings and are saddled with normative labels. Until now, strength, power, and dispassionate analysis were associated with male leadership and seen as inherently good. Femininity has been construed as weak, submissive, and emotional and normatively less desirable in leadership. As organizational life evolves and more women exercise political leadership, the labels will also change. Both men and women will experience more personal freedom to define and establish a leadership style that is less encumbered by gendered assumptions and meanings.

The lesson from Colorado is that individuation free from gender stereotypes comes only after gender near parity has achieved a certain ordinariness, when women are no longer "the first" this or that. In Colorado, the significant presence of women in the General Assembly must be seen as the cumulative impact of the positions women hold and their sheer staying power. The recent experience in Ohio under Speaker Jo Ann Davidson also suggests that a single, strategically prominent woman can have a powerful influence on the leadership philosophy of an institution. That is not to dismiss the impact of Oklahoma women on their legislature but rather to acknowledge that their performance is still evaluated as aberrant, exceptions to be explained rather than considered part of the normative definition of leadership behavior.

An example from history suggests how subtly institutional images change. Women's early activist voices in politics and the administrative state were often at odds with dominant values. Social feminists of the late 1800s and early 1900s—

whether part of the abolitionist, suffrage, or settlement house movements—practiced private benevolence based on compassion, communitarian activism, and a highly personal understanding of social policy.[23] Women contributed uniquely to the social services that were part of the new administrative state, yet in many ways their roles were paradoxical to the turn-of-the-century vision of bureaucratic efficiency, universalism, and scientific management. By the 1930s, however, a new era of management thinking was coming to the fore, an era emphasizing human relations. The direct connection between women's role and visibility in social welfare services and the emergent human relations paradigm may be tenuous, but as part of a broader sweep of cultural change the linkage seems plausible.

In sum, when women hold a substantial proportion of legislative leadership roles over a sustained period, perhaps our lawmaking institutions will be free of gendered conceptions of what constitutes appropriate legislative leadership. At a minimum, the talent pool of integrative leaders will be enlarged and granted a legitimacy and status comparable to a long tradition of aggregative leaders.

## A Cautionary Note

Speculation about a future of gender parity in politics must be accompanied by a note of realism: Institutional reforms, which are being proposed for and imposed upon legislatures, will do nothing to nurture the soil from which integrative leadership will grow. Limitations on state legislative terms have been adopted in twenty states (including the three featured here) and are contributing to higher turnover, membership instability, declining followership, and foreshortened policy horizons.[24] Initiatives and referenda are increasingly popular but tend to reduce complex policy questions to sound bites and slogans. These so-called reforms further undermine the processes of deliberation. For example, Claremont Graduate School political scientist Sherry Jeffe Bebitch observed about the California Assembly, "This once great deliberative body has sunk to the level of a petulant sand-box fight, except little kids aren't as mean and hateful as some of these folks."[25]

At risk is the "quiet work" of integrative politics. A former California assemblywoman described female committee chairs whom she has known and respected as specializing in the quiet work of legislatures.[26] With this term, she captures the key elements of institutions based on integrative politics and appropriateness, and of women's ways of leadership. For her, "quiet work" involves listening, foregoing publicity, defining the boundaries of mutual commitments, teasing out shared values, and seeking modest solutions to vexing problems.

In the cacophony of contemporary politics, the quiet work is at risk. We would do well to sustain and celebrate it as Lao-Tzu does:

For governing a country well
there is nothing better than moderation.

The mark of a moderate man
is freedom from his own ideas.
Tolerant like the sky,
all-pervading like sunlight,
firm like a mountain,
supple like a tree in the wind,
he has no destination in view
and makes use of anything
life happens to bring his way.

Nothing is impossible for him.
Because he has let go,
he can care for the people's welfare
as a mother cares for her child.[27]

When women truly integrate all aspects of governing, then perhaps a mother's care and the quiet ways of leadership will become as much accepted and valued in politics as are competition and conflict.

# Appendix: Methodology

Because of a desire to understand committee leadership at both the indi-vidual level and in its organizational setting, the study employed a triangulated research strategy. The research consisted of three complementary elements: (1) a mailed survey of male and female committee chairs from fifty state legislatures, (2) focused peer-group interviews with women committee chairs, and (3) interviews, fieldwork, and direct observation of committee chairs in three state legislatures.

## The Survey

The questionnaire was mailed in March 1994 to all 353 women and a random sample of 516 men who chaired standing or statutory committees at that time. Along with questions on demographic characteristics, pre–political, career and legislative career history, the survey consisted of seventy-five Likert-scale items, designed for factor analysis or development of scales. The items covered leadership traits, motivations, committee operations, use of information, decision-making strategies, and attitudes about conflict, power, ambition, and peer relationships.

The design of the questionnaire was shaped by previous research as well as semistructured interviews with women committee chairs. These interviews were conducted in 1992 in Oklahoma and in 1992 in conjunction with the Women's Network at the annual meeting of the National Conference of State Legislatures (NCSL). Prior to mailing, the questionnaire was administered to twelve individuals and then revised on the basis of their input. Copies of the questionnaire can be obtained from the author.

To enhance the survey's reliability, items were used from previous studies. First, questions on leadership traits were borrowed from several recent studies of male and female public administrators in state governments.[1] In addition, the survey included Fielder's Least Preferred Coworker instrument, which has proven highly reliable in assessing a person's underlying orientation toward task goals versus relationship objectives.[2] Finally, the questionnaire included several scales developed from the Thomas-Killmann conflict management instrument. The Thomas-Kilmann Conflict Mode Instrument is well established in the field of organizational behavior. The authors of the instrument report reliability coefficients for each of the five styles of .60 or higher. The authors also report evidence of substantive validity based on concurrent tests of four conflict-handling instruments that suggest convergence around the five modes in Thomas's theory. According to reviews of the instrument in *The Tenth Mental Measurements Yearbook,* the Thomas-Kilmann instrument when compared to similar organizational behavior instruments has the highest reliability coefficients and the lowest variance in scores that can be attributed to factors of social desirability.[3]

The sample was drawn from mailing lists of standing committee chairs used by the NCSL and from the directory of the Council of State Governments, *State Legislative Leadership, Committees & Staff 1993–1994,* which includes chairs of statutory committees. To maximize returns, letters of endorsement were obtained from prominent legislators and officials of the NCSL, surveys also included personalized notes, and follow-up contact and mailings were done.[4]

Completed surveys were received from 135 women, a response rate of 39 percent, and 156 men, a response rate of 30.5 percent. The response rate is based on the original sample minus questionnaires returned as undeliverable or from an individual who was no longer a committee chair. One additional follow-up letter probably is the primary factor contributing to the higher response rate among women than among men. The usable responses (after incomplete surveys are excluded) is 289 committee chairs (135 women and 154 men).

## The Sample

Respondents are representative of the population of committee chairs. Generally, the number of respondents is proportionate to the number of chairs in each state. Only Tennessee had no respondents in the survey. Low response rates from some states seem to be associated with timing or special circumstances. For example, the low response rate from Florida is most likely attributable to the timing of the survey and its follow-up, which coincided with Florida's compressed session schedule in April and May. No gender bias is evident among the states in terms of responses. The number of women who completed the survey in a state was significantly and positively correlated with the number of men who responded ($r = .308$, $p = .038$).

Female committee chairs in forty states responded to the study. Nine of the ten states with no female survey respondents are among twelve states with the lowest percentage of women chairs, and five of these states have two or fewer women chairs. The number of female respondents was positively and significantly correlated with the number of female chairs in a state ($r = .512$, $p = .000$).

In terms of party affiliation, committees chaired, and type of legislature, the survey respondents match generally the total population of committee chairs as calculated by the author.[5] See Table A.1.

With respect to age, race, educational attainment, and marital status, the committee chair respondents also parallel a 1994 profile of state legislators based on 900 lawmakers from sixteen states.[6] For example, 32.3 percent chairs in the sample have at least an undergraduate degree (compared with 35 percent of Woo's 900 legislators), 79.2 percent are married (compared with 83 percent), the average age of committee chairs is 53.6 years (compared to 50). Almost 95 percent of chairs report their racial background as Caucasian (compared with 90 percent of legislators).

Diagnostic tests for heteroskedasticity in the sample were performed, and no problems were found.

Table A.1.  Comparison of Overall Committee Population and Survey Respondents

|  | Women | | Men | |
|---|---|---|---|---|
|  | % of All Female Chairs | % of Survey Respondents | % of All Male Chairs | % of Survey Respondents |
| *Committee Chaired* | | | | |
| health & social services | 16.6% | 21.1% | 6.9% | 10.4% |
| education | 8.7 | 9.0 | 5.5 | 9.1 |
| natural resources & agri. | 6.7 | 6.8 | 12.6 | 16.9 |
| business, labor, & | | | | |
|   consumer affairs | 14.0 | 18.0 | 9.2 | 11.7 |
| budget & tax | 9.6 | 13.5 | 11.3 | 14.3 |
| general government | 27.2 | 12.0 | 21.6 | 14.9 |
| judiciary & crim. justice | 8.1 | 10.5 | 9.0 | 15.6 |
| leadership & rules | 2.8 | 1.5 | 6.6 | 4.5 |
| other | 6.5 | 7.5 | 7.1 | 2.6 |
| *Type of Legislature* | | | | |
| Citizen | 33.7 | 34.1 | 32.5 | 36.4 |
| Hybrid | 46.1 | 47.4 | 43.9 | 37.7 |
| Professional | 20.2 | 18.5 | 23.6 | 26.0 |
| *Political Party* | | | | |
| Democrat | 64.4 | 54.1 | 69.5 | 60.4 |
| Republican | 35.6 | 45.9 | 30.5 | 39.6 |

*Note.* Committee assignments and type of legislature for the overall population of state legislative committee chairs are based on author's calculation from Council of State Governments' *Directory.* Party data is from CAWP.

## The Focus Groups

The baseline survey was a necessary first step in delineating gender-based differences, but focused peer-group interviews and participant observation were designed to provide elaboration and insight into the survey results.[7] The term "focused peer-group interviews" is borrowed from William A. Gamson, a political scientist specializing in political communication, to distinguish the format as a variant of focus groups.[8] The key distinction, which Gamson identifies, is the selection of participants who already know each other.

The focus groups were conducted in conjunction with two annual conventions of the NCSL, held July 1994 in New Orleans, Louisiana, and July 1996 in St. Louis, Missouri. In all, thirty-eight chairs participated in the focus groups. The twenty-six women and twelve men represented twenty-four states, both parties (twenty-one Republicans and eighteen Democrats), and a range of legislative tenures (two to thirty years). The participants included one Asian-American and two African-American legislators.

Convenience sampling was used to select the participants; in other words, the participants were drawn from the attendance list of the meeting. Because of state budget constraints on travel, different state procedures for selecting attendees to the meeting, and personal schedules, the NCSL attendees may not reflect the universe of committee chairs. Nonetheless, an effort was made to involve a diverse group of participants. Each focus group lasted ninety minutes, was recorded and transcribed, and then coded by selected topics for analysis.[9] Participants spoke with the understanding that they would not be quoted by name.

The focus questions dealt with their experiences as committee chairs, factors in their states that shape leadership style, and differences among the states. In 1995, the focus groups included only women who discussed the preliminary survey findings and thus helped "to triangulate" the different forms of data collection. Of particular import, the focus groups were questioned about how and why the survey findings may vary in different settings. Morgan notes that focus groups are "useful when it comes to investigating *what* participants think, but they excel at uncovering *why* participants think as they do."[10] In 1996, the three focus groups (an all-female group, an all-male group, and one mixed group) discussed similar questions to facilitate comparison between the three groups. The second wave of focus groups drew out the discussants on committee decision-making practices, the meaning of consensus, and perceptions about gender differences.

Through the focus groups and individual interviews, the study reached all fifty states but did not include any women from Florida, Kentucky, Louisiana, New Jersey, New York, and South Carolina.

## Fieldwork

The three field states (Colorado, Ohio, and Oklahoma) were selected based on a number of factors including the number of women in the legislature, the extent of legislative professionalization, and a variety of political culture factors. (See appendix table 2.) In addition, considerations of access were also taken into account. Each of the three states received at least two field visits of one week each. Initial semistructured interviews were conducted with at least eight committee chairs (four male and four female) in each state. All committee chairs were asked about their personal goals for the session, the membership of their committees, key characteristics of their leadership style, formative leadership experiences or preparation, and whether they had encountered circumstances or treatment that was sex specific or sex related. Follow-up interviews obtained the committee chairs' explanations and elaboration of events that transpired in committees meetings during the observation period.[11]

The participating committee chairs were identified on the basis of recommendations by informed observers and were contacted in advance by letter to solicit their cooperation. Efforts were made to get a mix of tenure, experiences, committee jurisdictions, and styles. Interviews with others (i.e., staff, journalists, lobbyists, and scholars) were arranged as time allowed. Although all the participants spoke freely and candidly, the interviews were confidential. All direct quotes come from open public forums and published reports or are used with the respondent's approval.

In addition, committee hearings were monitored using the Sequential Analysis of Verbal Interaction (SAVI) coding system to track the communication behaviors of the chairs.[12] The SAVI observation system captures communication behaviors along "task" and "maintenance" of interpersonal relations dimensions. The communication patterns of the meetings were coded and tallied. Because I had no second coder with whom to compare results for reliability purposes, the results of these tabulations were used primarily as confirmation of other observations of committee behavior rather than as a principal source of data.

## The Data Analysis

The regression results in the appendix tables 4 through 9 report four models. The first covers the whole sample and includes demographic, personality, and contextual variables. I included all personality variables that had significant bivariate correlations with the dependent variable in the regression equation. The second and third models report the same variables in separate analyses for women and men. The fourth model includes interaction terms for sex and culture, sex and percentage of women legislators, sex and percentage of women-held leadership positions, and sex and legislative professionalization.

State environmental and social variables have been implicated as inhibiting female representation in state legislatures. Using regression analysis, Nelson explains 41 percent of the variance in female state legislative membership using twenty-two independent variables.[13] Five variables significantly predict the number of women serving in state legislatures consistent with intuitive expectations. These include the percentage of women employed in the labor market, two religious variables (the percentage of conservative Protestants and Catholics), traditional support for antidiscrimination legislation, and the proportion of a state's population located in metropolitan areas. Nelson found more women legislators in states in which a greater percentage of the population lives in metropolitan areas and more women work outside of the home and states that have a history of early adoption of antidiscrimination laws.[14] By contrast, states with a larger number of religious conservatives elect fewer women lawmakers.

Initial analyses of the committee chair surveys included the five key variables suggested by Nelson's analysis. These variables, however, generally added no more explanatory power to the analysis than already provided by the variables for female legislators and leaders and Sharkansky's adaptation of Elazar's three political cultures. In addition, problems of multicollinearity were evident. In the interests of parsimony, only political culture, legislative professionalization, and women in the legislature were used in the contextual analysis.

Because all the leadership-style variables except the inclusiveness scale are based on standardized scales, the "b" in the regression tables approximates a standard deviation of variation. On the inclusiveness scale, a "b" of one represents one response category on one of the five-point questions (five questions made up the overall measure). Therefore, a "b" of 3.5 (e.g., the interaction model in Table 4) indicates that women on average scored three and a half increments out of a possible twenty-five higher than the men. Since the standard deviation for the scale is 3.49, the results indicate women chairs on average score one standard deviation higher than men.

Figure 5.1 was developed by regressing only the power variable, sex and the interaction term on the dependent variables. The pattern and magnitude of results shown in Figure 5.1 are substantially the same as in Appendix tables 6 and 8 for accommodating and collaborating scales. For the inclusiveness scale, the results shown in figure 5.1 and Appendix table 4 reflect how men's and women's scores differ significantly; however the table reveals even more pronounced effects of women's power on men's behavior when other variables are included as controls.

Table A.2. Selected Characteristics of Colorado, Ohio, and Oklahoma

| State | Elazar's Political Culture[a] | Type of Legislature[b] | % Women in 1994 Legislature | % Women Leader and Chairs | % Women in Labor Force | % Pop. in Metro Areas | % Catholic or Conservative Protestants[c] |
|---|---|---|---|---|---|---|---|
| Colorado | M | 2 | 35.0 | 29.4 | 62.5 | 81.5 | 25.1%/ 13.0% |
| Ohio | IM | 3 | 21.2 | 11.8 | 54.7 | 79.0 | 24.2%/ 21.7% |
| Oklahoma | TI | 2 | 9.4 | 7.8 | 53.5 | 59.4 | 8.0%/ 44.1% |
| US Ave. | NA | NA | 20.5 | 17.6 | 56.8 | 77.5 | 26.2%/ 24.7% |

[a]"M" stands for moralistic, "IM" for individualistic and moralistic, and "TI" for the blend of traditionalistic and individualistic cultures.

[b]A "3" represents the most professionalized, full-time, highly staffed legislatures in Kurtz's typology. A "2" represents the hybrid category of more part-time legislatures with some professional staff resources.

[c]The first number shown represents those who identify their religious affiliation as Roman Catholic. The second number represents those identifying their religious preference as Baptist, Pentecostal, Church of Christ, Assemblies of God, Jehovah's Witness, Seventh-Day Adventist, Holiness, Evangelical, and Nazarene.

Sources: Elazar (1972), Kurtz (1992), 1990 U.S. Census, and Center for American Women in Politics (1993), Kosmin and Lachman (1993).

Table A.3. Influence of Female Mentoring on Leadership Styles

|  | Committee Chairs | | | | | |
|---|---|---|---|---|---|---|
|  | Women (N = 134) | | Men identifying 1+ female mentors (N = 62) | | Men identifying no female mentors (N = 91) | |
|  | Mean | Std Deviation | Mean | Std Deviation | Mean | Std Deviation |
| Collaborative Style***+++ | .221 | .98 | −.037 | .83 | −.289 | 1.06 |
| Competing Style | −.068 | 1.08 | −.047 | .82 | .127 | .98 |
| Avoidance Style | −.120 | .97 | .074 | 1.13 | .122 | .95 |
| Inclusive Style*+ | .132 | .93 | .084 | 1.00 | −.228 | 1.05 |
| People Motivation***+++ | .203 | .95 | .059 | .89 | −.340 | 1.05 |
| Policy Motivation* | .171 | .92 | −.204 | 1.00 | −.113 | 1.08 |
| Dominator Traits*+ | −.168 | .96 | .125 | .97 | .165 | 1.05 |
| Nurturer Traits**++ | .207 | .92 | −.131 | 1.13 | −.219 | .97 |
| Innovator Traits*+ | .145 | .87 | −.041 | 1.03 | −.188 | 1.13 |
| Competent Traits*** | .235 | .93 | −.394 | 1.05 | −.083 | .98 |

*p < .050, **p < .010, and ***p < .001 denotes a significant difference in means between one or more of the groups in one way analysis of variance using Student-Newman-Keuls test.

+denotes a significant weighted linear trend in oneway analysis of variance with an F-ratio probability of < .050, ++denotes an F-ratio probability of < .010, and +++denotes an F-ratio probability of < .001. Although the linear trends are significant on the policy motivation and competent traits, the pattern does not conform to the expected direction.

Table A.4. Regression Models for Inclusive Behaviors

| Variable | All Chairs | Men Only | Women Only | Interaction Model |
|---|---|---|---|---|
|  | (Unstandardized b reported) | | | |
| Female | .22 | — | — | 3.62** |
| Age | −.03 | −.02 | −.03 | −.02 |
| Years in legislature | .10*** | .09** | .13** | .08** |
| Democrat | .60* | .25 | 1.15** | .93** |
| Professional legislature | −1.16**** | −1.15**** | −1.29**** | −1.43**** |
| Female × prof. legis. | — | — | — | .02 |
| Moralistic culture | .09 | .06 | .19 | .13 |
| Female × moralistic | — | — | — | .02 |
| % Female legislators | .01 | .01** | −.01 | .01** |
| Female × % female | — | — | — | −.01* |
| Female power | .00 | −.71* | 1.11** | −.65* |
| Female × female power | — | — | — | 1.66** |
| Personality traits: | | | | |
| Nurturer | .43** | .23 | .78*** | — |
| Innovator | .75**** | .58** | 1.08**** | — |
| Dependable | .46** | .29 | .68*** | — |
| Dominator | −.40** | −.26 | −.50** | — |
| R-square | .28 | .23 | .42 | .21 |
| Adj R | .24 | .16 | .35 | .17 |
| F | 7.75**** | 3.57**** | 6.37**** | 5.50**** |
| N | 256 | 146 | 111 | 258 |

*p < .10, **p < .05, ***p < .01, ****p < .001, one-tailed significance test.

Table A.5. Regression Models for People Motivation

| Variable | All Chairs | Men Only | Women Only | Interaction Model |
|---|---|---|---|---|
| | (Unstandardized b reported) | | | |
| Female | .20** | — | — | 1.10** |
| Age | .00 | .01 | .00 | −.00 |
| Years in legislature | −.01 | −.02 | .01 | −.02* |
| Democrat | .05 | .11 | −.04 | .13 |
| Professional legislature | −.07 | −.04 | −.13* | −.10* |
| Female × prof. legis. | — | — | — | −.13 |
| Moralistic culture | −.04 | −.04 | −.04 | −.03 |
| Female × moralistic | — | — | — | .03 |
| % Female legislators | .00** | .00** | .00 | .01** |
| Female × % female | — | — | — | −.01* |
| Female power | −.05 | −.08 | −.08 | −.15 |
| Female × female power | — | — | — | .16 |
| Personality traits: | | | | |
| Share Power | .30**** | .26*** | .40**** | — |
| Nurturer | .25**** | .26**** | .21*** | — |
| Processor | .11** | .09 | .10 | — |
| R-square | .22 | .18 | .23 | .09 |
| Adj R | .18 | .12 | .16 | .05 |
| F | 6.49**** | 3.04*** | 3.41**** | 2.22** |
| N | 274 | 150 | 125 | 278 |

*p < .10, **p < .05, ***p < .01, ****p < .001, one-tailed significance test.


Table A.6. Regression Models for Policy Motivation

| Variable | All Chairs | Men Only | Women Only | Interaction Model |
|---|---|---|---|---|
| | (Unstandardized b reported) | | | |
| Female | .17* | — | — | .06 |
| Age | .01* | .01 | .01 | .01 |
| Years in legislature | .01* | .01 | .12* | .01 |
| Democrat | .01 | −.17 | .17 | .09 |
| Professional legislature | .17*** | .20*** | .13* | .12** |
| Female × prof. legis. | — | — | — | .06 |
| Moralistic culture | −.01 | −.01 | −.01 | .03 |
| Female × moralistic | — | — | — | −.07 |
| % Female legislators | .00** | .00 | .00** | .00 |
| Female × % female | — | — | — | .00 |
| Female power | −.04 | −.06 | −.03 | −.07 |
| Female × female power | — | — | — | −.06 |
| Personality traits: | | | | |
| Innovator | .26**** | .22*** | .31**** | — |
| Nurturer | .18**** | .24*** | .10 | — |
| R-square | .17 | .15 | .21 | .09 |
| Adj R | .14 | .09 | .15 | .05 |
| F | 5.52**** | 2.61*** | 3.37**** | 2.22**** |
| N | 276 | 148 | 127 | 278 |

*p < .10, **p < .05, ***p < .01, ****p < .001, one-tailed significance test.

Table A.7. Regression Models for Collaborative Style

| Variable | All Chairs | Men Only | Women Only | Interaction Model |
|---|---|---|---|---|
| | (Unstandardized b reported) | | | |
| Female | .31** | — | — | 1.15** |
| Age | −.01** | .00 | −.03*** | −.01 |
| Years in legislature | .01 | −.01 | .01 | −.01 |
| Democrat | −.20* | −.07 | −.24* | −.07 |
| Professional legislature | .03 | .01 | −.03 | −.08 |
| Female × prof. legis. | — | — | — | −.02 |
| Moralistic culture | −.05* | −.02 | −.03 | −.08 |
| Female × moralistic | — | — | — | −.01 |
| % Female legislators | −.00 | .00 | −.00* | .00 |
| Female × % female | — | — | — | −.00 |
| Female power | −.03 | −.18 | .19 | −.12 |
| Female × female power | — | — | — | .42** |
| Personality traits: | | | | |
|   Share power | .33**** | .30*** | .24** | — |
|   Dependable | .13** | .13* | .13* | — |
|   Competent | .10** | .12* | .06 | — |
|   Innovator | .07 | .03 | .28*** | — |
|   Nurturer | .13** | .06 | .20** | — |
| R-square | .19 | .12 | .30 | .08 |
| Adj R | .15 | .04 | .23 | .04 |
| F | 4.70**** | 1.50 | 4.03**** | 1.90* |
| N | 250 | 140 | 110 | 270 |

*$p < .10$, **$p < .05$, ***$p < .01$, ****$p < .001$, one-tailed significance test.

Table A.8. Regression Models for Competitive Style

| Variable | All Chairs | Men Only | Women Only | Interaction Model |
|---|---|---|---|---|
| | (Unstandardized b reported) | | | |
| Female | .07 | — | — | −.24 |
| Age | −.02*** | −.02** | −.02** | −.02**** |
| Years in legislature | .00 | .01 | −.01 | .01 |
| Democrat | −.05 | −.29* | .18 | −.10 |
| Professional legislature | .17*** | .17* | .17** | .14** |
| Female × prof. legis. | — | — | — | .17* |
| Moralistic culture | .01 | −.06 | .10** | −.04 |
| Female × moralistic | — | — | — | .06 |
| % Female legislators | −.00 | −.00 | −.00** | −.00 |
| Female × % female | — | — | — | −.00 |
| Female power | .04 | −.04 | .29** | −.02 |
| Female × female power | — | — | — | .26 |
| Personality traits: | | | | |
|   Share power | .00 | .04 | −.19** | — |
|   Dominator | .25**** | .23*** | .30*** | — |
|   Competent | .17*** | .16** | .17** | — |
|   Innovator | .17*** | .16** | .22** | — |
| R-square | .20 | .20 | .28 | .10 |
| Adj R | .16 | .14 | .21 | .07 |
| F | 5.27**** | 3.10*** | 3.95**** | 2.47*** |
| N | 264 | 149 | 123 | 269 |

*$p < .10$, **$p < .05$, ***$p < .01$, ****$p < .001$, one-tailed significance test.

Table A.9. Regression Models for Accommodative Style

| Variable | All Chairs | Men Only | Women Only | Interaction Model |
|---|---|---|---|---|
| | (Unstandardized b reported) | | | |
| Female | −.12 | — | — | 1.26** |
| Age | −.01 | −.00 | −.00 | −.01 |
| Years in legislature | .02*** | .02* | .01 | .02** |
| Democrat | .18* | .17 | .23 | .27** |
| Professional legislature | −.08 | −.13** | −.11 | −.15** |
| Female × prof. legis. | — | — | — | −.03 |
| Moralistic culture | .00 | −.03 | .07* | −.02 |
| Female × moralistic | — | — | — | .11** |
| % Female legislators | −.00 | .00 | −.01*** | .00 |
| Female × % female | — | — | — | −.01**** |
| Female power | .12 | −.22* | .65** | −.22* |
| Female × female power | — | — | — | 1.02**** |
| Personality traits: | | | | |
|   Share power | .15** | −.06 | .28*** | — |
|   Nurturer | .12** | .11* | .09 | — |
|   Dependable | .12** | .07 | .15** | — |
|   Processor | .15*** | .19*** | .11 | — |
| R-square | .12 | .16 | .26 | .13 |
| Adj R | .08 | .10 | .19 | .09 |
| F | 2.97*** | 2.40*** | 3.60**** | 3.37**** |
| N | 271 | 149 | 123 | 275 |

$*p < .10$, $**p < .05$, $***p < .01$, $****p < .001$, one-tailed significance test.

# Notes

## Chapter 1

1. Lois R. Shea, "Donna Sytek, Now Madam Speaker, Is Seen by Her Colleagues as a Consensus Builder Who Does Homework," *Boston Globe*, December 15, 1996 (New Hampshire weekly section), 1.

2. Donna Sytek, telephone interview, July 1, 1997, Concord, N.H.

3. Richard Fenno, *Home Style* (New York: HarperCollins Publishers, 1978).

4. Donna Sytek, personal interview, July 27, 1996, St. Louis, MO.

5. Sytek, telephone interview, July 1, 1997.

6. Ibid.

7. James MacGregor Burns, *Leadership* (New York: Harper & Row, 1978), 434–435.

8. Georgia Duerst-Lahti and Rita Mae Kelly, eds., *Gender Power, Leadership and Governance* (Ann Arbor: University of Michigan Press, 1995), 32.

9. An emerging field of feminist research focuses on gendered organizations or institutions. See, for example, Joan Acker, "Hierarchies, Jobs, Bodies: A Theory of Gendered Organizations," *Gender & Society* 4(2) (June 1990): 139–158; Sally J. Kenney, "New Research on Gendered Political Institutions," *Political Research Quarterly* 49(2) (June 1996): 445–466; Silvia Gherardi, "The Gender We Think, the Gender We Do in Our Everyday Organizational Lives," *Human Relations* 47(6) (June 1994): 591–610.

10. Joan Acker, "Gendered Institutions: From Sex Roles to Gendered Institutions," *Contemporary Sociology* 21 (1992): 565–569, as quoted in Sally Kenney, "New Research on Gendered Political Institutions," 446.

11. I must acknowledge my indebtedness to James G. March and Johan P. Olsen, *Rediscovering Institutions: the Organizational Basis of Politics* (New York: Free Press, 1989), for the terms "integrative" and "aggregative" to describe two institutionally embedded ideologies. I elaborate on these two concepts in chapter 2 (this volume).

12. Burns, *Leadership*, 344.

13. See, for example, Alice H. Eagly and Blair T. Johnson, "Gender and Leadership Style: A Meta-Analysis," *Psychological Bulletin* 108(2) (September 1990): 233–256; Judy B. Rosener, "Ways Women Lead," *Harvard Business Review* 68 (November/December 1990): 119–125; Margaret Hennig and A. Jardim, *The Managerial Woman* (New

York: Pocket Books, 1977); Marilyn Loden, *Feminine Leadership, or How to Succeed in Business Without Being One of the Boys* (New York: Times Books, 1985); Patricia Lunneborg, *Women Changing Work* (Westport, CT: Greenwood Press, 1990); and Sally Helgesen, *The Female Advantage* (New York: Doubleday, 1990.)

14. Nancy Schwartz, *The Blue Guitar: Political Representation and Community* (Chicago: University of Chicago Press, 1988), 1.

15. Hanna Pitkin, *The Concept of Representation* (Berkeley: University of California Press, 1967)

16. Schwartz, *The Blue Guitar*, chaps. 2, 3, provides an excellent description of this linkage and the court decisions that adopt what she calls the "transmission belt theory of representation."

17. Heinz Eulau, "Changing Views of Representation," in *Contemporary Political Science: Towards Empirical Theory*, ed. Ithiel de Sola Pool (New York: McGraw-Hill, 1967), quoted in Schwartz, *The Blue Guitar*, 62.

18. Schwartz, *The Blue Guitar*, 23.

19. John Adams, "Letter to John Penn," *Works IV*, Boston (1852–1865): 205, cited in Pitkin, *The Concept of Representation*, 60.

20. M. E. Hawkesworth, *Beyond Oppression: Feminist Theory and Political Strategy* (New York: Continuum Publishing, 1990), 183–184.

21. See, for example, Sue Thomas, "The Impact of Women on State Legislative Policies," *Journal of Politics* 53(4) (November 1991): 958–976; Susan J. Carroll and Ella Taylor, "Gender Differences in Committee Assignments of State Legislators: Preferences or Discrimination?" (Paper presented at the annual meeting of the Midwest Political Science Association, Chicago); Sue Thomas, *How Women Legislate* (New York: Oxford University Press, 1994); Debra L. Dodson, ed., *Gender and Policymaking: Studies of Women in Politics* (New Brunswick: Rutgers University Center for the American Woman and Politics, 1991); Debra L. Dodson and Susan J. Carroll, *Reshaping the Agenda: Women in State Legislatures* (New Brunswick, NJ: Rutgers University Center for the American Woman and Politics, 1991).

22. Susan J. Carroll and Linda M. G. Zerilli, "Feminist Challenges to Political Science," in *State of the Discipline II*, ed. Ada Finifter (Washington DC: American Political Science Association, 1993), 56–59.

23. Elizabeth C. Cox, "The Three Who Came First," *State Legislatures*, 20 (November 1994): 12–19.

24. Center for the American Women and Politics (CAWP), "Women in the U.S. Senate 1922–1995." Fact sheet (New Brunswick, NJ: Eagleton Institute of Politics, Rutgers University, 1994).

25. Ruth Mandel, Kathy Kleeman, and Lucy Baruch, "No Year of the Woman, Then or Now," *Extensions* (Spring 1995): 7–10.

26. CAWP, "Women in State Legislatures 1997." Fact sheet from the National Information Bank on Women in Public Office (New Brunswick, NJ: Eagleton Institute of Politics, Rutgers University, 1997). http://www.rci.rutgers.edu/~cawp/stleg97.html.

27. Marilyn Guttromson, North Dakota legislative librarian, personal E-mail correspondence, June 17, 1997.

28. National Conference of State Legislatures, "Women Legislative Leaders 1977–1997," typescript (Denver, CO: National Conference of State Legislatures, 1997).

29. Top leaders are defined as majority and minority leaders or the presiding

officers of a state house or senate. National Conference of State Legislatures, "More Women Legislators and Leaders," *State Legislatures* 23 (April 1997): 5.

30. Calculations made by the author based on rosters from the states. At the time of calculation, some states reported a number of vacancies, particularly on joint statutory committees. The numbers do not include vacancies, and individuals who chair more than one committee are counted only once.

31. CAWP, "Women State Legislators: Leadership Positions and Committee Chairs 1993," and "Women State Legislators: Leadership Positions and Committee Chairs 1991." Fact sheets from the National Information Bank on Women in Public Office (New Brunswick, NJ: Eagleton Institute of Politics, Rutgers University, 1993, 1991). The author's methods of calculating committee chairs may vary slightly from those of the CAWP.

32. Eagly and Johnson, "Gender and Leadership Style," 244.

33. Vera Katz, "Women Chart New Legislative Course," *Journal of State Government* 60(5) (September/October 1987): 213–216; Madeleine Kunin, "Lessons from One Woman's Career," *Journal of State Government* 60(5) (September/October 1987): 209–213; Hazel Frank Gluck, "The Difference," *Journal of State Government* 60(5) (September/October 1987): 223–226; Norma Paulus, "Women Find Political Power in Unity," *Journal of State Government* 60(5) (September/October 1987): 5–10.

34. Dorothy W. Cantor and Toni Bernay with Jean Stoess, *Women in Power: The Secrets of Leadership* (Boston: Houghton-Mifflin, 1992).

35. Malcolm Jewell and Marcia Lynn Whicker, *Legislative Leadership in the American States* (Ann Arbor: University of Michigan Press, 1994), chap. 6.

36. Ibid., chap. 7.

37. Ibid., 179.

38. Robert L. Peabody, "Leadership in Legislatures: Evolution, Selection, Functions," *Legislative Studies Quarterly* IX(3) (1984): 441–473.

39. Malcolm Jewell and Marcia Lynn Whicker, "The Feminization of Leadership in State Legislatures," *PS* 26(4) (December 1993): 711.

40. Thomas, *How Women Legislate*, 155.

41. Leroy N. Rieselbach, "'Fools Rush In . . .': Thinking about Power and Leadership in Congressional Committees" (Paper presented at the annual meeting of the American Political Science Association, Chicago, 1992), 2.

42. Burns, *Leadership*.

43. Malcolm J. Jewell and S. Patterson, *The Legislative Process in the United States*, 3rd ed. (New York: Random House, 1977); Alan Rosenthal, *Legislative Life* (New York: Harper & Row, 1981); Lucinda S. Simon and Carl Tubbesing, eds., *A Guide to Legislative Leadership* (Denver, CO: National Conference of State Legislatures, 1981).

44. Janice Petty, *A Chairman's Guide to Effective Committee Management* (Denver, CO: National Conference of State Legislatures, 1981); Rosenthal, *Legislative Life*.

45. David T. Canon, *Actors, Athletes, and Astronauts: Political Amateurs in the United States Congress* (Chicago: University of Chicago Press, 1990).

46. Kenney, "New Research on Gendered Political Institutions," 455–456.

47. Focus group, July 30, 1996, St. Louis, MO.

48. Kenney, "New Research on Gendered Institutions," 456.

49. Robert Lipsyte, "Married to the Game," *New York Times*, 1 June 1997, 19.

50. Focus group, July 27, 1994, New Orleans, LA.

51. Ibid.

52. Carol Nechemias, "Changes in the Election of Women to U.S. State Legislative Seats," *Legislative Studies Quarterly* 12 (February 1987): 125–142.

53. Kenney, "New Research on Gendered Political Institutions," 457–461.

54. Kathleen Hall Jamieson, *Beyond the Double Bind* (New York: Oxford University Press, 1995), 121.

55. Author's survey of legislative rules and state Web sites.

56. Feminist epistemologists call for and embrace multiple methods for understanding gendered phenomenon. For a discussion of this emphasis, see Carroll and Zerilli, "Feminist Challenges to Political Science." Carroll and Zerilli urge empirical political scientists to be more contextual and more historical in their analyses in order to achieve "depth and richness"(72).

57. Focus groups are a useful means of overcoming limitations of self-reports. For further information on the use of focus groups, see, for example, Robert K. Merton, Marjorie Fiske, and Patricia L. Kendall, *The Focused Interview*, 2nd ed. (New York: Macmillan, 1990); David L. Morgan, *Focus Groups: A Qualitative Research* (Newbury Park, CA: Sage Publications, 1988); and David W. Stewart and Prem N. Shamdasani, *Focus Groups: Theory and Practice* (Newbury Park, CA: Sage Publications, 1990).

58. Daniel J. Elazar, *American Federalism: A View from the States* (New York: Thomas Y. Crowell, 1966).

59. Kenney, "New Research on Gendered Political Institutions," 456–457.

60. Rosabeth Moss Kanter, *Men and Women of the Corporation*, (New York: Basic Books, 1977).

61. Peter M. Blau, "A Macrosociological Theory of Social Structure," *American Journal of Sociology* 83(1) (1977): 26–54.

62. Janice D. Yoder, "Rethinking Tokenism: Looking beyond Numbers," *Gender and Society*, 5 (June 1991): 178–192.

63. As used in this study, the cases do not explicitly test hypotheses but, rather, use existing theory to interpret the particular case and to build new theory. This dual purpose combines aspects of what Harry Eckstein describes as "disciplined-configurative studies" and "heuristic case studies." See Harry Eckstein, "Case Study and Theory in Political Science" in *Handbook of Political Science*, vol. 7, ed. Fred Greenstein and Nelson Polsby (Reading, MA: Addison-Wesley, 1975).

64. The iceberg metaphor is not my own but rather was inspired by Mary E. Guy, ed., *Women and Men of the States: Public Administrators at the State Level* (Armonk, NY: M. E. Sharpe, 1992), 205.

65. Ruth B. Mandel, "Doing It Whose Way? Women in Leadership," in *Our Vision and Values: Women Shaping the 21st Century*, ed. Frances C. Hutner (Westport, CT: Praeger Publishers, 1994).

66. Kenney, "New Research on Gendered Political Institutions," 456.

*Chapter 2*

1. Harold Lasswell, *Politics, Who Gets What, When and How* (New York: Peter Smith, 1936).

2. See, for example, David Mayhew, *Congress: The Electoral Connection* (New Haven, CT: Yale University Press, 1974); and Morris Fiorina, *Congress: Keystone of the Washington Establishment* (New Haven, CT: Yale University Press, 1989).

3. March and Olsen, *Rediscovering Institutions*.

4. Ibid., 160.

5. Ibid., 120.

6. Burns, *Leadership*, 344.

7. Ibid., 434.

8. Ibid., 18.

9. Ibid., 50.

10. Ralph M. Stogdill, *Handbook of Leadership* (New York: Free Press, 1974).

11. Tom Peters and Nancy Austin, *A Passion for Excellence: The Leadership Difference* (New York: Random House, 1985).

12. See, for instance, Rensis Likert, *New Patterns of Management* (New York: McGraw-Hill, 1961); and R. Blake and J. S. Mouton, *Managerial Grid III* (Houston, TX: Gulf, 1985). Behavioral theories typically share two main dimensions: a concern for task and a focus on interpersonal relations.

13. See, for example, Fred E. Fiedler, *A Theory of Leadership Effectiveness* (New York: McGraw-Hill, 1967); and Paul Hersey and Kenneth T. Blanchard, *The Management of Organizational Behavior*, 3rd ed. (Englewood Cliffs, NJ: Prentice-Hall, 1977).

14. See, for example, Burns, *Leadership*; and Max Weber, *Essays in Sociology*, trans. H. H. Gerth and C. Wright Mills (New York: Oxford University Press, 1946).

15. See, for example, Kanter, *Men and Women of the Corporation*; Henry Mintzberg, *Power in and around Organizations* (Englewood Cliffs, NJ: Prentice-Hall, 1983), and Jeffrey Pfeffer, *Power in Organizations* (Boston: Pitman, 1981).

16. See, for instance, Edgar Schein, *Organizational Culture and Leadership* (San Francisco: Jossey-Bass, 1985).

17. See, for example, Richard E. Neustadt, *Presidential Power and the Modern Presidents* (New York: Macmillan Publishing, 1990); and Ronald M. Peters, Jr., *The American Speakership: The Office in Historical Perspective* (Baltimore: Johns Hopkins University Press, 1990).

18. The theories in this last category tend to be somewhat eclectic, synthesizing useful elements from the other theories into a multidimensional perspective. See, for example, Peter Vaill, *Managing as Performing Art: New Ideas for a World of Chaotic Change* (San Francisco: Jossey-Bass, 1989); Robert E. Quinn, *Beyond Rational Management* (San Francisco: Jossey-Bass, 1988); and Lee G. Bolman and Terrence E. Deal, *Reframing Organizations: Artistry, Choice, and Leadership* (San Francisco: Jossey-Bass, 1991).

19. Four similar approaches (trait, behavior, situational, and power-influence) are used by Gary Yukl, *Leadership in Organizations*, 2nd ed. (Englewood Cliffs, NJ: Prentice-Hall, 1989).

20. Bernard M. Bass, *Bass and Stogdill's Handbook of Leadership*, 3rd ed. (New York: Free Press, 1990).

21. Peter F. Drucker, "Foreword: Not Enough Generals Were Killed," in *The Leader of the Future*, ed. Frances Hesselbein, Marshall Goldsmith, and Richard Beckhard (San Francisco: Jossey-Bass, 1996), xii (emphasis in the original).

22. Ibid., xii–xiii.

23. Camilla Stivers, *Gender Images in Public Administration* (Newbury Park, CA: Sage Publications, 1993): 59.

24. Ibid., 72.

25. Duerst-Lahti and Kelly, eds., *Gender Power, Leadership and Governance*, 261.

26. Cheryl Simrell King, "Sex Role Identity and Decision Styles: How Gender Helps Explain the Paucity of Women at the Top," in *Gender Power, Leadership and Governance*, ed. Duerst-Lahti and Kelly.

27. Natasha Josefowitz, *Paths to Power* (Reading, MA: Addison-Wesley, 1980).

28. Georgia Duerst-Lahti and Cathy Johnson, "Gender and Style in Bureaucracy," *Women and Politics*, 10(1) (1990): 67–120.

29. Lao-tzu, *Tao Te Ching*, trans. Stephen Mitchell (New York: HarperCollins Publishers, 1988): viii–ix. I prefer Mitchell's translation, but my understanding of the *Tao* as it relates to the art of government, leadership, and management behavior also is informed by Vaill, *Managing as Performing Art*, and John Heider, "The Leader Who Knows How to Make Things Happen," in *Contemporary Issues in Leadership*, ed. William E. Rosenbach and Robert L. Taylor (Boulder, CO: Westview Press, 1984).

30. Lao-tzu, verse 68.

31. Mary Parker Follett, *The New State* (New York: Longmans, Green & Co., 1920).

32. The notion of servant leadership has been fostered by Robert K. Greenleaf, *The Servant as Leader* (Indianapolis, IN: Robert K. Greenleaf Center for Servant-Leadership, 1970, 1991); *On Becoming a Servant Leader* (San Francisco: Jossey-Bass, 1996).

33. Mary Parker Follett, *Prophet of Management: A Celebration of Writings from the 1920s*, ed. Pauline Graham (Boston: Harvard Business School Press, 1996), 188. See chap. 2, in *Prophet of Management*.

34. March and Olsen, *Rediscovering Institutions*, 118.

35. Ibid., 163.

36. Ibid., 126.

37. Burns, *Leadership*, 426–427. Burns associates transformational leadership with the charismatic figures of Gandhi and Mao but also acknowledges its simple, more humble form in parents and teachers.

38. Ibid., 20.

39. Sue Carroll, "Feminist Scholarship on Political Leadership," in *Leadership: Multi-disciplinary Perspectives*, ed. Barbara Kellerman (Englewood Cliffs, NJ: Prentice-Hall, 1984).

40. Stivers, *Gender Images*, 59–72. Although the source of this portrayal is a feminist standpoint, the perspective has also been espoused by proponents of participative management, total quality management and other innovations in management, and the concept of servant leadership.

41. I do not want to overstate the distributive paradigm and I acknowledge that it is not universally endorsed. See, for example, Steven Kelman, *Making Public Policy: A Hopeful View of American Government* (New York: Basic Books, 1987); Peters, *The American Speakership*; and Erwin C. Hargrove, "Two Conceptions of Institutional Leadership," in *Leadership and Politics*, ed. Bryan D. Jones (Lawrence: University Press of Kansas, 1989). Kelman argues that politics need not be dominated by "the imagery of jousting" but rather can be conceived as "a common problem-solving venture" (42–43). Peters emphasizes the cultural roots of political leadership and argues that modern leadership is "therapeutic" rather than transactional, responding to demands for participation and an emphasis on interpersonal communication. Hargrove combines the rational actor and neoinstitutionalist perspectives with Burns' transactional and transforming leadership into a useful typology of political leaders. Many of the critiques or alternatives come from the feminist standpoint. See, for

example, Jane J. Mansbridge, ed., *Beyond Self-Interest* (Chicago: University of Chicago Press, 1988).

42. Thomas S. Kuhn, *The Structure of Scientific Revolutions*, 2nd ed. (Chicago: University of Chicago Press, 1970).

43. Among the most prominent feminist writers on this point are Christine DiStefano, *Configurations of Masculinity: A Feminist Perspective on Modern Political Theory* (Ithaca, NY: Cornell University Press, 1991), and Wendy Brown, *Manhood and Politics: A Feminist Reading in Political Theory* (Totowa, NJ: Rowman & Littlefield, 1988).

44. DiStefano, *Configurations of Masculinity*, 4.

45. Paula Johnson, "Women and Power: Towards a Theory of Effectiveness," *Journal of Social Issues*, 32(3) (Summer 1976): 99–110.

46. Duerst-Lahti and Kelly, eds., *Gender Power, Leadership and Governance*, 22.

47. Kenneth Thomas, "Conflict and Conflict Management," in *The Handbook of Industrial and Organizational Psychology*, ed. Marvin Dunnette (Chicago: Rand McNally, 1975.)

48. Thomas actually proposes two models: a structural model of conflict resolution that focuses on the factors in a conflict situation and a process model that traces the sequence of events in a conflict episode. The five conflict-handling orientations are found in both models. Thomas acknowledges the contribution of Robert Blake and J. S. Mouton, *Managerial Grid* (Houston, TX: Gulf, 1964) in his scheme.

49. Christine DeGregorio, "Leadership Approaches in Congressional Committee Hearings," *Western Political Quarterly* 45:4 (December 1992): 971–984.

50. Ibid., 972.

51. DeGregorio uses the three types of committees identified by Richard Fenno, *Congressmen in Committees* (Boston: Little, Brown, 1973).

52. DeGregorio, "Leadership Approaches in Congressional Committee," 973

53. Christine DeGregorio, E-mail correspondence, June 28, 1997. DeGregorio's original sampling frame included a female subcommittee chair who subsequently declined to be interviewed. Interviews were conducted with female staff directors who worked for male chairs. DeGregorio speculates that region and career background (i.e., women with small business experience) may have as much influence as gender on accommodation styles.

54. Ibid., 980.

55. Lyn Kathlene, "Power and Influence in State Legislative Policymaking: The Interaction of Gender and Position in Committee Hearing Debates," *American Political Science Review* 88: 3 (September 1994): 560–576.

56. Thomas, "Conflict and Conflict Management," 902–903.

57. Ibid., 897.

58. Talcott Parsons and Robert F. Bales, *Family, Socialization and Interaction Process* (Glencoe, IL: Free Press, 1955).

59. For example, the cultural view of communication behavior as studied by sociolinguists emphasizes children's play groups as the originating source of gender behavior differences. In other words, children learn a style of talk through their typical play group, not from modeling adult behavior. See the discussion of Lynn Smith-Lovin and Dawn T. Robinson, "Gender and Conversational Dynamics," in *Gender, Interaction and Inequality*, ed. Cecilia L. Ridgeway (New York: Springer-Verlag, 1992).

60. See Sylvia Junko Yanagisako and Jane Fishburn Collier, eds., *Gender and Kinship: Essays toward a Unified Analysis* (Stanford, CA: Stanford University Press, 1987).

61. Nancy Chodorow, "Family Structure and Feminine Personality," in *Women, Culture, and Society*, ed. Michelle Zimbalist Rosaldo and Louise Lamphere (Stanford, CA: Stanford University Press, 1974).

62. Carol Gilligan, *In a Different Voice: Psychological Theory and Women's Development* (Cambridge, MA: Harvard University Press, 1982).

63. Smith-Lovin and Robinson, "Gender and Conversational Dynamics," 125–126.

64. Acker, "Hierarchies, Jobs, Bodies," 146–147.

65. For an excellent review of this research, see Patricia Yancey Martin, "Gender, Interaction and Inequality in Organizations," in *Gender, Interaction and Inequality*, ed. Ridgeway. See also Christine Williams, *Gender at Work: Women and Men in Nontraditional Occupations* (Berkeley: University of California Press, 1989).

66. U.S. Bureau of the Census, "American Women: A Profile," *Statistical Brief* (Washington DC: U.S. Department of Commerce, Economics and Statistics Administration, July 1995).

67. Arlie Russell Hochschild, *The Managed Heart: Commercialization of Human Feeling* (Berkeley: University of California Press, 1983), 7.

68. Ibid., 235.

69. Ibid., chap. 7.

70. Elaine J. Hall, "Waitering/Waitressing: Engendering the Work of Table Servers," *Gender and Society* 7 (September 1993): 330.

71. Christine Williams, *Gender at Work: Women and Men in Nontraditional Occupations* (Berkeley: University of California Press, 1989), 142.

72. Candace West and Don H. Zimmerman, "Doing Gender," *Gender and Society* 1 (June 1987): 125. The term "doing gender" comes out of research on the sociology of work. Other works associated with this literature include Elaine J. Hall, "Smiling, Deferring and Flirting: Doing Gender by Giving 'Good Service.'" *Work and Occupations*, 20 (November 1993): 452–471.

73. Loden, *Feminine Leadership*, 120–131.

74. Lunneborg, *Women Changing Work*, 47.

75. Rosener, "Ways Women Lead," 119–125.

76. Mary M. Hale and Rita Mae Kelly, eds., *Gender, Bureaucracy and Democracy* (Westport, CT: Greenwood Press, 1989).

77. Rosener, "Ways Women Lead."

78. David C. McClelland, *Power: The Inner Experience* (New York: Irvington Publishers, 1975), chap. 3.

79. Fiedler, *Leadership Effectiveness*. Fiedler specifically argues that three factors are key: (1) leader-member relations (e.g., the degree of friendliness, trust, and cooperation), (2) position power of the leader (e.g., the amount of formal authority held), and (3) task structure (e.g., the clarity and specificity of what must be done). Leadership situations vary from favorable to unfavorable on all three dimensions. Fiedler asserts that task-oriented leaders do best in very favorable and very unfavorable situations, whereas relationship-oriented leaders perform most effectively in mixed situations.

80. March and Olsen, *Rediscovering Institutions*, 17.

81. Duerst-Lahti and Kelly, eds., *Gender Power, Leadership and Governance*, 32.

82. Duerst-Lahti and Kelly conceptualize the layers of influence on leaders as concentric circles, the outermost being national culture, then organizational culture, followed by career interactions, and, finally, individual-level factors. The impact of

culture raises a fundamental question: does culture affects gender understandings or vice versa? In *The American Speakership*, Peters emphasizes a "therapeutic" culture in which followers want to be included more, consulted frequently, and allowed greater participation. Because both the therapeutic culture and the integrative style emphasize participation, the question of causality arises (i.e., cultural influences or women's impact).

83. Duerst-Lahti and Kelly, eds., *Gender Power, Leadership and Governance*.

84. Ibid., 20–21. Political scientist Robert Darcy has found that women are not underrrepresented as committee chairs, if one looks just at the pools of majority party members or more senior members from which chairs are selected. Darcy's finding suggests women are not discriminated against or barred from obtaining power, but nonetheless the resulting distribution of power is clearly gendered. See R. Darcy, "Women in State Legislative Power Structure: Committee Chairs," *Social Science Quarterly* 77 (December 1996): 888–898.

85. Kanter, *Men and Women of the Corporation*.

86. Ibid.

87. Cynthia Fuchs Epstein, *Women in Law* (New York: Anchor Books, 1983), 265.

88. Noelle Norton, "Women, It's Not Enough to Be Elected: Committee Position Makes a Difference," in *Gender Power, Leadership and Governance*, ed. Duerst-Lahti and Kelly, 115–140.

89. Meredith Ann Newman, "The Gendered Nature of Lowi's Typology; or Who Would Guess You Could Find Gender Here?" in *Gender Power, Leadership and Governance*, ed. Duerst-Lahti and Kelly, 141–164.

90. Mary Ellen Guy, "Hillary, Health Care, and Gender Power," in *Gender Power, Leadership, and Governance*, ed. Duerst-Lahti and Kelly, 239–256.

91. Georgia Duerst-Lahti and Dayna Verstegen, "Making Something of Absence: The 'Year of the Woman' and Women's Political Representation," in *Gender Power, Leadership and Governance*, ed. Duerst-Lahti and Kelly, 213–238.

92. Kanter, *Men and Women of the Corporation*, chap. 8.

93. Rosabeth Moss Kanter, "Some Effects of Proportions on Group Life: Skewed Sex Ratios and Responses to Token Women," *American Journal of Sociology* 82(5) (1977): 965–990; and Kanter, *Men and Women of the Corporation*, chap. 8.

94. A good review of this literature is provided by Yoder, "Rethinking Tokenism."

95. Ibid., 181.

96. Janice D. Yoder, "Looking beyond Numbers: The Effects of Gender Status, Job Prestige, and Occupational Gender Typing on Tokenism Processes," *Social Psychology Quarterly* 57(2) (1994): 150–159.

97. Yoder attributes the intrusiveness theory to Hubert Blalock, *Toward a Theory of Minority-Group Relations* (New York: Wiley, 1967). Her own research on women in the military lends empirical support to the effects of intrusiveness. See Janice D. Yoder, "Women at West Point: Lessons for women in Male-Dominated occupations," in *Women: A Feminist Perspective*, 4th ed., ed. Jo Freeman (Mountain View, CA: Mayfield, 1989).

98. Judith Long Laws, "The Psychology of Tokenism: An Analysis," *Sex Roles* 1(January 1975): 51–52, cited in Yoder, "Rethinking Tokenism," 185.

99. Blau, "A Macrosociological Theory of Social Structure."

*Chapter 3*

1. Explicating the causes of underrepresentation is not the purpose of this review, but for readers who want a good overview of these questions, see Marianne Githens, "Women and State Politics: An Assessment," in *Political Women: Current Roles in State and Local Government*, ed. Janet Flammang (Beverly Hills, CA: Sage Publications, 1984); Janet Clark, "Getting There: Women in Political Office," *The Annals of the American Academy of Political and Social Science* 515 (May 1991): 63–76; Robert Darcy, Susan Welch, and Janet Clark, *Women, Elections, and Representation* (New York: Longman, 1987); Jewell and Whicker, *Legislative Leadership in the American States*, chap. 7; and Albert J. Nelson, *Emerging Influentials in State Legislatures* (New York: Praeger Publishers, 1991). This chapter also does not deal with the issue of overt discrimination or gender bias either among voters or in electoral systems.

2. Jeane Kirkpatrick, *Political Woman* (New York: Basic Books, 1974): 219.

3. Ibid.

4. From the extant literature, the primary reference points are Kirkpatrick, *Political Woman*; Irene Diamond, *Sex Roles in the State House* (New Haven, CT: Yale University Press, 1977); Sue Thomas, *How Women Legislate*; and a three-decade longitudinal analysis by Kathleen Dolan and Lynne E. Ford, "Change and Continuity among Women State Legislators: Evidence from Three Decades," *Political Research Quarterly* 50 (March 1997): 137–151. Other research is cited as well. The cohorts from the major studies noted previously are not necessarily identical. For example, Diamond targeted legislators serving in four New England states and Thomas drew her 1987 sample of lawmakers from a geographically diverse selection of twelve states. The sample by Dolan and Ford includes all women and a stratified random of men from fifteen states.

5. Dolan and Ford, "Change and Continuity," 147.

6. See, for example, Diamond, *Sex Roles*; Kirkpatrick, *Political Woman*; Susan Welch, "Recruitment of Women to Office: A Discriminant Analysis," *Western Political Quarterly* 31(2) (1978): 372–380; Marianne Githens and Jewel L. Prestage, eds., *A Portrait of Marginality: The Political Behavior of the American Woman* (New York: David McKay Publishers, 1977); Githens, "Women and State Politics"; and Emmy E. Werner, "Women in State Legislatures," *Western Political Quarterly* 21:1 (1968): 40–50.

7. Diamond, *Sex Roles*, 38.

8. Thomas, *How Women Legislate*, 45.

9. Dolan and Ford, "Change and Continuity," 143. See also Laurie Zink, "Three Decades of Elite Participation: Women in Oregon State Politics 1960–1990" (Paper presented at the annual meeting of the Western Political Science Association, Albuquerque, N.M.).

10. Diamond, *Sex Roles*; Thomas, *How Women Legislate*, 45.

11. Dolan and Ford, "Continuity and Change," 142, 146.

12. Sara E. Rix, ed., *The American Woman, 1987–88: A Report in Depth* (New York: W. W. Norton, 1987).

13. Diamond, *Sex Roles*.

14. Dolan and Ford, "Change and Continuity," 142, 146.

15. Ibid.

16. Ibid., 142, 146.

17. Mary E. Guy and Lois Lovelace Duke, "Personal and Social Background as Determinants of Position," in *Women and Men of the States*, ed. Mary E. Guy, 45.

18. Kirkpatrick, *Political Woman*.

19. Dolan and Ford, "Change and Continuity," 142, 146.

20. Guy, ed., *Women and Men of the States*, 49.

21. Woodrow Jones and Albert J. Nelson, "Correlates of Women's Representation in Lower State Legislative Chambers," *Social Behavior and Personality* 9:1 (1981): 9–15.

22. Guy, ed., *Women and Men of the States*, 50–52.

23. Marcia M. Lee, "Toward Understanding Why Few Women Hold Public Office: Factors Affecting the Participation of Women in Local Politics," in *A Portrait of Marginality*, ed. Githens and Prestage, 124.

24. Githens and Prestage, eds., *A Portrait of Marginality*, 5.

25. Marilyn Johnson and Susan Carroll with Kathy Stanwyck and Lynn Korenblit, *Profile of Women Holding Office II* (New Brunswick, NJ: Center for the American Woman and Politics, 1978).

26. Diamond, *Sex Roles*.

27. See Thomas, *How Women Legislate*, 66–67; Carroll and Taylor, "Gender Differences in Committee Assignments of State Legislators"; and Dolan and Ford, "Change and Continuity," 142.

28. Dolan and Ford, "Change and Continuity," 142.

29. Kirkpatrick, *Political Woman*, 212.

30. Diamond, *Sex Roles*, 55.

31. See Thomas, *How Women Legislate*, 50; and Edmond Constantini, "Political Women and Political Ambition: Closing the Gender Gap," *American Journal of Political Science* 34:3 (1990): 741–770.

32. Thomas, *How Women Legislate*, 50,

33. Githens and Prestage, eds., *A Portrait of Marginality*, 8.

34. Johnson et al., *Profile of Women Holding Office II*.

35. Thomas, *How Women Legislate*, 53.

36. Ibid., 48. The concern over legislative bargaining again reflects the paradigmatic assumption that "normal" legislative behavior is aggregative behavior.

37. Significance levels in this table and table 3.2 are based on calculation of *t* tests for independent samples for the continuous variables such as age and length of time in office. Significance levels for categorical variables such as level of education, family social class, full-time legislator, or ambition for higher office use the chi-square statistic. In addition, hierarchical loglinear regression analysis and analysis of variance were used to determine whether significant interactions or trends were evident for men and women across all three types of legislatures. For purposes of simplicity, only the significance levels for each category are reported in the table. Significant interactions or trends are indicated in subsequent notes.

38. For an excellent discussion of the distinctions between professionalization and institutionalization in legislatures, see Alan Rosenthal, "State Legislative Development: Observations from Three Perspectives," *Legislative Studies Quarterly* 21:2 (May 1996): 169–198. The three-part typology is from Karl T. Kurtz, *State Legislatures: Progress, Problems, and Possibilities* (Denver, CO: National Conference of State Legislatures and the Eagleton Institute of Politics, 1992).

39. States with professional legislatures include California, Illinois, Massachusetts, Michigan, New Jersey, New York, Ohio, Pennsylvania, and Wisconsin.

40. States with hybrid legislatures include Alabama, Alaska, Arizona, Colorado, Connecticut, Delaware, Florida, Hawaii, Indiana, Iowa, Kansas, Louisiana, Mary-

land, Minnesota, Missouri, Nebraska, Oklahoma, Oregon, South Carolina, Tennessee, Texas, Virginia, and Washington.

41. States with citizen legislatures include Arkansas, Georgia, Idaho, Kentucky, Maine, Mississippi, Montana, Nevada, New Hampshire, New Mexico, North Carolina, North Dakota, Rhode Island, South Dakota, Utah, Vermont, West Virginia.

42. Arlie Russell Hochschild with Anne Machung, *The Second Shift* (New York: Avon Books, 1990).

43. Personal correspondence, June 16, 1994.

44. Peggy Kerns, personal interview, January 30, 1995, Denver, Colo.

45. Jane Campbell, personal interview, February 21, 1995, Columbus, Ohio.

46. Helgesen, *The Female Advantage*, 31–32.

47. Focus group, July 28, 1994, New Orleans, La.

48. Focus group, July 27, 1995, New Orleans, La.

49. Hochschild, *The Managed Heart*, 165.

50. Sytek, telephone interview, July 1, 1997.

51. Personal interview, January 10, 1995, Denver, Colo.

52. Personal interview, February 22, 1995, Columbus, Ohio.

53. Answers were coded to multiple categories when appropriate. Among the respondents, 112 men provided 160 different responses; and 98 women provided 183 separate responses.

54. Putnam explores the decline of social capital in several articles, among these are "The Prosperous Community: Social Capital and Public Life," *The American Prospect* (Spring 1993): 35–42; "Bowling Alone: America's Declining Social Capital," *Journal of Democracy* 6 (January 1995): 65–78; and "Tuning in, Tuning out: The Strange Disappearance of Social Capital in America," *PS: Political Science and Politics* (December 1995): 664–683.

55. Putnam, "Bowling Alone," 67.

56. Ibid.

57. Cindy Simon Rosenthal and Jana Vogt, "Collaborative Leadership: Is It Gender, Civic Engagement, Legislative Norms, or None of the Above?" (Paper presented at the annual meeting of the Western Political Science Association, Tucson, Ariz., 1997).

58. Sidney Verba, Kay Lehman Schlozman, and Henry E. Brady, *Voice and Equality: Civic Voluntarism in American Politics*, (Cambridge, MA: Harvard University Press, 1995), 310.

59. Peverill Squire, "Legislative Professionalization and Membership Diversity in State Legislatures," *Legislative Studies Quarterly* 17:1 (1992): 69–79.

60. In the case of age when first elected, women chairs in citizen legislatures run at a younger age than those in professional legislatures, a pattern that borders on significance in one-way analysis of variance ($p = .082$). For additional analysis, see Cindy Simon Rosenthal, "A View of Their Own: Women's Committee Leadership Styles and State Legislatures," *Policy Studies Journal* 25(4) (1997): 585–600. Bivariate associations between professionalization, sex, and educational background are statistically significant and substantively interesting, but the three-way interaction does not reach statistical significance in hierarchical loglinear analysis.

61. Citizens Conference on State Legislatures, *The Sometime Governments* (New York: Bantam Books, 1971), 138.

62. Hierarchical loglinear analysis reveals that the three-way interaction between sex, social class, and type of legislature approaches significance (LR $\chi^2 = 8.38$, df 4, $p = .079$).

63. Hierarchical loglinear analysis reveals a strong and significant association between sex and civic volunteer experience (LR $\chi^2$ = 37.122, df 2, $p$ = .000), and type of legislature also has a modest association with civic and volunteer background (LR $\chi^2$ = 4.822, df 2, $p$ = .090), but the three-way interaction with type of legislature does not reach statistical significance.

64. Again, hierarchical loglinear analysis reveals a strong and significant association between sex and political or government experience, but the three-way interaction with type of legislature does not reach statistical significance. Hierarchical loglinear analysis does not reveal a significant three-way interaction between sex, professional experience, and type of legislature. The data are substantively intriguing but not robust enough to reach statistical significance because of limitations of sample size.

65. Focus group, July 27, 1996, St. Louis, Mo.

66. Using multiple regression with total years of legislative service as a control variable, sex does not have a significant association with total years as a committee chair ($T$ = .540, $p$ = .590).

67. For a discussion of committee appointment processes in state legislatures, see Wayne Francis, *The Legislative Committee Game: A Comparative Analysis of 50 States* (Columbus: Ohio State University Press, 1989); Alan Rosenthal, *Legislative Life* (New York: Harper & Row, 1981); and Ronald D. Hedlund and Keith E. Hamm, "Political Parties as Vehicles for Organizing U.S. State Legislative Committees," *Legislative Studies Quarterly* 21:3 (1966): 383–408.

68. Focus group, July 29, 1996, St. Louis, Mo.

69. Ibid.

70. Ibid.

71. Focus group, July 28, 1994, New Orleans, La.

72. Ibid.

73. Personal interview, February 21, 1995, Columbus, Ohio.

74. See especially Peverill Squire, "Career Opportunities and Membership Stability in Legislatures," *Legislative Studies Quarterly* 13:1 (1988). 65–82, and "Legislative Professionalization and Membership Diversity in State Legislatures."

75. This pattern might undergo considerable change as legislatures adapt to term limits and legislators weigh their opportunities in light of determinate legislative tenure.

76. Hierarchical log linear analysis of this three-way interaction between sex, type of legislature, and ambition for higher office is statistically significant (LR $\chi^2$ = 11.188, df 4, $p$ = .025)

77. Alan Ehrenhalt, *The United States of Ambition: Politicians, Power and the Pursuit of Office* (New York: Times Books, 1991).

78. A larger percentage of the women (53.3 percent compared with 44 percent of the men) would choose an influential policy job over continuing their political careers. The difference, however, does not reach statistical significance.

79. Focus group, July 28, 1994, New Orleans, La.

80. Ibid.

81. Women chairs said they spent on average 21 hours during the session and more than 7 hours during the interim on committee business. Men chairs reported spending an average of 20 hours during the session and 6.6 hours during the interim.

82. Personal interview, December 15, 1994, Norman, Okla.

83. Focus group, July 28, 1994, New Orleans, La.

84. Focus group, July 27, 1995, New Orleans, La.

85. Using the percentage of women serving in leadership and as legislators and a chair's total years of service as control variables, ordinary least squares (OLS) regres-sion analysis of the question dealing with strategic information and logistic regression of the yes/no question indicating whether a chair feels included were performed.

86. Focus group, July 28, 1995, New Orleans, La.

87. Personal interview, July 28, 1996, St. Louis, Mo.

88. Personal interview, February 23, 1995, Columbus, Ohio.

89. Maxine Berman, *The Only Boobs in the House Are Men* (Troy, MI: Momen-tum Books, 1994).

90. Ibid., 124.

91. Thomas, *How Women Legislate*, 33.

92. Jean Bethke Elshtain, *Public Man, Private Woman: Women in Social and Political Thought* (Princeton, NJ: Princeton University Press, 1981), 335.

93. Focus group, July 29, 1996, St. Louis, Mo.

## Chapter 4

1. Nancy D. Kates, "The Saga of Vera Katz," Kennedy School of Government Case Program (Cambridge: Harvard University Press, 1988), 2.

2. Ibid.

3. Ibid., 6.

4. Vera Katz, "Women Chart New Legislative Course," and "The Leader and the Public," *Journal of State Government* 60:6 (November/December 1987): 262–264.

5. Katz, "The Leader and the Public," 262.

6. Ellen Perlman, "Vera Katz and Beverly Stein: The Friendly Art of Collabora-tion," *Governing* 8:3 (1994): 34.

7. Ibid.

8. Foster Church, "Vera Katz: Just Like a Woman," *Governing* 3 (September 1990): 26–30.

9. See, for instance, Virginia Sapiro, *The Political Integration of Women* (Urbana: University of Illinois Press, 1983); Githens and Prestage, eds. *A Portrait of Marginal-ity*; and Elshtain, *Public Man, Private Woman*.

10. See Thomas, "The Impact of Women on State Legislative Policies"; Carroll and Zerilli, "Feminist Challenges to Political Science"; and Michelle A. Saint-Germain, "Does Their Difference Make a Difference? The Impact of Women on Public Policy in the Arizona Legislature," *Social Science Quarterly* 70(4) (December 1989): 956–968.

11. See Dodson, *Gender and Policymaking*; Dodson and Carroll, *Reshaping the Agenda*.

12. Sue Thomas, "The Effects of Race and Gender on Constituency Service," *Western Political Quarterly* 45:1 (1992): 169–180.

13. See Diane D. Blair and Jeanie R. Stanley, "Personal Relationships and Leg-islative Power: Male and Female Perceptions," *Legislative Studies Quarterly* 17(4) (1991): 495–507; and Carol Mueller, "Women's Organizational Strategies in State Legisla-tures," in *Political Women*, ed. Flammang.

14. Kathleen A. Frankovic, "Sex and Voting in the U. S. House of Representa-tives, 1961–1975," *American Politics Quarterly* 5(3) (July 1977): 315–330; Freida Gehlen, "Women Members of Congress: A Distinctive Role," in *A Portrait of Marginality*, ed. Githens and Prestage; Shelah Leader, "The Policy Impact of Elected Women Offi-

cials," in *The Impact of the Electoral Process*, ed. Louis Maisel and Joseph Cooper (Beverly Hills, CA: Sage Publications, 1977); Susan Welch, "Are Women More Liberal Than Men in the U. S. Congress," *Legislative Studies Quarterly* 10(1) (1985): 125–134; and Sue Thomas, "Voting Patterns in the California Assembly: The Role of Gender," *Women and Politics* 9(1) (1989): 43–53; Dodson and Carroll, *Reshaping the Agenda*.

15. Beth Reingold, "Concepts of Representation among Female and Male State Legislators," *Legislative Studies Quarterly* 17(4) (1992): 509–537.

16. Lyn Kathlene, "Exploring the Political Impacts of Gender: An Exploratory Study," *Western Political Quarterly* 44(2) (1991): 387–421.

17. Kathlene, "Power and Influence in State Legislative Policymaking."

18. Eagly and Johnson, "Gender and Leadership Style."

19. Gilligan, *In a Different Voice*.

20. Loden, *Feminine Leadership*, 120–131.

21. Lunneborg, *Women Changing Work*, 47.

22. A few studies found no significant differences between men and women in their power orientations, drive, and style. See, for example, D. C. Jones, "Power Structures and Perceptions of Powerholders in Same-Sex Groups of Young Children," *Women and Politics* 3(2) (1983): 147–164; and I. E. Deutchman, "Socialization to Power: Questions about Women and Politics," *Women and Politics* 5(1) (1986): 79–89. For an overview of different gender perspectives on power, see Cynthia L. Miller and A. Gaye Cummins, "An Examination of Women's Perspectives on Power," *Psychology of Women Quarterly* 16(4) (December 1992): 415–428; and Janice D. Yoder and Arnold S. Kahn, "Toward a Feminist Understanding of Women and Power," *Psychology of Women Quarterly* 16(4) (December 1992): 381–388.

23. See, for example, Rosener, "Ways Women Lead"; Hale and Kelly, *Gender, Bureaucracy and Democracy*; and McClelland, *Power: The Inner Experience*.

24. Miller and Cummins, "Women's Perspectives on Power," 426–427.

25. Katz, "The Leader and the Public," 262–263.

26. Alice H. Eagly and S J. Karau, "Gender and the Emergence of Leaders: A Meta-Analysis," *Journal of Personality and Social Psychology* 60(5) (May 1991): 685–710.

27. Alice H. Eagly, *Sex Differences in Social Behavior: A Social Role Interpretation* (Hillsdale, NJ: Erlbaum Publishers, 1987).

28. Ann M. Morrison, Randall P. White, and Ellen Van Velson, *Breaking the Glass Ceiling* (Reading, MA: Addison-Wesley, 1987).

29. Rita Mae Kelly, M. M. Hale, and J. Burgess, "Gender and Managerial/Leadership Styles: A Comparison of Arizona Public Administrators," *Women and Politics* 11(1) (1991): 129.

30. Quinn, *Beyond Rational Management*, 97–109.

31. Jewell and Whicker, *Legislative Leadership*, 178.

32. Eagly and Johnson, "Gender and Leadership Style."

33. Rosener, "Ways Women Lead."

34. See Hennig and Jardim, *The Managerial Women*; Loden, *Feminine Leadership*; and Lunneborg, *Women Changing Work*.

35. Helgesen, *The Female Advantage*.

36. Eagly and Johnson, "Gender and Leadership Style."

37. The analysis, using principal components method and varimax rotation, extracted four factors with eigenvalues of 3.702, 2.163, 1.258, and 1.062, respectively. The four factors explain 63.0 percent of the variance in the sample. The final rotated

factor matrix produced loadings of greater than .500 on all items and substantially stronger loadings (above .670 to .821) on ten of the items. The mean scores for men and women and significance levels on *t* tests for each of the four motivational factors are: (1) policy-oriented, x̄ = .171 for women, −.150 for men, *p* = .007; (2) people-oriented, x̄ = .204 for women, −.178 for men, *p* = .001; (3) power/status, x̄ = .012 for women, −.011 for men, *p* = .846; (4) constituent interest, x̄ = .037 for women, −.032 for men, *p* = .558.

38. Gilligan, *In a Different Voice*.

39. The scale scores on all four motivational factors do in fact follow normal bell-curve distributions. The effect size of the gender difference is modest, .39. The use of effect sizes and their interpretation as small, modest, or strong is based on Jacob Cohen, *Statistical Power Analysis for the Social Sciences* (Hillsdale, NJ: Erlbaum Publishers, 1988), 25–27.

40. Focus group, July 28, 1994, New Orleans, La.

41. The gender difference on the policy leadership motivation has a modest effect size of .33. Interpretation of the effect size is based on Cohen, *Statistical Power Analysis*.

42. Kaye Steinmetz, telephone interview, January 15, 1996; and focus group, July 27, 1994, New Orleans, La.

43. Belle Rose Ragins and Eric Sundstrom, "Gender and Power in Organizations: A Longitudinal Perspectives," *Psychological Bulletin* 105(1) (January 1989): 51–88.

44. Focus group, July 28, 1994, New Orleans, La.

45. All four motivational factor scores were correlated with demographic variables on which male and female chairs differed significantly, specifically age when first elected, total years served in the legislature, and years as committee chair. The correlations on the three other factors reveal similar patterns for men and women. Specifically, the motivation for greater status and power declines with age ($r = −.109$ for women; $r = −.287$, $p < .001$, for men) and legislative experience ($r = −.036$ for women; $r = -.240$, $p < .001$, for men). The emphasis on involving people in the process shows the same declining pattern with age ($r = −.145$ for women; $r = −.041$ for men). The focus on policy leadership increases slightly as total years of service rise ($r = .136$ for women; $r = .107$ for men) and remains essentially unchanged in relationship to a chair's age ($r = .092$ for women; $r = −.086$ for men).

46. The interaction of years as chair and the constituent-interests motivation has a statistical probability of occurring by chance less than 1 time in 1,000. The association between number of years as chair and the motivation for women is $r = −.228$, $p = .009$; for men, the association is $r = .109$, $p = .181$.

47. Focus group, July 29, 1996, St. Louis, Mo.

48. McClelland, *Power: The Inner Experience*.

49. Ibid., 265.

50. See Duerst-Lahti and Johnson, "Gender and Style in Bureaucracy"; Georgia Duerst-Lahti and Cathy Johnson, "Management Styles, Stereotypes, and Advantages," in *Women and Men of the States*, ed. Guy; and Rita Mae Kelly and Mary E. Guy with Jane Bayes, Georgia Duerst-Lahti, Mary M. Hale, Cathy Johnson, A. Kawar, and Jean R. Stanley, "Public Managers in the States: A Comparison of Career Advancement by Sex," *Public Administration Review* 51 (1991): 402–412.

51. The factor analysis, using principal-components method and varimax rotation, extracted six factors with eigenvalues of 4.926, 2.131, 1.743, 1.432, 1.328, and 1.062, respectively. The six factors explain 57.4 percent of the variance in the sample. The

final rotated factor matrix produced loadings of greater than .500 on all but three of the items and substantially stronger loadings (above .670) on ten of the items. The factor analysis was performed on the whole sample and on the separate samples of men and women. Although there are some differences in the clustering of traits and the factor loadings for women and men separately, the resulting factors are not markedly distinct from the factors produced from the whole sample. Theoretically, the factors from the whole sample reflect the strong institutional norms of behavior that are expected to be present in legislatures and reinforced by leadership appointment of committee chairs. In other words, behavioral styles (although diverse for both men and women) are constrained by legislative norms. In other research using the same question, the results show that sex differences in leadership styles are most pronounced in middle-management civil service positions and style conformity to organizational norms is greater among higher-level executive appointees. See Duerst-Lahti and Johnson, "Gender and Style in Bureaucracy."

52. The mean scores and significance levels on $t$ tests for the the six factors are: dominator, $\bar{x} = .149$ for men, $-.168$ for women, $p = .007$; innovator, $\bar{x} = -.128$ for men, $.145$ for women, $p = .021$; nurturer, $\bar{x} = -.183$ for men, $.207$ for women, $p = .001$; processor, $\bar{x} = -.093$ for men, $\bar{x} = .104$ for women, $p = .097$; competent, $\bar{x} = -.209$ for men, $\bar{x} = .235$ for women, $p < .001$; dependable, $\bar{x} = .026$ for men, $\bar{x} = -.030$ for women, $p = .638$.

53. The distributions on the three trait scores approximate normal bell curves.

54. Fiedler, *Leadership Effectiveness.*

55. Fred E. Fiedler and Joseph E. Garcia, *New Approaches to Effective Leadership: Cognitive Resources and Organizational Performance* (New York: John Wiley & Sons, 1987), chap. 7.

56. For a brief review of the history of the score, its reliability and interpretation, and both corroborating and critical research, see Fiedler and Garcia, *New Approaches to Effective Leadership.* In completing the "least preferred coworker" (LPC) instrument, a person is asked to think about the most difficult coworker with whom he or she has had to work. Then, the respondent rates that coworker on eighteen personality features (kindness, warmth, disposition, openness, etc.) using an eight-point scale. Negative assessments of a coworker yield a low score, whereas a positive evaluation of the person produces a high score. A high score on the LPC (73 or above) is interpreted as an orientation to personal relationships, a low score (63 or less) reflects task motivation and is interpreted as a high need to accomplish the task. Interpretations of a middle score (64–72) indicate a person who is flexible with regard to task and "socioindependent" or less concerned about opinions of others. See Fiedler and Garcia, *New Approaches to Effective Leadership,* 76–77.

57. For both male and female committee chairs, the LPC scores fall slightly below the norms established for the scale (Fiedler's norms: $\bar{x} = 68.8$, sd 21.8; committee chairs: $\bar{x} = 66.9$, sd 20.47 for men; $\bar{x} = 62.2$, sd 19.29 for women.)

58. The significance level is $p = .057$, based on the mean scores for men and women chairs in $t$ tests for independent samples.

59. The $\chi^2 = 4.719$, df 2, $p = .094$.

60. I elaborate on this argument in Cindy Simon Rosenthal, "Getting the Job Done: A Strategy for Overcoming Gender Inequality," in *Women and Elective Office: Past, Present and Future,* ed. Sue Thomas and Clyde Wilcox (New York: Oxford University Press, 1998).

61. J. Goodchilds, "Power: A Matter of Mechanics?," *SASP Newsletter* 5 (1979):

3, quoted in Hilary M. Lips, *Women, Men, and the Psychology of Power* (Englewood Cliffs, NJ: Prentice-Hall, 1981), 37–38.

62. To determine whether there was a discrepancy between a chair's self-description and the indirect measure of task versus people orientation, correlations were run between the LPC score and the clusters of traits identified by the committee chairs. For women, the correlation between "competent" traits and the LPC score was statistically significant ($p$ = .034, one-tailed significance test) and was in the expected direction. In other words, female chairs who identify themselves as task oriented, independent, and managerial are consistent in their self-assessment and in the indirect LPC measure. An orientation to personal relations (i.e., a high LPC) showed no correlation with the "nurturer" traits, which suggests that some female chairs hold contradictory self-perceptions and actual orientations. Among the men, the orientation to personal relations is positively and significantly correlated with the "dependable" traits ($p$ = .019), but is negatively correlated with "nurturer" traits for men ($p$ = .044). These results suggest that gender stereotypes influence some chairs' self-assessment of leadership traits. Men who are inclined toward maintenance of personal relations consider it okay to present themselves as trusting and loyal yet not appropriate to describe themselves as affectionate. Some women may demonstrate a similar tendency to rate themselves as affectionate even when they are inclined to be more task oriented than relationship oriented.

63. Focus group, July 29, 1997, St. Louis, Mo.

64. Focus group, July 28, 1994, New Orleans, La.

65. "Tough Work Still Remains on Trauma Care Network," *Denver Post*, June 11, 1995, E2.

66. Focus group, July 28, 1994, New Orleans, La.

67. Ohio House Minority Leader Jo Ann Davidson, "Women in Legislative Leadership" (Panel presentation at the annual meeting of the National Conference of State Legislatures, New Orleans, July 25, 1994).

68. Focus group, July 28, 1994, New Orleans, La.

69. Focus group, July 29, 1996, St. Louis, Mo.

70. The scale of possible responses for the first questions ranges from "1" for "almost never" to "3" for "sometimes" to "5" for "almost always." Responses for the last question range on a five-point scale from "1" for "strongly disagree" to "5" for "strongly agree." The items were summed and standardized for a scale score of inclusive behavior. Reliability analysis for the six-item scale produced a standardized item Alpha coefficient of .635 for the whole sample. The reliability of the scale is substantially similar for both men (Alpha = .668) and women (Alpha = .576).

71. On the individual item, $\bar{x}$ = 3.51 for men and 3.81 for women $p$ = .005.

72. On the individual item, $\bar{x}$ = 3.80 for men and 4.02 for women, $p$ = .031.

73. On the individual item, $\bar{x}$ = 3.66 for men and 3.84 for women, $p$ = .031.

74. On the scale, the mean score for women equals .142, compared to –.112 for men, $p$ = .039.

75. The distributions on the three trait scores approximate normal bell curves.

76. Thomas, "Conflict and Conflict Management." The Thomas-Kilmann instrument consists of three pages of forced-choice questions. For this survey, the questions were converted to fifteen individual questions with a five-point response scale ranging from "1" for "almost never" to "3" for "sometimes" to "5" for "almost always."

77. The factor analysis, using principal-components method and varimax rotation, extracted five factors with eigenvalues of 3.490, 1.961, 1.193, 1.096, and 1.013. The

factors explains 58.4 percent of the variance in the sample. The Alpha reliability of the scales comprising the principle items is .667 for accommodation, .581 for collaboration, .645 for compromise, .502 for avoidance, and .497 for competing. The Alpha reliability was substantially the same for both men and women except on the competing scale. The items constituting the "competing" scale have a reliability for men of Alpha = .425 and for women of Alpha = .567. Elimination of the item "I make every effort to get my way" would increase the reliability of the scale for women (Alpha = .635) but would decrease the scale's reliability for men (Alpha = .192). In the factor analysis for men, only this item loads strongly, whereas for women, two items load on the competitive style ("I make every effort to get my way," .800, and "I try hard to convince others of the merits of my position," .774).

78. A chair's dominant style was determined by his or her highest score on the five factors. The percentage of women distributed among the five styles was 15.9 percent accommodate, 29.4 percent collaborate, 22.2 percent compromise, 13.5 percent avoid, and 19 percent compete; for the men, the distribution was 21.8 percent accommodate, 15.6 percent collaborate, 21.1 percent compromise, 21.8 percent avoid, and 19.7 percent compete. Cross-tabs calculated for the five conflict-resolution styles produced a Pearson's $\chi^2$ 9.694, df 4, $p$ =.046.

79. Personal interview, February 23, 1995, Columbus, Ohio.

80. Focus group, July 27, 1994, New Orleans, La.

81. Focus group, July 27, 1994, New Orleans, La.

82. Focus group, July 28, 1994, New Orleans, La.

83. Personal interview, January 10, 1995, Denver, Colo.

84. Focus group, July 29, 1996, St. Louis, Mo.

85. Focus group, July 27, 1996, St. Louis, Mo.

86. Focus group, July 30, 1996, St. Louis, Mo.

87. Mary M. Hale, "Mentoring," in *Women and Men of the States*, ed. Guy.

88. See R. A. Noe, "Women and Mentoring: A Review and Research Agenda," *Academy of Management Review* 13(1) (1988): 65–78; and K. E. Kram, *Mentoring at Work: Developmental Relationships in Organizational Life* (Glenview, IL: Scott, Foresman, 1985).

89. Hale, "Mentoring," 89.

90. See Hale, "Mentoring"; Noe, "Women and Mentoring"; Belle Rose Ragins, "Barriers to Mentoring: The Female Manager's Dilemma," *Human Relations* 42(1) (1989): 1–22.; Kathy E. Kram and Lynn A. Isabella, "Mentoring Alternatives: The Role of Peer Relationships in Career Development," *Academy of Management Journal* 28(1) (1985) 110– 132; Gerald R. Roche, "Much Ado About Mentors," *Harvard Business Review* (January/February 1979), 14–28.; Dee W. Henderson, "Enlightened Mentoring: A Characteristic of Public Management Professionalism," *Public Administrative Review* 49 (November/December 1985), 857–864; Kelly et al., "Public Managers in the States."

91. The survey asked committee chairs to identify important mentors by sex in six categories: legislative leaders, senior legislators, other legislative peers, professional colleagues, friends or political advisers, and family members. The category "family members" contained the greatest number of opposite-sex mentors because many respondents identified their spouse as a key mentor. Spousal relationships, although extremely important to politicians, are distinctly different from the kind of organizational mentoring considered here and therefore were not included in the analysis.

92. Significance levels are computed for the dichotomous dummy variable indi-

cating an important female or male mentor in each category. The $\chi^2$ statistic for all the items on which there is a significant sex difference is as follows: female mentors: "senior legislator" $\chi^2 = 6.784$, df 1, $p = .009$; "legislator peer" $\chi^2 = 30.118$, df 1 , $p < .000$; "professional colleague" $\chi^2 = 11.755$, df 1, $p < .001$; "Friend/political adviser" $\chi^2 = 34.400$, df 1, $p < .001$.

93. Kelly et al., "Public Managers in the States."

94. One-way analysis of variance was used to examine the association between mentoring and leadership styles, behaviors, traits, and motivations. On all six measures reported in the table, the weighted linear trend is statistically significant at a .05 level or less. On two of the other measures (i.e., competent traits and policy motivation), the weighted linear trend is statistically significant, but the data in actuality do not conform to the expected linear pattern. In other words, the male committee chairs who identified female mentors are less like the female subgroup than the other male committee chairs. Arguably, mentoring is more likely to influence one's specific behaviors than to change motivations and traits; thus the deviation of these two factors from the hypothesized expectations does not negate the overall trend apparent in these results.

95. Focus group, July 27, 1996, St. Louis, Mo.

96. Variables included in the logistic regression model were the conflict and behavioral styles and motivational orientations that proved significant in the previous analyses and are theoretically associated negatively or positively with integrative leadership. The model also includes demographic control variables discussed in chapter 3 (this volume) and female mentorship. All variables were entered into the equation initially and then, to identify a more parsimonious model, backward regression was performed using .05 as the standard for removal of variables. The full model of thirteen variables improves on the predictive power of the reduced model only marginally from 75.2 percent to 78.5 percent. The reduced model with predictors variables significant at $p < .05$ includes: policy motivation, nurturer traits, competent traits, a dummy variable for a female legislative mentor, and age when first elected.

97. Personal interview, July 27, 1994, New Orleans, La.

98. Focus group, July 28, 1994, New Orleans, La.

99. Eagly and Johnson, "Gender and Leadership Style."

100. Such tendencies pose risks. Research shows that leaders who display consistent sex-role behaviors, regardless of whether female or male, tend to be judged more effective. See Stephen M. Bushardt, Aubrey Fowler, and Regina Coveny, "Sex Role Behavior and Leadership: An Empirical Investigation," *Leadership and Organizational Journal* 8:1 (1987): 13–16; and Anne Statham, "Women Managers: Leadership Style, Development, and Misunderstandings," in *Women and Work: Selected Papers*, ed. Knezek, La Verne (Arlington: University of Texas, Arlington, 1985).

## Chapter 5

1. Karen Hansen, "Legislator Pay: Baseball It Ain't," *State Legislatures* 23(7) (July/August 1997), 22.

2. Diane Watson, personal interview, July 27, 1994, New Orleans, La.

3. Beverly Evans, telephone interview, July 13, 1997.

4. Focus group, July 30, 1996, St. Louis, Mo.

5. Watson, personal interview, July 27, 1994.

6. Ibid.

7. Focus group, July 30, 1996, St. Louis, Mo.

8. Evans, telephone interview, July 13, 1997.

9. Fenno, *Home Style*.

10. Evans, telephone interview, July 13, 1997.

11. Elected in 1978, Senator Watson is the first African-American woman and only the second female to serve in the California State Senate. She points out that in 1994, every office in her district from U.S. Congress to state legislature to local school board was occupied by a black woman. Watson, personal interview, July 27, 1994.

12. Ibid.

13. Francis, *The Legislative Committee Game*.

14. Committee differences are detailed in Rosenthal, *Legislative Life*, chap. 9, and Council of State Governments, *Book of the States: 1992–93 Edition* (Lexington, KY: Council of State Governments, 1992).

15. An extensive literature documents the importance of norms and their contribution to institutional stability in the U.S. Congress. See, for example, Donald Matthews, "The Folkways of the United States Senate: Conformity to Group Norms and Legislative Effectiveness," *American Political Science Review* 53 (1959): 1064–1089; Herbert Asher, "The Learning of Legislative Norms," *American Political Science Review* 67(3) (1973): 499–513; and Barbara Hinckley, *Stability and Change in Congress*, 4th ed., (New York: Harper & Row, 1988). A parallel literature focusing on state legislatures also exists. See, e.g., John C. Wahlke, Heinz Eulau, William Buchanan, and LeRoy C. Ferguson, *The Legislative System* (New York: Wiley Publishers, 1962); Charles M. Price and Charles G. Bell, "The Rules of the Game: Political Fact or Academic Fancy?" *Journal of Politics* 32(4) (November 1970): 839–855; F. Ted Hebert and Lelan E. McLemore, "Character and Structure of Legislative Norms: Operationalizing the Norm Concept in the Legislative Setting," *American Journal of Political Science* 17(2) (1973): 506–527; and Rosenthal, *Legislative Life*, 123–125.

16. Schein, *Organizational Culture and Leadership*.

17. See, for example, Anthony Downs, *Inside Bureaucracy* (Boston: Little, Brown, 1967); James Q. Wilson, *Bureaucracy. What Government Agencies Do and Why They Do It* (New York: Basic Books, 1989); and Hugh Heclo, *A Government of Strangers: Executive Politics in Washington* (Washington, DC: The Brookings Institution, 1977).

18. Burns, *Leadership*, 434–435.

19. Cathleen Decker and Jenifer Warren, "Sexism Still Alive in Sacramento," *Los Angeles Times*, June 12, 1995, 1.

20. Watson, personal interview, July 27, 1994.

21. Kanter, *Men and Women of the Corporation*, chap. 9.

22. Kanter, "Some Effects of Proportions on Group Life."

23. Blau, "A Macrosociological Theory of Social Structure."

24. See Kanter, "Some Effects of Proportions on Group Life," 985; and *Men and Women of the Corporation*, 233–237.

25. Kanter, *Men and Women of the Corporation*, 6.

26. Kanter, "Some Effects of Proportions on Group Life," 966.

27. Kanter, *Men and Women of the Corporation*, 209.

28. Blau, "A Macrosociological Theory of Social Structure," 37–40.

29. Yoder, "Rethinking Tokenism," 188.

30. Yoder, "Looking beyond Numbers," 151.

31. Duerst-Lahti and Kelly, eds., *Gender Power, Leadership and Governance*, chap. 2. See also Norton, "Women, It's Not Enough to Be Elected"; and Lyn Kathlene,

"Position Power versus Gender Power: Who Holds the Floor?" in *Gender Power, Leadership and Governance*, ed. Duerst-Lahti and Kelly.

32. Kanter identifies power and opportunity as determinants of organizational behavior but treats them as separate concepts. Power refers to the capacity to mobilize resources, for example, the structural elements of job discretion, visibility, the relevance of a function to current organizational priorities, and status. By opportunity, Kanter means expectations and future prospects that are shaped by such structural components as mobility prospects, career paths, and access to decision-making centers. Clearly, a greater proportion of women would seem to be a necessary antecedent of increased gender power and opportunity.

33. Rosenthal, in "State Legislative Development," points out the difference between institutional professionalism and careerism among individual legislators. Nonetheless, careerists, as Rosenthal describes them, are more likely to be found in the more professionalized legislatures. For purposes of this discussion, the association between professionalization and careerism is critical.

34. Ibid., 185–186.

35. Josefowitz, *Paths to Power*.

36. Rosenthal, "State Legislative Development," 176–177.

37. Philip Selznick, *Leadership in Administration: A Sociological Interpretation*, (Evanston, IL: Row, Peterson, 1957); and Herbert Kaufman, *The Forest Ranger* (Baltimore: Johns Hopkins University Press, 1960).

38. See Stivers, *Gender Images*, 51.

39. Citizens Conference on State Legislatures, *The Sometime Governments*.

40. Ibid., 104–109.

41. Rita Mae Kelly, *The Gendered Economy: Work, Careers, and Success* (Newbury Park, CA: Sage Publications, 1991).

42. Stivers, *Gender Images*, 58–59.

43. Ibid., chap. 4.

44. Ibid.

45. Jamieson, *Beyond the Double Bind*, chap. 4.

46. Duerst-Lahti and Johnson, "Gender and Style in Bureaucracy."

47. See Kelly et al., "Public Managers in the States"; and Loden, *Feminine Leadership*.

48. Duerst-Lahti and Johnson, "Gender and Style in Bureaucracy."

49. Morrison, White, and Van Velson, *Breaking the Glass Ceiling*, 56.

50. Joseph Cooper and David W. Brady, "Institutional Context and Leadership Style: The House from Cannon to Rayburn," *American Political Science Review* 75(2) (1981): 411–425.

51. Elazar, *American Federalism*.

52. Although Elazar's initial work was impressionistic and descriptive, Sharkansky found empirical utility to the concept, particularly the association between low popular political participation and "traditionalism" as contrasted with high participation and "moralism." See Ira Sharkansky, "The Utility of Elazar's Political Culture," *Polity* 2(1) (1969): 67–83. He transforms Elazar's three categories into a nine-point continuum reflecting blends of the three.

53. Barry A. Kosmin and Seymour P. Lachman, *One Nation under God* (New York: Harmony Books, 1993).

54. Nelson, *Emerging Influentials*.

55. Kwang Shik Shin, "Innovation Adoption and Diffusion in the Political Systems of States: A Focus on Taxation and Antidiscrimination" (Ph. D. diss., Southern Illinois University, 1979).

56. Nelson, *Emerging Influentials*, identifies six variables that consistently and significantly predict the number of women in state legislatures: the percentage of women employed in the labor force, the percentage of the population with a college education or more, the percentage of population living in metropolitan areas, the percentages of Roman Catholics and conservative Protestants, and historical support for antidiscrimination legislation.

57. For those interested in looking at analyses of the other leadership variables, see Rosenthal, "A View of Their Own"; and Cindy Simon Rosenthal, "Women's Ways of Political Leadership: Gender Differences in a Cross-Jurisdictional Study of State Legislative Committee Chairs" (Paper presented at the annual meeting of the American Political Science Association, Chicago, 1995.)

58. The variable measuring legislative professionalization is derived from three separate indices developed by Kurtz, *State Legislatures: Progress, Problems, and Possibilities*; Squire, "Legislative Professionalization and Membership Diversity in State Legislatures"; and Ann O'M. Bowman and Richard Kearney, "Dimensions of State Government Capability," *Western Political Quarterly* 41(2) (1988): 341–362. From Bowman and Kearney, I use only the measure of state government staffing and spending that is principally based on five measures of legislative compensation, staffing, session length, and expenditures.

The number of women members, chairs, and leaders are for 1993–1994 and are taken from the CAWP, "Women State Legislators: Leadership Positions and Committee Chairs 1993–94." Women's power is calculated by adding the z-scores of the percentage of chairs and leadership jobs held by women in a state and then computing a z-score of that sum. The indices were standardized and summed.

Only Elazar's moralistic-traditionalistic continuum is used in this analysis. Specifically, I use Sharkansky's conversion of political culture into a linear continuum. Initial analyses included the variables suggested by Nelson's analysis (e.g., 1990 U.S. Census Bureau data for percentage of state population living in metropolitan areas and the percentage of women employed in the labor force) and conservative religious variables taken from Kosmin and Lachman, *One Nation under God*. These additional variables did not add explanatory power and were dropped for the analysis in the interests of parsimony.

59. Personality variables that are entered into the regression equation include all those that had a significant bivariate relationship.

60. See Duerst-Lahti and Kelly, eds., *Gender Power, Leadership and Governance*, chap. 1, for a more detailed discussion of conceptualizing gender as a variable.

61. For more detail, see Rosenthal, "A View of Their Own."

62. The categories shown in table 5.2 deviate somewhat from Kanter's specifications of skewed, tilted, and balanced groups. In part, the categories were defined by the data and the need for sufficiently similar-size groups to facilitate analysis. The exact cutoff points between skewed, tilted, and balanced groups remain something of a term of art, but the categorization made here does not deviate from the essence of Kanter's theory. Legislatures are categorized into three groups: those where women constitute less than 18 percent of the members, those where women number 18 to 28 percent of the members, and those where women number more than 28 percent of the membership.

63. Focus group, July 28, 1994, New Orleans, La.

64. Ibid.

65. Focus group, July 30, 1996, St. Louis, Mo.

66. Mindy Greiling and Alice Hausman, "Minnesota House DFL Must Oust Its Abusive Leadership," April 14, 1996, *Saint Paul Pioneer Press*, 23A; and Becky Sisco, "Loud and Clear: Women Legislators Speak Out against House Leadership," May 15–28, 1996, *Minnesota Women's Press*, 5.

67. Greiling and Hausman, 23A.

68. Ibid.

69. Focus group, July 29, 1996, St. Louis, Mo.

70. Morrison, White, and Van Velson, *Breaking the Glass Ceiling*, 56.

71. Perhaps it is no coincidence that among the most professional legislatures where women seem most likely to conform to the male norms, the number of women legislators generally is less than 25 percent. Among the nine most professional legislatures, the proportion of women legislators in 1994 was as follows: Pennsylvania (9.9 percent), New Jersey (12.5 percent), New York (16.6 percent), Michigan (20.3 percent), Ohio (21.2 percent), Massachusetts (23 percent), Illinois (23.2 percent), and Wisconsin (27.3 percent).

72. Ellen Goodman, quoted in Stivers, *Gender Image*, 89.

*Chapter 6*

1. David R. Morgan, Robert E. England, and George G. Humphreys, *Oklahoma Politics and Policies: Governing the Sooner State* (Lincoln, NB: University of Nebraska Press, 1991), 6–7.

2. Evidence is drawn from related research, semistructured personal interviews with nineteen current or former legislators, legislative staff and others, and direct observation of fourteen committee meetings.

3. Robert Darcy, Margaret Brewer, and Judy Clay, "Women in the Okla Political System: State Legislative Elections," *Social Science Journal* 21(1) (January 1984): 67–78.

4. Mildred Ladner, "State's First Congresswoman," *Tulsa World*, July 26, 1984, D-1. Ironically, Robertson won election as a vocal vice president of the state's antisuffragette forces and with a platform proclaiming "I am a Christian—I am an American—I am a Republican."

5. Legislative Reference Division, "Women in Government," typescript memorandum, 1972, Oklahoma State Library.

6. Darcy, Brewer, and Clay, "Women in the Oklahoma Political System," 76.

7. Ibid.

8. Ibid.

9. Dianna Gordon, "Republican Women Make Gains," *State Legislatures* (February 1995): 15.

10. Anne Firor Scott, *The Southern Lady: From Pedestal to Politics, 1830–1930* (Chicago: University of Chicago Press, 1970).

11. Eleanor C. Main, Gerard S. Gryski, and Beth S. Schapiro, "Different Perspectives: Southern State Legislators' Attitudes about Women in Politics," *Social Science Journal* 21 (March 1984): 21–28.

12. Darcy, Brewer, and Clay, "Women in the Oklahoma Political System," 75–76.

13. Ibid., 76.

14. Oklahoma Senate debate, audiotape, floor session of March 6, 1997.

15. Ellen Knickmeyer, "Boyd Tests Her Own Style of Politics in State House," *Daily Oklahoman*, April 10, 1994, 10.

16. Ibid.

17. Personal interview, February 15, 1995, Oklahoma City, Okla.

18. After her career in the legislature, Deatherage made an unsuccessful run for lieutenant governor. Currently, she is legal counsel and director of Americans for Term Limits, based in Washington, D.C.

19. Joyce Peterson, "Deatherage Says Budgets Got Boring," *Daily Oklahoman*, August 28, 1983, 10.

20. John Greiner, "Democratic Caucus to Meet on Speaker," *Daily Oklahoman*, August 24, 1983, 1.

21. Jim Myers, "3 Women Break Male Hold on Education Policy Clout," *Tulsa World*, May 29, 1990, A-1.

22. Ronald M. Peters Jr. and Elizabeth Himmerich, "Policy Shift and Leadership Coalition: The Revolt Against Speaker Barker in Oklahoma" (Paper presented at the annual meeting of the American Political Science Association, San Francisco, 1990).

23. Personal interviews, March 7, 1992, Norman, Okla.; and December 16, 1994 and January 25, 1995, Oklahoma City, Okla.

24. Frosty Troy, "Those Wondrous Women," *The Oklahoma Observer*, September 10, 1993, 1.

25. Elazar, *American Federalism*.

26. Morgan, England, and Humphreys, *Oklahoma Politics and Policies*, 9.

27. Ibid., 15.

28. Kosmin and Lachman, *One Nation under God*, 88–93. Denominations categorized as fundamentalist include Baptist, Pentecostal, Church of Christ, Seventh-Day Adventist, Assemblies of God, Holiness Church, Nazarene, and born-again evangelicals.

29. For example, the manufacturing sector remains small, making up little more than 14 percent of the state's nonagricultural employment compared with 18 percent nationally. See Oklahoma Futures, *Oklahoma's Strategic Economic Development Plan 1988–1993* (Oklahoma City: Oklahoma Department of Commerce, 1990), 19.

30. Morgan, England, and Humphreys, *Oklahoma Politics and Policies*, 15.

31. I rely on James R. Scales and Danney Goble, *Oklahoma Politics* (Norman: University of Oklahoma Press, 1982); Danney Goble, "Oklahoma Politics and the Sooner Electorate," in *Oklahoma: New Views*, ed. Anne Hodges Morgan and H. Wayne Morgan (Norman: University of Oklahoma Press, 1982); and Morgan, England, and Humphreys, *Oklahoma Politics and Policies*, for much of the historical data provided in this chapter.

32. Samuel A. Kirkpatrick, *The Legislative Process in Oklahoma* (Norman: University of Oklahoma Press, 1978), 138–140.

33. Steven D. Gold and Judy Zelio, *State-Local Fiscal Indicators* (Denver, CO: National Conference of State Legislatures, 1990), 64–71. Measures of tax effort are often subject to considerable dispute over taxes compared and methods of computation that are beyond the subject of this discussion. However, in a recent state ranking developed by the Center for the Study of States, Oklahoma was twenty-fifth among the forty-three states with a personal income tax. Penelope Lemov, "A Mild Case of Tax-cut Fever," *Governing* 8 (June 1995): 20.

34. Cindy Simon Rosenthal, "The Case of Oklahoma Futures," *Oklahoma Politics* 2 (1993): 13–32.

35. Nancy L. Bednar and Allen D. Hertzke, "The Christian Right and Republican Realignment in Oklahoma," *PS: Political Science and Politics* 28 (March 1995): 11–15.

36. Goble, "Oklahoma Politics and the Sooner Electorate," 167.

37. Scales and Goble, *Oklahoma Politics*, 344.

38. Morgan, England, and Humphreys, *Oklahoma Politics and Policies*, 152.

39. Scales and Goble, *Oklahoma Politics*, 344–345.

40. Democrats went from 92.5 percent of House seats in 1959 to 75.2 percent of House seats in 1975. See Kirkpatrick, *The Legislative Process in Oklahoma*, 21–25.

41. Ibid., 29.

42. Citizens Conference on State Legislatures, *The Sometime Governments*, 49.

43. Ibid., 38.

44. Morgan, England, and Humphreys, *Oklahoma Politics and Policies*, 97.

45. Francis, *The Legislative Committee Game*, 42–44.

46. Alan Ehrenhalt, "Even Among the Sooners, There Are More Important Things Than Football," *Governing* 2(2) (November 1988), 44.

47. Peters and Himmerich, "Policy Shift and Leadership Coalition," 7.

48. Morgan, England, and Humphreys, *Oklahoma Politics and Policies*, 109–111.

49. Ibid., 97.

50. Peters and Himmerich, "Policy Shift and Leadership Coalition," 9.

51. Chuck Ervin, "Keating Picks Try to Buck Tradition," *Daily Oklahoman*, January 15, 1995, N15.

52. Morgan, England, and Humphreys, *Oklahoma Politics and Policies*, 82.

53. Peters and Himmerich, "Policy Shift and Leadership Coalition"; "Oklahoma Ousts Speaker," *State Legislatures*, July 1989, 9; *Daily Oklahoman* coverage April–May 1989; and *Oklahoma Legislative Weekly Reporter*, May 30, 1989, 4–5.

54. Gary W. Copeland and John David Rausch, Jr., "Sendin' 'Em Home Early: Oklahoma Legislative Term Limitations," *Oklahoma Politics*, 2 (1993): 33–50.

55. Kanter, *Men and Women of the Corporation*, 236.

56. Oklahoma House of Representatives, *Legislative Manual*, 6th ed. (Oklahoma City: Oklahoma House of Representatives, 1994), 25.

57. Ibid.

58. See Morgan, England, and Humphreys, *Oklahoma Politics and Policies*, 98, for the colorful assessment of former Senator David Riggs.

59. *Legislative Manual*, 6th ed., 39.

60. Personal interviews, 24 January 1995, Oklahoma City, Okla.

61. Personal interviews, January and February 1995, Oklahoma City, Okla.

62. A typical shell bill is a one-page document that appears in official form and is assigned a number. In reality, the draft is little more than an enacting clause that gives a member the ability to introduce a fully developed bill at a later time.

63. To ensure that one house does not relinquish its opportunity for input to the other house, a committee will "strike the title" and thus ensure that a bill will end up in conference committee.

64. *Legislative Manual*, 6th ed., 26.

65. Kanter, *Men and Women of the Corporation*, 210–242.

66. Bernice McShane, "Women Serving in the House, Senate," *Daily Oklahoman*, February 15, 1987, 1 (Women's section).

67. Kelly Haney, personal interview, January 17, 1995, Oklahoma City, Okla.

68. Personal interview, February 15, 1995, Oklahoma City, Okla.

69. Kanter, *Men and Women of the Corporation*, 213.

70. Ibid., 219–221.

71. Ibid., 216.

72. Personal interview, January 25, 1995, Oklahoma City, Okla.

73. Personal interview, February 16, 1995, Oklahoma City, Okla.

74. Myers, A-1.

75. Troy, 1.

76. Kanter, *Men and Women of the Corporation*, 223.

77. Personal interview, January 25, 1995, Oklahoma City, Okla.

78. Committee hearing, January 23, 1995, Oklahoma City, Okla.

79. Committee hearing, January 16, 1995, Oklahoma City, Okla.

80. Committee hearing, February 14, 1995, Oklahoma City, Okla.

81. Ibid.

82. Kanter, *Men and Women of the Corporation*, 224.

83. Personal interview, January 25, 1995, Oklahoma City, Okla.

84. Personal interview, January 25, 1995, Oklahoma City, Okla.

85. Telephone interview, April 1992, Oklahoma City, Okla.

86. Kanter, *Men and Women of the Corporation*, 229.

87. Personal interview, January 17, 1995, Oklahoma City, Okla.

88. Personal interview, December 15, 1994, Norman, Okla.

89. Kanter, *Men and Women of the Corporation*, 236.

90. Personal interview, February 16, 1995, Oklahoma City, Okla.

91. Personal interview, December 15, 1994, Norman, Okla.

92. Knickmeyer, "Boyd Tests Her Own Style of Politics."

93. Personal interview, January 24, 1995, Oklahoma City, Okla.

94. Kanter, *Men and Women of the Corporation*, 239.

95. Personal interview, February 16, 1995, Oklahoma City, Okla.

96. Personal interview, March 11, 1992, Oklahoma City, Okla.

97. Personal interview, December 13, 1995, Norman, Okla.

98. March and Olsen, *Rediscovering Institutions.*

99. Personal interview, January 17, 1995, Oklahoma City, Okla.

100. Personal interview, January 23, 1995, Oklahoma City, Okla.

101. This practice is now prohibited under the Oklahoma House Rules.

102. Committee hearing, January 24, 1995, Oklahoma City, Okla.

103. Personal interview, January 24, 1995, Oklahoma City, Okla.

104. Personal interview, January 17, 1995, Oklahoma City, Okla.

105. Personal interview, January 23 and 24, 1995, Oklahoma City, Okla.

106. Personal interview, January 23, 1995, Oklahoma City, Okla.

107. Personal interview, February 16, 1995, Oklahoma City, Okla.

108. Personal interviews, January 23 to 25, 1995, Oklahoma City, Okla.

109. *Legislative Manual*, 31.

110. In fact, the collaborative method of combining similar bills into a broader, more sweeping legislative proposal has earned a pejorative label based on the name of a House member who has been known to attempt such an approach. The other members view his efforts as coopting their own ideas.

111. A good example of this process took place in 1993–1994 when a consensus emerged around the reorganization of the state's juvenile justice system.

112. Personal interview, January 25, 1995, Oklahoma City, Okla.

113. Personal interview, January 17, 1995, Oklahoma City, Okla.

114. Personal interview, January 17, 1995, Oklahoma City, Okla.
115. Personal interview, January 25, 1995, Oklahoma City, Okla.
116. Personal interview, January 23, 1995, Oklahoma City, Okla.
117. Of those women interviewed, almost half (44.4 percent) have some kind of background in teaching.
118. Personal interview, March 11, 1992, Norman, Okla.
119. Personal interview, February 16, 1995, Oklahoma City, Okla.
120. Personal interview, March 11, 1992, Norman, Okla.
121. Yoder, "Rethinking Tokenism."

*Chapter 7*

1. Committee hearings, February 1995, 21 and 22, Columbus, Ohio.
2. Thomas Suddes, "The New Guard: House Speaker an Ohio First," *Cleveland Plain Dealer*, December 11, 1994, 1B; Lee Leonard, "An Era Ends with 120th Assembly," *Columbus Dispatch*, December 25, 1994, 1E; and Andrew Zajac, "1st Woman Takes Over Ohio House," *Akron Beacon Journal*, January 4, 1995, D1.
3. Lee Leonard, "Vernal G. Riffe Jr.: The Definitive House Speaker," *Columbus Dispatch*, December 25, 1994, 1C.
4. Ibid., 1E.
5. This chapter draws on other research; interviews with eighteen legislators, legislative staff, and other knowledgeable observers; direct observation of fifteen committee proceedings; and news reports to develop an understanding of the Ohio General Assembly.
6. Data on the number of female legislators is drawn from several sources, including Ohio Women's Policy and Research Commission, "Ohio Women as Elected Officials," press release, typescript, n.d.; Anita R. Young, Legislative Reference Bureau, "Women Who Have Served in the Ohio General Assembly," typescript, January 1979; Marilyn G. Hood, Legislative Reference Bureau, "Women Who Have Served in the Ohio General Assembly," typescript, December 1970; and Legislative Service Commission, "Women of the Ohio General Assembly: Standing Committee Assignments," n.d. Some of the fluctuation in numbers of women legislators parallels changes in the size of the legislature. Until the mid-1960s, the House membership ranged as high as 149 seats with 34 Senate seats. In the wake of the mid-1960s reapportionment revolution brought on by *Baker v. Carr*, the size of the House was reduced from 130 to its current 99 seats and the Senate from 34 to its current 33.
7. Ibid.
8. Catherine Candisky, "GOP Women Take the Majority from Democratic Peers," *Columbus Dispatch*, December 25, 1994, 1C.
9. Personal interview, February 24, 1995, Columbus, Ohio.
10. Kanter, *Men and Women of the Corporation*.
11. Personal interview, February 21, 1995, Columbus, Ohio.
12. Personal interview, February 22, 1995, Columbus, Ohio.
13. Mary Yost, "Women Move In on Statehouses," *Columbus Dispatch*, March 26, 1989, 4C.
14. Ohio Women's Policy and Research Commission, "Focusing on Women," *Ohio Women* 4:2 (Summer/Fall 1996): 3.
15. Ann Fisher, "Ohio's Democratic Women Expand Their Quest for Unity," *Toledo Blade*, March 19, 1995, B1.

16. Ibid.

17. Personal interviews, February 22, 1995, Columbus, Ohio.

18. See Hugh C. McDiarmid, "The Gilligan Interlude, 1971–1975," and George Knepper, "Ohio Politics: A Historial Perspective," 12, both in *Ohio Politics*, ed. Alexander P. Lamis, with Mary Anne Sharkey (Kent, OH: Kent State University Press, 1994), 12.

19. John J. Gargan and James G. Coke, *Political Behavior and Public Issues in Ohio* (Kent, OH: Kent State University Press, 1972), 8–16.

20. Lamis, ed., *Ohio Politics*, 3.

21. John Fenton, *Midwest Politics* (New York: Holt, Rinehart, & Winston, 1966), 117–154.

22. Ibid., 146.

23. Ibid.

24. Knepper, "Ohio Politics," 5.

25. Fenton, *Midwest Politics*.

26. Ibid., 117.

27. Ibid.

28. Lawrence Baum and Samuel C. Patterson, "Ohio: Party Change without Realignment," in *Party Realignment and State Politics*, ed. Maureen Moakley, (Columbus, OH: Ohio State University Press, 1992), 195.

29. Ibid., 304.

30. Elazar, *American Federalism*.

31. Fenton (*Midwest Politics*, 115) terms political motivations "job oriented."

32. Leonard, "Vernal Riffe," 1C.

33. Knepper, "Ohio Politics," 12–14.

34. Thomas Suddes, "Panorama of Ohio Politics in the Voinovich Era, 1991–," in *Ohio Politics*, ed. Lamis, 162–163.

35. Samuel C. Patterson, "Legislative Politics in Ohio," in *Ohio Politics*, ed. Lamis, 242.

36. Lee Leonard, "Republicans Risk Losing Their Unity," *Columbus Dispatch*, February 14, 1995, 9A.

37. Sandy Theis, "House Freshmen Seizing the Day," *Cincinnati Enquirer*, March 5, 1995, B1; Sandy Theis, "In Power, Not Always in Agreement," *Cincinnati Enquirer*, April 10, 1995, A1; and Lee Leonard, "House's Budget Game Left Out Some Key Players," *Columbus Enquirer*, April 10, 1995, 9A.

38. Catherine Candisky and Jonathan Riskind, "School Repairs, Crime Top GOP's Agenda," *Columbus Dispatch*, December 29, 1994, 1A.

39. Leonard, "Vernal Riffe," 1C.

40. Patterson, "Legislative Politics in Ohio," 236.

41. Kurtz, *State Legislatures*. The others include California, Illinois, Massachusetts, Michigan, New Jersey, New York, Pennsylvania, and Wisconsin.

42. Council of State Governments, *Book of the States*. Only four other states do not pay legislators any expense allowance or per diem. The four include New Mexico, New Hampshire, and two commuter legislatures (Rhode Island and New Jersey).

43. Patterson, "Legislative Politics in Ohio," 239–240.

44. Ibid., 253.

45. Ibid., 246–247.

46. Vernal Riffe, personal interview, May 2, 1995, Columbus, Ohio.

47. Patterson, "Legislative Politics in Ohio," 256.

48. Ibid., 245.

49. 121st Genderal Assembly, *Rules of Ohio House of Representatives*, State of Ohio, adopted January 11, 1996.

50. Personal interview, February 25, 1995, Columbus, Ohio.

51. Personal interview, February 23, 1995, Columbus, Ohio.

52. Theis, March 5, 1995, B1.

53. Personal interview, May 4, 1995, Columbus, Ohio.

54. Personal interview, February 22, 1995, Columbus, Ohio.

55. Leonard, "An Era Ends," 1E.

56. Candisky and Riskind, December 29, 1994, 1A; and Leonard, February 14, 1995, 9A.

57. The Ohio General Assembly has, since the 1960s, followed the practice of holding committee hearings on separate days for sponsor presentation, proponent testimony, and opponent input. On noncontroversial bills, proponent and opponent testimony may be combined into a single hearing. On highly controversial issues, the number of hearings may total a dozen of more in the house of origin. Patterson, "Legislative Politics in Ohio," 253.

58. Dennis J. Willard, "House to Vote on Abortion Bill," *Akron Beacon Journal*, April 7, 1995, 1B.

59. Thomas Suddes, "House Panel Short-Circuits Anti-Abortion Bill," *Cleveland Plain Dealer*, April 20, 1995, 5B; and Catherine Candisky, "Bill to Ban Some Late-Term Abortions Forced to House Vote," *Columbus Dispatch*, April 7, 1995.

60. Personal interview, May 5, 1995, Columbus, Ohio.

61. Leonard, February 14, 1995, 9A.

62. Sandy Theis, "House Speaker Eases Latest Spat, but Abortion Bill Debate Continues," *Cincinnati Enquirer*, April 25, 1995, C1.

63. Catherine Candisky, "GOP's Unity Shatters Over Abortion Bill," *Columbus Dispatch* May 2, 1995, 9A; Tom Suddes, "Paper Bag Fund in Ohio House," *Cleveland Plain Dealer*, 13 April 1995, 15B; and Ann Fisher, "Abortion Is a Hot Issue for Garcia," *Toledo Blade*, May 7, 1995, B1.

64. Riffe, personal interview May 2, 1995.

65. Gongwer News Service, "Negotiations Continue on Abortion Bill," *Ohio Report*, May 9, 1995, 1; Thomas Suddes, "House Republicans Debate Abortion Bill," *Cleveland Plain Dealer*, May 10, 1995, 6B; Thomas Suddes, "House Delays Vote on Abortion Bill," *Cleveland Plain Dealer*, May 11, 1995, 1B; and Associated Press, "House GOP Scrambles to Find Compromise on Abortion Bill," *Akron Beacon Journal*, May 10, 1995.

66. Thomas Suddes, "House GOP Hashes over Abortion Proposal," *Cleveland Plain Dealer*, May 17, 1995, 5B; Stephanie Warsmith, "Abortion Bill a Balancing Act," *Akron Beacon Journal*, May 11, 1995, C1; and Catherine Candisky, "Abortion Bill Is Changed," *Columbus Dispatch*, May 11, 1995, 6C.

67. Debra Jasper, "House Likely to Pass Curb on Abortions," *Dayton Daily News*, June 1, 1995, 10A; and Catherine Candisky, "House OKs Bill Limiting Abortions," *Columbus Dispatch*, June 2, 1995, 1C.

68. The bill essentially codified portions of the U.S. Supreme Court's 1973 decision, *Roe v. Wade*, by banning third-trimester and postviability abortions except to protect the health of the mother. The bill allowed pro-life advocates to claim a reduction in late-term abortions and to require viability testing to determine whether a fetus in the twenty-second week of gestation could live outside the womb. For pro-choice supporters, the bill was heralded as no erosion of current rights, and the com-

promise bill eliminated inflammatory language and limited civil liability provisions that were in the original proposal.

69. Candisky, June 2, 1995, 1C.

70. Warsmith, May 11, 1995, C1.

71. Ann Fisher, "Ohio Ban on Abortion Procedure First of Kind," *Toledo Blade*, June 29, 1995, 1.

72. Personal interview, February 22, 1995, Columbus, Ohio.

73. Personal interview, February 23, 1995, Columbus, Ohio.

74. JoAnn Davidson, personal interview, February 3, 1995, Columbus, Ohio.

75. Ibid.

76. Ohio House Minority Leader Jo Ann Davidson, "Women in Legislative Leadership" (Panel presentation at the annual meeting of the National Conference of State Legislatures, July 25, 1994, New Orleans).

77. Christopher Davey, "Ohio Might Loosen Grip on Hospitals," *Cincinnati Enquirer*, April 19, 1995, C1.

78. Adrienne Bosworth, "Rating the Legislators," *Columbus Monthly*, October 1988, 38–46; and "Rating the Legislators," *Columbus Monthly*, September 1986, 51–137.

79. Personal interviews, February 21 to 25, 1995, Columbus, Ohio.

80. Catherine Candisky, "Proposal Stirs Tragic Memory," *Columbus Dispatch*, March 16, 1995, B1.

81. Personal interview, May 3, 1995, Columbus, Ohio.

82. Personal interview, May 3, 1995, Columbus, Ohio.

83. Patrick Field, "State Legislators Use Consensus-Building to Resolve Issues, Involve Citizens, Develop Legislation," *Consensus*, July 1994.

84. Committee hearing, May 2, 1995, Columbus, Ohio.

85. Personal interview, February 23, 1995, Columbus, Ohio.

86. Committee hearings, February 21, 1995, and May 2, 1995, Columbus, Ohio.

87. Personal interview, May 5, 1995, Columbus, Ohio.

88. Personal interview, February 22, 1995, Columbus, Ohio.

89. Committee hearing, February 22, 1995; and personal interview, February 23, 1995, Columbus, Ohio.

90. Ibid.

91. Ibid.

92. Committee hearing, May 2, 1995, Columbus, Ohio.

93. Personal interview, May 3, 1995, Columbus, Ohio.

94. Bosworth, September 1986, 51–137.

95. Personal interview, May 3, 1995, Columbus, Ohio.

96. Peters, *The American Speakership*.

97. Sandy Theis, April 10, 1995, A1.

98. Personal interview, May 4, 1995, Columbus, Ohio. The group has adopted the name B.O.O.B.S. (Babes Of OCLA Bonding Socially).

99. Personal interview, May 4, 1995, Columbus, Ohio.

*Chapter 8*

1. Steve Lipsher, "GOP Women Gain Clout in Colorado," *Denver Post*, April 18, 1993, 1A.

2. John Sanko, "Key Players Bringing Different Agendas," *Rocky Mountain News*, January 11, 1995, 7.

3. Washington, Nevada, Colorado, Arizona, New Hampshire, Vermont, and Maryland are states that currently or in recent years have had women elected to 30 percent or more of the state legislative seats.

4. This chapter draws on interviews with fifteen legislators, legislative staff, and lobbyists; direct observation of a dozen committee hearings; and other analyses of Colorado politics.

5. Thomas E. Cronin and Robert D. Loevy, *Colorado Politics and Government: Governing the Centennial State* (Omaha: University of Nebraska Press, 1993), xxxi.

6. Kanter, *Men and Women of the Corporation*, 209.

7. Cox, "The Three Who Came First." Utah and Idaho were the only other states to elect women in the nineteenth century to serve in their state legislatures. Ibid., 14.

8. Cronin and Loevy, *Colorado Politics and Government*, 91.

9. Ibid.

10. Cox, "The Three Who Came First," 13–19.

11. Ibid., 19.

12. CAWP, *Women in Public Office* (New York: R. R. Bowker, 1976), xv.

13. CAWP, "Roster of Women State Legislators," typescript (New Brunswick, NJ: Eagleton Institute of Politics, Rutgers University, 1979).

14. Ehrenhalt, *The United States of Ambition*, 197.

15. CAWP, 1993.

16. Lipsher, April 18, 1993, A12.

17. Ehrenhalt, *The United States of Ambition*, 203–205.

18. Bob Ewegen, "Overlooked amid Political Thunder, Colorado's Quiet Revolution Continues," *Denver Post*, November 16, 1992, B7; and Lipsher, April 18, 1993, A12.

19. Personal interview, January 30, 1995, Denver, Colo.

20. Personal interview, July 27, 1996, St. Louis, Mo.

21. Michelle Dally Johnston, "Majority Leader Receives Rare Bipartisan Ovation," *Denver Post*, May 8, 1997, B1.

22. Ibid.

23. Thomas Frank, "Wham Respected, Feared at Capitol," *Denver Post*, April 1997, A1.

24. Lipsher, April 18, 1993, A12.

25. See Daniel J. Elazar, "Series Introduction," in Cronin and Loevy, *Colorado Politics and Government*, xxii.

26. Cronin and Loevy, *Colorado Politics and Government*, chap. 1.

27. The description of these five regions draws almost exclusively upon Cronin and Loevy, *Colorado Politics and Government*, chaps. 1 and 6; and, to a lesser extent, John A. Straayer, *The Colorado General Assembly* (Niwot: University Press of Colorado, 1990), chap. 1.

28. Cronin and Loevy, *Colorado Politics and Government*, 169–170.

29. John P. McIver and Walter J. Stone, "Stability and Change in Colorado Politics," in *Party Realignment and State Politics*, ed. Maureen Moakley, 65.

30. Cronin and Loevy, *Colorado Politics and Government*, 19.

31. Ehrenhalt, *The United States of Ambition*, 203; and Straayer, *The Colorado General Assembly*, 11.

32. McIver and Stone, "Stability and Change in Colorado Politics," 71.

33. Cronin and Loevy, *Colorado Politics and Government*, 144–145.

34. Ibid., 129.
35. Ibid., 26.
36. Ibid., 19.
37. Ibid., 186–190.
38. Ibid., 29.
39. Litigation is still under way to settle a host of legal questions about the scope and interpretation of Amendment 1.
40. Ehrenhalt, *The United States of Ambition.*
41. Ibid., 190.
42. Ibid., 191.
43. Ibid.
44. Ibid., 190.
45. Ibid., 192–197.
46. Ibid., 192.
47. Straayer, *The Colorado General Assembly,* 81.
48. Ehrenhalt, *The United States of Ambition,* 197.
49. Council of State Governments, *Book of the States,* 104.
50. Hansen, "Legislator Pay," 22.
51. Ehrenhalt, *The United States of Ambition,* 198–199.
52. Colorado Legislative Council, "The Legislative Process," staff memorandum, 1 December 1988, cited in Cronin and Loevy, *Colorado Politics and Government,* 91.
53. Quoted in Ehrenhalt, *The United States of Ambition,* 199.
54. Cronin and Loevy, *Colorado Politics and Government,* 194. The governor is not without significant powers even though the office has been characterized as weak. Colorado's governor is one of the few who controls the expenditure of federal funds as a result of several court cases, including *MacManus v. Love.* The governor also appoints the entire Colorado judiciary, subject only to popular retention vote. Only Texas and South Carolina are viewed as having stronger legislative budget powers. By statute, the chairs of the House and Senate Appropriations Committees, which hear bills that have a fiscal impact, serve on the JBC.
55. Straayer, *The Colorado General Assembly,* chap. 8 provides a detailed description of how the Colorado budget process works.
56. Ibid., 214.
57. Francis, *The Legislative Committee Game.*
58. Ibid., 185.
59. Straayer, *The Colorado General Assembly,* 136–137.
60. There are mechanisms for getting around the five-bill limit, but most legislators are at or below that number.
61. Council of State Governments, *Book of the States,* 183–184.
62. Cronin and Loevy, *Colorado Politics and Government,* 181.
63. Ibid., 182.
64. Carl Miller, "Bledsoe: The Real Bad Guy," *Denver Post,* March 12, 1988, cited in Straayer, *The Colorado General Assembly,* 96.
65. Cronin and Loevy, *Colorado Politics and Government,* 182.
66. Fred Brown, Jennifer Gavin, and Steve Lipsher, "Mad Dash Leaves Some Loose Ends," *Denver Post,* May 10, 1995, A1.
67. Straayer, *The Colorado General Assembly,* 86. The major difference in leadership power is that the Senate president shares the power of appointing committees with the Committee on Committees.

68. Cronin and Loevy, *Colorado Politics and Government*, 184.

69. Dan Luzadder, "Leaders' Styles Serve as Tip-off to Discerning Voters," *Rocky Mountain News*, March 29, 1997, 5A.

70. Straayer, *The Colorado General Assembly*, 102.

71. Ibid.

72. Cronin and Loevy, *Colorado Politics and Government*, 28.

73. Personal interview, January 12, 1995, Denver, Colo.

74. Straayer, *The Colorado General Assembly*.

75. Personal interview, January 12, 1995, Denver, Colo.

76. Personal interview, January 12, 1995, Denver, Colo.

77. Francis, *The Legislative Committee Game*.

78. Straayer, *The Colorado General Assembly*, 116–122.

79. Robert S. Lorch, *Colorado's Government* (Niwot: Colorado Associated University Press, 1983), 173.

80. Personal interview, January 10, 1995, Denver, Colo.

81. Three types of committees—policy, service oriented, and prestige—are described by Fenno, *Congressmen in Committees*. The distinction between policy and service-oriented committees may have had more relevance in Colorado in an earlier era, but in the contemporary General Assembly diverse interests are overseen by committees of broad jurisdiction.

82. Personal interview, January 12. 1995, Denver, Colo.

83. Fawn Germer, "The Education Lawmakers: Pair of Republicans Wield Great Power over Legislation Governing Public Schools," *Denver Post*, February 19, 1995, 28A.

84. Personal interview, January 12, 1995, Denver, Colo.

85. Personal interview, January 12, 1995, Denver, Colo.

86. Personal interview, January 12, 1995, Denver, Colo.

87. Personal interview, January 10, 1995, Denver, Colo.

88. Germer, 28A.

89. Tustin Amole, "The Education Lawmakers: Pair of Republicans Wield Great Power over Legislation Governing Public Schools," *Denver Post*, February 19, 1995, 28A.

90. Michelle Dally Johnston, "Far-Right Agenda Faltering," *Denver Post*, April 13, 1997, 1A.

91. Ibid.

92. Straayer, *The Colorado General Assembly*, 116.

93. Personal interview, January 10, 1995, Denver, Colo.

94. Personal interview, January 11, 1995, Denver, Colo.

95. Personal interview, January 10, 1995, Denver, Colo.

96. Straayer, *The Colorado General Assembly*, 94.

97. Lipsher, April 18, 1993, 12A; and Ewegen, B7.

98. Carl Hilliard, "Capitol Close-Up," *Associated Press*, May 5, 1995, writing about Representative Jeanne Adkins.

99. Ibid.

100. Carl Hilliard, "Capitol Close-Up," *Associated Press*, May 12, 1995.

101. Jennifer Gavin, "Gun Bill Loses Last Round, Chlouber Refuses 'Local Control' Change," *Denver Post*, May 9, 1995, B1.

102. Ewegen, November 16, 1992, B7.

103. Hilliard, "Capitol Close-Up," May 5, 1995.

104. Personal interview, January 10, 1995, Denver, Colo.

105. Personal interview, January 11, 1995, Denver, Colo.

106. Kathlene, "Power and Influence in State Legislative Policymaking," 572–573.

107. Kathlene, "Position Power versus Gender Power," in *Gender Power, Leadership and Governance*, ed. Duerst-Lahti and Kelly, 183.

108. Personal interview, January 10, 1995, Denver, Colo.

109. Personal interview, January 11, 1995, Denver, Colo.

110. Johnston, May 8, 1997.

111. Personal interview, January 10, 1995, Denver, Colo.

112. Personal interview, January 30, 1995, Denver, Colo.

113. Personal interviews, January 10 and 12, 1995, Denver, Colo.

114. Personal inteview, January 11, 1995, Denver, Colo.

115. Personal interview, January 11, 1995, Denver, Colo.

116. Straayer, *The Colorado General Assembly*, 117–118.

117. Personal interview, January 10, 1995, Denver, Colo.

118. Personal interview, January 10, 1995, Denver, Colo.

119. Committee hearing, February 2, 1995, Denver, Colo.

120. Ehrenhalt, *United States of Ambition*, 203; and Straayer *Colorado General Assembly*, 326. See also Bob Ewegen, "BEVERLY's List Salutes Rising Stars of Republican Women in Colorado," *Denver Post*, July 27, 1992, 5B; and Ewegen, November 16, 1992, 7B.

121. Personal interview, January 10, 1995, Denver, Colo.

122. "Tough Work Still Remains on Trauma Care Network," *Denver Post*, June 11, 1995, E2.

123. Personal interview, January 10, 1995, Denver, Colo.

124. Personal interview, January 12, 1995, Denver, Coloradp.

125. Personal interview, January 11, 1995, Denver, Colo.

126. Burns, *Leadership*, 43–44.

127. Ibid., 425–426.

128. Ehrenhalt, *The United States of Ambition*, 206.

129. Ibid.

Chapter 9

1. Berman, *The Only Boobs*, 62–63.

2. Kirkpatrick, *Political Woman*.

3. See Peter Drucker, "Introduction," in *Follett, Prophet of Management*, 4–7.

4. Follett, *The New State*, 229–230.

5. Stivers, *Gender Images*, 79.

6. Jody Newman, *Perception and Reality: A Study Comparing the Success of Men and Women Candidates* (Washington, DC: National Women's Political Caucus, 1994).

7. DeGregorio, "Leadership Approaches in Congressional Committee Hearings."

8. James David Barber, *The Lawmakers* (New Haven, CT: Yale University Press, 1965).

9. Wahlke et al., *The Legislative System*.

10. Kirkpatrick, *Political Woman*.

11. Diamond, *Sex Roles in the State House*.

12. Cynthia Fuchs Epstein, "Ways Men and Women Lead" *Harvard Business Review* 69 (March/April 1991): 150–151.

13. Stivers, *Gender Images.*

14. March and Olsen, *Rediscovering Institutions.*

15. Robert N. Bellah, Richard Madsen, William M. Sullivan, Ann Swidler, and Steven M. Tipton, *Habits of the Heart: Individualism and Commitment in American Life* (New York: Harper & Row, 1985), 200.

16. Ibid., chap. 11.

17. Cooper and Brady, "Institutional Context and Leadership Style."

18. Peters, *The American Speakership.*

19. Hawkesworth, *Beyond Oppression,* 197.

20. Peter F. Drucker, "The Age of Social Transformation" *Atlantic* 274 (1994): 77.

21. Burns, *Leadership,* chap. 13.

22. Stiver, *Gender Images.*

23. John Mack Faragher, Mari Jo Buhle, Daniel Czitrom, and Susan H. Armitage, *Out of Many: A History of the American People,* vol. II (Englewood Cliffs, NJ: Prentice-Hall, 1994).

24. See, for example, Arlene Levinson, "So Much to Do, So Little Time," *State Legislatures* 21 (1995): 36–45; and Steven Stark, "Too Representative Government" *Atlantic* 275 (1995): 104.

25. B. Drummond Ayres, Jr., "California's Squabbling Legislature Just Stumbles Along," *New York Times,* July 9, 1995, 12.

26. Focus group, July 27, 1995, New Orleans, La.

27. Lao-Tzu, verse 59.


*Appendix*

1. See, for example, Mary E. Guy, ed., *Women and Men of the States.*

2. Fiedler, *Leadership Effectiveness.*

3. Jane Close Conoley, Jack J. Kramer and James V. Mitchell, *The Tenth Mental Measurement Yearbook* (Lincoln: University of Nebraska Press and the Buros Institution of Mental Measurements, 1990).

4. The survey methods follow those suggested by Don A. Dillman et al., "Increasing Mail Questionnaire Response: A Four-State Comparison," *American Sociological Review* 39:5 (October 1974): 744–756.

5. These numbers are calculated from data provided by the Center for the American Woman and Politics, the National Conference of State Legislatures, the Council of State Governments, *Book of the States* and Kurtz, *State Legislatures.*

6. Lillian Woo, "Today's Legislators: Who They Are and Why They Run," *State Legislatures* 20(4) (April 1994): 28–33.

7. Focus groups were organized and guided by the work of Morgan, *Focus Groups;* Stewart and Shamdasani, *Focus Groups: Theory and Practice;* and Merton, Fiske, and Kendall, *The Focused Interview.*

8. William A. Gamson, *Talking Politics* (Cambridge: Cambridge University Press, 1992).

9. The coding of focus group comments used qualitative methods suggested by Anselm Strauss and Juliet Corbin, *Basics of Qualitative Research: Grounded Theory, Procedures and Techniques* (Newbury Park, CA: Sage Publications, 1990); and Matthew B. Miles and A. Michael Huberman, *Qualitative Data Analysis,* 2nd ed. (Thousand Oaks, CA: Sage Publications, 1994).

10. Morgan, "Focus Groups," 25.

11. Richard Fenno, *Watching Politicians* (Berkeley, CA: Institute of Governmental Studies, 1990).

12. A. Simon and E. Boyer, *Mirrors for Behavior* (Philadelphia: Research for Better Schools, 1970).

13. Nelson, *Emerging Influentials.*

14. Nelson used an antidiscrimination policy index developed by Shin, "Innovation Adoption and diffusion in the Political Systems of States."

# References

Acker, Joan. "Gendered Institutions: From Sex Roles to Gendered Institutions." *Contemporary Sociology* 21(4) (1992): 565-569.

Acker, Joan. "Hierarchies, Jobs, Bodies: A Theory of gendered Organizations." *Gender and Society* 4(2) (June 1990): 139–158.

Asher, Herbert. "The Learning of Legislative Norms." *American Political Science Review* 67(3) (1973): 499–513.

Asplund, Gisele. *Women Managers: Changing Organizational Cultures*. Chichester, England: John Wiley & Sons, 1988.

Astin, Helen S., and Carole Leland. *Women of Influence, Women of Vision*. San Francisco: Jossey-Bass, 1991.

Barber, James David. *The Lawmakers*. New Haven, CT: Yale University Press, 1965.

Bass, Bernard M. *Bass and Stodgill's Handbook of Leadership*, 3rd. ed. New York: Free Press, 1990.

Baum, Lawrence, and Samuel C. Patterson. "Ohio: Party Change without Realignment." In *Party Realignment and State Politics*, ed. Maureen Moakley, Columbus: Ohio State University Press, 1992.

Beattie, Geoffrey. *Talk: An Analysis of Speech and Non-verbal Behavior in Conversation*. Milton Keynes, England: Open University Press, 1983.

Becker, Robin A. "Explaining Sex Roles of Women State Legislators in the Mid-Atlantic Region." Paper presented at the annual meeting of the Midwest Political Science Association, Chicago, 1989.

Bednar, Nancy L., and Allen D. Hertzke. "The Christian Right and Republican Realignment in Oklahoma." *PS: Political Science and Politics* 28 (March 1995): 11–15.

Bellah, Robert N., Richard Madsen, William M. Sullivan, Ann Swidler, and Steven M. Tipton. *Habits of the Heart: Individualism and Commitment in American Life*. Berkeley: University of California Press, 1985.

Berman, Maxine. *The Only Boobs in the House Are Men*. Troy, MI: Momentum Books, 1994.

Blair, Diane D., and Jeanie R. Stanley. "Personal Relationships and Legislative Power: Male and Female Perceptions." *Legislative Studies Quarterly* 17(4) (1991): 495–507.

Blake, Robert, and Mouton J. S. *Managerial Grid*. Houston, TX: Gulf, 1964.

Blalock, Hubert. *Toward a Theory of Minority-Group Relations*. New York: Wiley, 1967.

Blau, Peter M. "A Macrosociological Theory of Social Structure." *American Journal of Sociology* 83(1) (1977): 26–54.

Bolman, Lee G., and Terrence E. Deal. *Reframing Organizations: Artistry, Choice, and Leadership*. San Francisco: Jossey-Bass, 1991.

Bowman, Ann O'M., and Richard Kearney. "Dimensions of State Government Capability." *Western Political Quarterly* 41(2) (1988): 341–362.

Brown, Wendy. *Manhood and Politics: A Feminist Reading in Political Theory*. Totowa, NJ: Rowman & Littlefield, 1988.

Burns, James MacGregor. *Leadership*. New York: Harper & Row, 1978.

Bushardt, Stephen M., Aubrey Fowler, and Regina Coveny. "Sex Role Behavior and Leadership: An Empirical Investigation." *Leadership and Organizational Journal* 8(1) (1987): 13–16.

Canon, David T. *Actors, Athletes, and Astronauts: Political Amateurs in the United States Congress*. Chicago: University of Chicago Press, 1990.

Cantor, Dorothy W., and Toni Bernay with Jean Stoess. *Women in Power: The Secrets of Leadership*. Boston: Houghton-Mifflin, 1992.

Carroll, Susan J. "Feminist Scholarship on Political Leadership." In *Leadership: Multidisciplinary Perspectives*, ed. Barbara Kellerman. Englewood Cliffs, NJ: Prentice-Hall, 1984.

Carroll, Susan J., and Ella Taylor. "Gender Differences in Committee Assignments of State Legislators: Preferences or Discrimination?" Paper presented at the annual meeting of the Midwest Political Science Association. Chicago, 1989.

Carroll, Susan J., and Linda M. G. Zerilli. "Feminist Challenges to Political Science." In *State of the Discipline II*, ed. Ada Finifter. Washington, DC: American Political Science Association, 1993.

Center for the American Woman and Politics (CAWP). "Roster of Women State Legislators." Typescript. New Brunswick, NJ: Eagleton Institute of Politics, Rutgers University, 1979.

Center for the American Woman and Politics (CAWP). *Women in Public Office*. New York: R. R. Bowker Company, 1976.

Center for the American Woman and Politics (CAWP). "Women State Legislators: Leadership Positions and Committee Chairs 1993." Fact sheet from the National Information Bank on Women in Public Office. New Brunswick, NJ: Eagleton Institute of Politics, Rutgers University, 1993.

Center for the American Woman and Politics (CAWP). "Women State Legislators: Leadership Positions and Committee Chairs 1991." Fact sheet from the National Information Bank on Women in Public Office. New Brunswick, NJ: Eagleton Institute of Politics, Rutgers University, 1991.

Center for the American Woman and Politics (CAWP). "Women in State Legislatures 1997." Fact sheet from the National Information Bank on Women in Public Office. New Brunswick, NJ: Eagleton Institute of Politics, Rutgers University, 1997.

Center for the American Women and Politics (CAWP). "Women in the U.S. Senate 1922–1995." Fact sheet. New Brusnwick, NJ: Eagleton Institute of Politics, Rutgers University, 1994.

Chodorow, Nancy. "Family Structure and Feminine Personality." In *Women, Culture, and Society*, ed. Michelle Zimbalist Rosaldo and Louise Lamphere. Stanford, CA: Stanford University Press, 1974.

Church, Foster. "Vera Katz: Just Like a Woman." *Governing* 3 (September 1990): 26–30.

Citizens Conference on State Legislatures. *The Sometime Governments.* New York: Bantam Books, 1971.

Clark, Janet. "Getting There: Women in Political Office." *The Annals of the American Academy of Political and Social Science* 515 (May 1991): 63–76.

Cohen, Jacob. *Statistical Power Analysis for the Social Sciences.* Hillsdale, NJ: Erlbaum Publishers, 1988.

Conoley, Jane Close, Jack J. Kramer, and James V. Mitchell. *The Tenth Mental Measurement Yearbook* (Lincoln: University of Nebraska Press and the Buros Institution of Mental Measurements, 1990).

Constantini, Edmond. "Political Women and Political Ambition: Closing the Gender Gap." *American Journal of Political Science* 34 (3) (1990): 741–770.

Cooper, Joseph, and David W. Brady. "Institutional Context and Leadership Style: The House from Cannon to Rayburn." *American Political Science Review* 75 (2) (1981): 411–425.

Copeland, Gary W., and John David Rausch Jr. "Sendin' 'Em Home Early: Oklahoma Legislative Term Limitations." *Oklahoma Politics* 2 (1993): 33–50.

Council of State Governments. *Book of the States: 1993–94 Edition.* Lexington, KY: Council of State Governments, 1993.

Council of State Governments. *State Legislative Leadership, Committees and Staff 1993–1994.* Lexington, KY: Council of State Governments, 1993.

Cox, Elizabeth C. "The Three Who Came First." *State Legislatures* 20 (November 1994): 12–19.

Cronin, Thomas E., and Robert D. Loevy. *Colorado Politics and Government: Governing the Centennial State.* Omaha: University of Nebraska Press, 1993.

Darcy, Robert, Margaret Brewer, and Judy Clay. "Women in the Oklahoma Political System: State Legislative Elections." *Social Science Journal* 21(1) (January 1984): 67–78.

Darcy, R., Susan Welch, and Janet Clark. *Women, Elections, and Representation.* New York: Longman, 1987.

Darcy, R. "Women in State legislative Power Structure: Committee Chairs." *Social Science Quarterly* 77(4) (December 1996): 888–898.

Davidson, Jo Ann. "Women in Legislative Leadership." Panel presentation at the annual meeting of the National Conference of State Legislatures, New Orleans, July, 25 1994.

DeGregorio, Christine. "Leadership Approaches in Congressional Committee Hearings." *Western Political Quarterly* 45(4) (December 1992): 971–983.

Deutchman, I. E. "Socialization to Power: Questions about Women and Politics." *Women and Politics* 5(1) (1986): 79–89.

Diamond, Irene. *Sex Roles in the State House.* New Haven, CT: Yale University Press, 1977.

Dillman, Don A., James A. Christenson, Edwin H. Carpenter, and Ralph M. Brooks. "Increasing Mail Questionnaire Response: A Four-State Comparison." *American Sociological Review* 39(5) (October 1974): 744–756.

DiStefano, Christine. *Configurations of Masculinity: A Feminist Perspective on Modern Political Theory.* Ithaca, NY: Cornell University Press, 1991.

Dodson, Debra L., ed. *Gender and Policymaking: Studies of Women in Politics.* New Brunswick, NJ: Rutgers University Center for the American Woman and Politics, 1991.

Dodson, Debra L., and Susan J. Carroll. *Reshaping the Agenda: Women in State Legislatures.* New Brunswick, NJ: Rutgers University Center for the American Woman and Politics, 1991.

Dolan, Kathleen, and Lynne E. Ford. "Change and Continuity Among Women State Legislators: Evidence from Three Decades." *Political Research Quarterly* 50 (March 1997): 137–151.

Downs, Anthony. *Inside Bureaucracy.* Boston: Little, Brown, 1967.

Drucker, Peter F. "The Age of Social Transformation." *Atlantic* 274 (November 1994): 53–80.

Drucker, Peter F. "Foreword: Not Enough Generals Were Killed." In *The Leader of the Future,* ed. Frances Hesselbein, Marshall Goldsmith, and Richard Beckhard. San Francisco: Jossey-Bass, 1996.

Duerst-Lahti, Georgia, and Cathy Johnson. "Management Styles, Stereotypes, and Advantages." In *Women and Men of the States,* ed. Mary E. Guy. Armonk, NY: M. E. Sharpe, 1992.

Duerst-Lahti, Georgia, and Cathy Johnson. "Gender and Style in Bureaucracy." *Women and Politics* 10(1) (1990): 67–120.

Duerst-Lahti, Georgia, and Rita Mae Kelly, eds. *Gender Power, Leadership, and Governance.* Ann Arbor: University of Michigan Press, 1995.

Duerst-Lahti, Georgia, and Dayna Verstegen. "Making Something of Absence: The 'Year of the Woman' and Women's Political Representation." In *Gender Power Leadership and Governance,* ed. Georgia Duerst-Lahti and Rita Mae Kelly. Ann Arbor: University of Michigan Press, 1995.

Eagly, Alice H. *Sex Differences in Social Behavior: A Social Role Interpretation.* Hillsdale, NJ: Erlbaum Publishers. 1987.

Eagly, Alice H., and Blair T. Johnson. "Gender and Leadership Style: A Meta-Analysis." *Psychological Bulletin* 108(2) (September 1990): 233–256.

Eagly, Alice H., and S. J. Karau. "Gender and the Emergence of Leaders: A Meta-analysis." *Journal of Personality and Social Psychology* 60(5)(May 1991): 685–710.

Eckstein, Harry. "Case Study and Theory in Political Science," In *Handbook of Political Science,* vol. 7, ed. Fred Greenstein and Nelson Polsby. Reading, MA: Addison-Wesley, 1975.

Ehrenhalt, Alan. "Even Among the Sooners, There are More Important Things Than Football." *Governing* 2(2) (November 1988): 40–45.

Ehrenhalt, Alan. *The United States of Ambition: Politicians, Power and the Pursuit of Office.* New York: Times Books, 1991.

Elazar, Daniel J. *American Federalism: A View from the States.* New York: Thomas Y. Crowell, 1966.

Elshtain, Jean Bethke. *Public Man, Private Woman: Women in Social and Political Thought.* Princeton, NJ: Princeton University Press, 1981.

Epstein, Cynthia Fuchs. *Deceptive Distinctions.* New Haven, CT: Yale University Press, 1988.

Epstein, Cynthia Fuchs. "Ways Men and Women Lead." *Harvard Business Review* 69(1) (January/February 1991): 150–151.

Epstein, Cynthia Fuchs. *Women in Law.* New York: Anchor Books, 1983.

Faragher, John Mack, Mari Jo Buhle, Daniel Czitrom, and Susan H. Armitage. *Out of Many: A History of the American People,* vol. II. Englewood Cliffs, NJ: Prentice-Hall, 1994.

Fenno, Richard. *Congressmen in Committees.* Boston: Little, Brown, 1973.

Fenno, Richard. *Home Style.* New York: HarperCollins, 1978.

Fenno, Richard. *Watching Politicians.* Berkeley, CA: Institute of Governmental Studies, 1990.

Fenton, John. *Midwest Politics.* New York: Holt, Rinehart, & Winston, 1966.

Fiedler, Fred E. *A Theory of Leadership Effectiveness.* New York: McGraw-Hill, 1967.

Fiedler, Fred E., and Joseph E. Garcia. *New Approaches to Effective Leadership: Cognitive Resources and Organizational Performance.* New York: John Wiley & Sons, 1987.

Fiorina, Morris. *Congress: Keystone of the Washington Establishment.* New Haven, CT: Yale University Press. 1989.

Follett, Mary Parker. *Prophet of Management: A Celebration of Writings from the 1920s,* ed. Pauline Graham. Boston: Harvard Business School Press, 1996.

Follett, Mary Parker. *The New State.* New York: Longmans, Green & Co, 1920.

Francis, Wayne. *The Legislative Committee Game: A Comparative Analysis of 50 States.* Columbus: Ohio State University Press, 1989.

Frankovic, Kathleen A. "Sex and Voting in the U.S. House of Representatives, 1961–1975." *American Politics Quarterly* 5(3) (July 1977): 315–330.

Gamson, William A. *Talking Politics.* Cambridge: Cambridge University Press, 1992.

Gargan, John J., and James G. Coke. *Political Behavior and Public Issues in Ohio.* Kent, OH: Kent State University Press, 1972.

Gehlen, Freida. "Women Members of Congress: A Distinctive Role." In *A Portrait of Marginality,* ed. Marianne Githens and Jewell L. Prestage. New York: Longman, 1977.

Gherardi, Silvia. "The Gender We Think, the Gender We Do in Our Everyday Organizational Lives." *Human Relations* 47(6) (June 1994): 591–610.

Gilligan, Carol. In a Different Voice: Psychological Theory and Women's Development. Cambridge, MA: Harvard University Press, 1982.

Githens, Marianne. "Women and State Politics: An Assessment." In *Political Women: Current Roles in State and Local Government,* ed. Janet Flammang, Beverly Hills, CA: Sage Publications, 1984.

Githens, Marianne, and Jewel L. Prestage, eds. *A Portrait of Marginality: The Political Behavior of the American Woman.* New York: David McKay Publishers, 1977.

Gluck, Hazel Frank. "The Difference." *Journal of State Government* 60(5) (September/October 1987): 223–226.

Goble, Danney. "Oklahoma Politics and the Sooner Electorate." In *Oklahoma: New Views,* ed Anne Hodges Morgan and H. Wayne Morgan, Norman: University of Oklahoma Press, 1982.

Gold, Steven D., and Judy Zelio. *State-Local Fiscal Indicators.* Denver, CO: National Conference of State Legislatures, 1990.

Gordon, Dianna. "Republican Women Make Gains." *State Legislatures* (February 1995): 15.

Greenleaf, Robert K. *On Becoming a Servant Leader.* San Francisco: Jossey-Bass, 1996.

Greenleaf, Robert K. *The Servant as Leader.* Indianapolis, IN: Robert K. Greenleaf Center for Servant-Leadership, 1970, 1991.

Guy, Mary E. "Hillary, Health Care, and Gender Power." In *Gender Power, Leadership, and Governance,* ed. Georgia Duerst-Lahti and Rita Mae Kelly. Ann Arbor: University of Michigan Press, 1995.

Guy, Mary E., ed. *Women and Men of the States: Public Administrators at the State Level.* Armonk, NY: M. F. Sharpe, 1992.

Guy, Mary E., and Lois Lovelace Duke. "Personal and Social Background as Determinants of Position." In *Women and Men of the States*, ed. Mary E. Guy. Armonk, NY: M. E. Sharpe, 1992.

Hale, Mary M. "Mentoring." In *Women and Men of the States*, ed. Mary E. Guy, Armonk, NY: M. E. Sharpe, 1992.

Hale, Mary M., and Rita Mae Kelly, eds. *Gender, Bureaucracy and Democracy*. Westport, CT: Greenwood Press, 1989.

Hall, Elaine J. "Smiling, Deferring and Flirting: Doing Gender by Giving 'Good Service.'" *Work and Occupations* 20 (November 1993): 452–471.

Hall, Elaine J. "Waitering/Waitressing: Engendering the Work of Table Servers." *Gender and Society* 7 (September 1993): 329–246

Hall, J. A. "Gender Effects in Decoding Nonverbal Cues," *Psychological Bulletin* 85(4) (July 1978): 845–857.

Hamm, Keith, and Alan Rosenthal. *Legislative Life*. New York: Harper & Row, 1981.

Hansen, Karen. "Legislator Pay: Baseball It Ain't." *State Legislatures* 23(7) (July/August 1997): 20–26.

Hargrove, Erwin C. "Two Conceptions of Institutional Leadership." In *Leadership and Politics*, ed. Bryan D. Jones. Lawrence: University Press of Kansas, 1989.

Hawkesworth, M. E. *Beyond Oppression: Feminist Theory and Political Strategy*. New York: Continuum Publishing, 1990.

Hebert, F. Ted, and Lelan E. McLemore, "Character and Structure of Legislative Norms: Operationalizing the Norm Concept in the Legislative Setting." *American Journal of Political Science* 17(2) (1973): 506–527.

Heclo, Hugh. *A Government of Strangers: Executive Politics in Washington*. Washington, DC: The Brookings Institution, 1977.

Hedlund, Ronald D., and Keith E. Hamm. "Political Parties as Vehicles for Organizing U.S. State Legislative Committees." *Legislative Studies Quarterly* 21:3 (1996): 383–408.

Heider, John. "The Leader Who Knows How to Make Things Happen." In *Contemporary Issues in Leadership*, ed. William E. Rosenbach and Robert L. Taylor, Boulder, CO: Westview Press, 1984.

Helgesen, Sally. *The Female Advantage*. New York: Doubleday, 1990.

Henderson, Dee W. "Enlightened Mentoring: A Characteristic of Public Management Professionalism." *Public Administrative Review* 49 (November/December 1985): 857–864.

Hennig, Margaret, and A. Jardim. *The Managerial Woman*. New York: Pocket Books, 1977.

Hersey, Paul, and Kenneth T. Blanchard, *The Management of Organizational Behavior*, 3rd ed. Englewood Cliffs, NJ: Prentice-Hall, 1977.

Hinckley, Barbara. *Stability and Change in Congress*, 4th ed. New York: Harper & Row, 1988.

Hochschild, Arlie Russell. *The Managed Heart: Commercialization of Human Feeling*. Berkeley: University of California Press, 1983.

Hochschild, Arlie Russell with Anne Machung. *The Second Shift*. New York: Avon Books, 1990.

Jamieson, Kathleen Hall. *Beyond the Double Bind: Women and Leadership*. New York: Oxford University Press, 1995.

Jewell, Malcolm J., and S. Patterson. *The Legislative Process in the United States*, 3rd. ed. New York: Random House, 1977.

Jewell, Malcolm, and Marcia Lynn Whicker. "The Feminization of Leadership in State Legislatures." *PS* 26(4) (December 1993): 705–711.

Jewell, Malcolm, and Marcia Lynn Whicker. *Legislative Leadership in the American States*. Ann Arbor: University of Michigan Press, 1994.

Johnson, Marilyn, and Susan Carroll, with Kathy Stanwyck and Lynn Korenblit. *Profile of Women Holding Office II*. New Brunswick, NJ: Center for the American Woman and Politics, 1978.

Johnson, Paula. "Women and Power: Toward a Theory of Effectiveness." *Journal of Social Issues* 32(3) (Summer 1976): 99–110.

Jones, D. C. "Power Structures and Perceptions of Powerholders in Same-Sex Groups of Young Children." *Women and Politics* 3(2) (1983): 147–164.

Jones, Woodrow, and Albert J. Nelson. "Correlates of Women's Representation in Lower State Legislative Chambers." *Social Behavior and Personality* 9(1) (1981): 9–15.

Josefowitz, Natasha. *Paths to Power*. Reading, MA: Addison-Wesley, 1980.

Kanter, Rosabeth Moss. *Men and Women of the Corporation*. New York: Basic Books, 1977.

Kanter, Rosabeth Moss. "Some Effects of Proportions on Group Life: Skewed Sex Ratios and Responses to Token Women." *American Journal of Sociology* 82(5) (1977): 965–990.

Kates, Nancy D. "The Saga of Vera Katz." Kennedy School of Government Case Program. Cambridge, MA: Harvard University Press, 1988.

Kathlene, Lyn. "Exploring the Political Impacts of Gender: An Exploratory Study." *Western Political Quarterly* 44(2) (1991): 387–421.

Kathlene, Lyn. "Position Power versus Gender Power: Who Holds the Floor?" In *Gender Power, Leadership, and Governance*, ed. Georgia Duerst-Lahti and Rita Mae Kelly, Ann Arbor: University of Michigan Press, 1995.

Kathlene, Lyn. "Power and Influence in State Legislative Policymaking: The Interaction of Gender and Position in Committee Hearing Debates." *American Political Science Review* 88(3) (September 1994): 560–576.

Katz, Vera. "The Leader and the Public." *Journal of State Government* 60(6) (November/December 1987): 262–264.

Katz, Vera. "Women Chart New Legislative Course." *Journal of State Government* 60(5) (September/October 1987): 213–216.

Kaufman, Herbert. *The Forest Ranger*. Baltimore: Johns Hopkins University Press, 1960.

Kelly, Rita Mae. *The Gendered Economy: Work, Careers, and Success*. Newbury Park, CA: Sage Publications, 1991.

Kelly, Rita Mae, and Mary E. Guy, with Jane Bayes, Georgia Duerst-Lahti, Mary M. Hale, Cathy Johnson, A. Kawar, and Jean R. Stanley. "Public Managers in the States: A Comparison of Career Advancement by Sex." *Public Administration Review* 51(5) (1991): 402–412.

Kelly, Rita Mae, M. M. Hale, and J. Burgess. "Gender and Managerial/Leadership Styles: A Comparison of Arizona Public Administrators." *Women & Politics* 11(1) (1991): 119–139.

Kelman, Steven. *Making Public Policy: A Hopeful View of American Government*. New York: Basic Books, 1987.

Kenney, Sally. 1996. "New Research on Gendered Political Institutions." *Political Research Quarterly* 49(2)(June 1996): 445–466.

King, Cheryl Simrell. "Sex Role Identity and Decision Styles: How Gender Helps Explain the Paucity of Women at the Top." In *Gender Power Leadership and Governance*, ed. Georgia Duerst-Lahti and Rita Mae Kelly. Ann Arbor: University of Michigan Press, 1995.

Kirkpatrick, Jeanne. *Political Woman*. New York: Basic Books, 1974.

Kirkpatrick, Samuel A. *The Legislative Process in Oklahoma*. Norman: University of Oklahoma Press, 1978.

Knepper, George. "Ohio Politics: A Historical Perspective." In *Ohio Politics*, ed. Alexander P. Lamis. Kent, OH: Kent State University Press, 1994.

Kosmin, Barry A., and Seymour P. Lachman. *One Nation under God*. New York: Harmony Books, 1993.

Kram, K. E. *Mentoring at Work: Developmental Relationships in Organizational Life*. Glenview, IL: Scott, Foresman, 1985.

Kram, Kathy E., and Lynn A. Isabella. "Mentoring Alternatives: The Role of Peer Relationships in Career Development." *Academy of Management Journal* 28(1) (1985) 110–132.

Kuhn, Thomas S. *The Structure of Scientific Revolutions*, 2nd ed. Chicago: University of Chicago Press, 1970.

Kunin, Madeleine. "Lessons from One Woman's Career." *Journal of State Government* 60(5) (September/October 1987): 209–213.

Kurtz, Karl T. *State Legislatures: Progress, Problems, and Possibilities*. Denver, CO: National Conference of State Legislatures and the Eagleton Institute of Politics, 1992.

Lamis, Alexander P., ed., with Mary Anne Sharkey. *Ohio Politics*. Kent, OH: Kent State University Press, 1994.

Lao-Tzu. *Tao Te Ching*, trans. Stephen Mitchell. New York: HarperCollins Publishers, 1988.

Lasswell, Harold. *Politics, Who Gets What, When and How*. New York: Peter Smith, 1936.

Laws, Judith Long. "Psychology of Tokenism: An Analysis." *Sex Roles* 1 (January 1975): 51–67.

Leader, Shelah. "The Policy Impact of Elected Women Officials." In *The Impact of the Electoral Process*, ed. Louis Maisel and Joseph Cooper. Beverly Hills, CA: Sage Publications, 1977.

Lee, Marcia M. "Toward Understanding Why Few Women Hold Public Office: Factors Affecting the Participation of Women in Local Politics." In *A Portrait of Marginality*, ed. Marianne Githens and Jewell Prestage. New York: David McKay Publishers, 1977.

Lemov, Penelope. "A Mild Case of Tax-cut Fever." *Governing* 8 (June 1995): 20–21.

Levinson, Arlene. "So Much to Do, So Little Time," *State Legislatures* 21(7) (July/August 1995): 36–45.

Likert, Rensis. *New Patterns of Management*. New York: McGraw-Hill, 1961.

Lips, Hilary M. *Women, Men, and the Psychology of Power*. Englewood Cliffs, NJ: Prentice-Hall, 1981.

Loden, Marilyn. *Feminine Leadership, or How to Succeed in Business Without Being One of the Boys*. New York: Times Books, 1985.

Lorch, Robert S. *Colorado's Government*. Niwot: Colorado Associated University Press, 1983.

Lunneborg, Patricia. *Women Changing Work*. Westport, CT: Greenwood Press, 1990.

Main, Eleanor C., Gerard S. Gryski, and Beth S. Schapiro. "Different Perspectives: Southern State Legislators' Attitudes about Women in Politics." *Social Science Journal* 21 (March 1984): 21–28.

Mandel, Ruth B., "Doing It Whose Way? Women in Leadership." In *Our Vision and Values: Women Shaping the 21st Century*, ed. Frances C. Hutner. Westport, CN: Praeger Publishers, 1994.

Mandel, Ruth B., Kathy Kleeman, and Lucy Baruch. "No Year of the Woman, Then or Now." *Extensions* (Spring 1995): 7–10.

Mansbridge, Jane J., ed. *Beyond Self-Interest*. Chicago: University of Chicago Press, 1988.

March, James G., and Johan P. Olsen. *Rediscovering Institutions: The Organizational Basis of Politics*. New York: Free Press, 1989.

Martin, Patricia Yancey. "Gender, Interaction and Inequality in Organizations." In *Gender, Interaction and Inequality*, ed. Cecilia L. Ridgeway. New York: Springer-Verlag, 1992.

Mayhew, David. *Congress: The Electoral Connection*. New Haven, CT: Yale University Press, 1974.

McClelland, David C. *Power: The Inner Experience*. New York: Irvington Publishers, 1975.

McDiarmid, Hugh C. "The Gilligan Interlude, 1971–1975." In *Ohio Politics*, ed. Alexander P. Lamis. Kent, OH: Kent State University Press, 1994.

McIver, John P., and Walter J. Stone. "Stability and Change in Colorado Politics." In *Party Realignment and State Politics*, ed. Maureen Moakley. Columbus: Ohio State University Press, 1992.

Merton, Robert K., Marjorie Fiske, and Patricia L. Kendall. *The Focused Interview*, 2nd ed. New York: Macmillan, 1990.

Miles, Matthew B., and A. Michael Huberman. *Qualitative Data Analysis*, 2nd ed. Thousand Oaks, CA: Sage Publications, 1994.

Miller, Cynthia L., and A. Gaye Cummins. "An Examination of Women's Perspectives on Power." *Psychology of Women Quarterly* 16(4) (December 1992): 415–428.

Mintzberg, Henry. *Power in and around Organizations*. Englewood Cliffs, NJ: Prentice-Hall, 1983.

Morgan, David L. *Focus Groups: A Qualitative Research*. Newbury Park, CA: Sage Publications, 1988.

Morgan, David R , Robert E. England, and George G. Humphreys. *Oklahoma Politics and Policies: Governing the Sooner State*. Lincoln: University of Nebraska Press, 1991.

Morrison, Ann M., Randall P. White, and Ellen Van Velson. *Breaking the Glass Ceiling*. Reading, MA: Addison-Wesley, 1987.

Mueller, Carol. "Women's Organizational Strategies in State Legislatures." In *Political Women: Current Roles in State and Local Government*, ed. Janet A. Flammang. Beverly Hills, CA: Sage Publications, 1984.

National Conference of State Legislatures. "More Women Legislators and Leaders." *State Legislatures* 23 (April 1997): 5.

National Conference of State Legislatures. "Women Legislative Leaders 1977–1997." Typescript. Denver, CO: National Conference of State Legislatures, 1997.

Nelson, Albert J. *Emerging Influentials in State Legislatures*. New York: Praeger Publishers, 1991.

Neustadt, Richard F. *Presidential Power and the Modern Presidents*. New York: Macmillan Publishing, 1990.

Newman, Jody. *Perception and Reality: A Study Comparing the Success of Men and Women Candidates.* Washington, DC: National Women's Political Caucus, 1994.

Newman, Meredith Ann. "The Gendered Nature of Lowi's Typology; or Who Would Guess You Could Find Gender Here?" In *Gender Power, Leadership, and Governance,* ed. Georgia Duerst-Lahti and Rita Mae Kelly. Ann Arbor: University of Michigan Press, 1995.

Noe, R. A. "Women and Mentoring: A Review and Research Agenda." *Academy of Management Review* 13(1) (1988): 65–78.

Norton, Noelle. "Women, It's Not Enough to Be Elected: Committee Position Makes a Difference." in *Gender Power, Leadership, and Governance.* ed. Georgia Duerst-Lahti and Rita Mae Kelly. Ann Arbor: University of Michigan Press, 1995.

Ohio Women's Policy and Research Commission. "Focusing on Women." *Ohio Women* 4(2) (Summer/Fall 1996): 3.

Oklahoma Futures. *Oklahoma's Strategic Economic Development Plan 1988–1993.* Oklahoma City: Oklahoma Department of Commerce, 1990.

Oklahoma House of Representatives. *Legislative Manual,* 6th ed. Oklahoma City: Oklahoma House of Representatives, 1994.

Parsons, Talcott, and Robert F. Bales. *Family, Socialization and Interaction Process.* Glencoe, IL: Free Press, 1955.

Patterson, Samuel C. "Legislative Politics in Ohio." In *Ohio Politics,* ed. Alexander P. Lamis. Kent, OH: Kent State University Press, 1994.

Paulus, Norma. "Women Find Political Power in Unity." *Journal of State Government* 60(5) (September/October 1987): 5–10.

Peabody, Robert L. "Leadership in Legislatures: Evolution, Selection, Functions." *Legislative Studies Quarterly* IX(3) (1984): 441–473.

Perlman, Ellen. "Vera Katz and Beverly Stein: The Friendly Art of Collaboration." *Governing* 8(3) (1994): 34.

Peters, Ronald M. Jr. *The American Speakership: The Office in Historical Perspective.* Baltimore: Johns Hopkins University Press, 1990.

Peters, Ronald M. Jr., and Elizabeth Himmerich. "Policy Shift and Leadership Coalition: The Revolt Against Speaker Barker in Oklahoma." Paper presented at the annual meeting of the American Political Science Association, San Francisco, 1990.

Peters, Tom, and Nancy Austin. *A Passion for Excellence: The Leadership Difference.* New York: Random House, 1985.

Petty, Janice. *A Chairman's Guide to Effective Committee Management.* Denver, CO: National Conference of State Legislatures, 1981.

Pfeffer, Jeffrey. *Power in Organizations.* Boston: Pitman, 1981.

Pitkin, Hanna. *The Concept of Representation.* Berkeley: University of California Press, 1967.

Price, Charles M., and Charles G. Bell. "The Rules of the Game: Political Fact or Academic Fancy?" *Journal of Politics* 32(4) (November 1970): 839–855.

Putnam, Robert D. "Bowling Alone: America's Declining Social Capital." *Journal of Democracy* 6 (January 1995): 65–78.

Putnam, Robert D. "The Prosperous Community: Social Capital and Public Life." *The American Prospect* (Spring 1993): 35–42.

Putnam, Robert D. "Tuning in, Tuning out: The Strange Disappearance of Social Capital in America." *PS: Political Science and Politics* 28 (December 1995): 664–683.

Quinn, Robert E. *Beyond Rational Management.* San Francisco: Jossey-Bass, 1988.

Ragins, Belle Rose. "Barriers to Mentoring: The Female Manager's Dilemma." *Human Relations* 42(1) (1989): 1–22.

Ragins, Belle Rose, and Eric Sundstrom. "Gender and Power in Organizations: A Longitudinal Perspective." *Pyschological Bulletin* 105(1) (January 1989): 51–88.

Reingold, Beth. "Concepts of Representation Among Female and Male State Legislators." *Legislative Studies Quarterly* 17(4) (1992): 509–537.

Rieselbach, Leroy N. "'Fools Rush In . . .': Thinking about Power and Leadership in Congressional Committees." Paper presented at the annual meeting of the American Political Science Association, Chicago, 1992.

Rix, Sara E., ed. *The American Woman, 1987–88: A Report in Depth.* New York: W. W. Norton, 1987.

Roche, Gerald R. "Much Ado about Mentors." *Harvard Business Review* (January/February 1979): 14–28.

Rosener, Judy B. "Ways Women Lead." *Harvard Business Review* 68 (November/December 1990): 119–125.

Rosenthal, Alan. *Legislative Life.* New York: Harper & Row, 1981.

Rosenthal, Alan. "State Legislative Development: Observations from Three Perspectives." *Legislative Studies Quarterly* 21(2) (May 1996): 169–198.

Rosenthal, Cindy Simon. "The Case of Oklahoma Futures," *Oklahoma Politics* 2 (1993): 13–32.

Rosenthal, Cindy Simon. "Explorations of the Impact of Legislative Mentoring." Unpublished manuscript, December 1997.

Rosenthal, Cindy Simon. "Getting the Job Done: A Strategy for Overcoming Gender Inequality." *Women and Elective Office: Past, Present and Future,* ed. Sue Thomas and Clyde Wilcox. New York: Oxford University Press, 1998.

Rosenthal, Cindy Simon. "A View of Their Own: Women's Committee Leadership Styles and State Legislatures." *Policy Studies Journal* 25(4) (1997): 585–600

Rosenthal, Cindy Simon. "Women's Ways of Political Leadership: Gender Differences in a Cross-Jurisdictional Study of State Legislative Committee Chairs." Paper presented at the annual meeting of the American Political Science Association, Chicago, 1995.

Rosenthal, Cindy Simon, and Jana Vogt. "Collaborative Leadership: Is It Gender, Civic Engagement, Legislative Norms, or None of the Above?" Presented at the annual meeting of the Western Political Science Association, Tucson, Arizona, 1997.

Saint-Germain, Michelle A. "Does Their Difference Make a Difference? The Impact of Women on Public Policy in the Arizona Legislature." *Social Science Quarterly* 70(4) (December 1989): 956–1968.

Sapiro, Virginia. *The Political Integration of Women.* Urbana: University of Illinois Press, 1983.

Scales, James R. and Danney Goble. *Oklahoma Politics.* Norman: University of Oklahoma Press, 1982.

Schein, Edgar. *Organizational Culture and Leadership.* San Francisco: Jossey-Bass, 1985.

Schwartz, Nancy L. *The Blue Guitar: Political Representation and Community.* Chicago: University of Chicago Press. 1988.

Scott, Anne Firor. *The Southern Lady: From Pedestal to Politics, 1830–1930.* Chicago: University of Chicago Press, 1970.

Selznick, Philip. *Leadership in Administration: A Sociological Interpretation*. Evanston, IL: Row, Peterson, 1957.

Sharkansky, Ira. "The Utility of Elazar's Political Culture," *Polity* 2(1) (1969): 67–83.

Shin, Kwang Shik. Innovation Adoption and Diffusion in the Political Systems of States: A Focus on Taxation and Antidiscrimination. Ph.D. diss., Southern Illinois University, 1979.

Simon, A., and E. Boyer. *Mirrors for Behavior*. Philadelphia: Research for Better Schools, 1970.

Simon, Lucinda S., ed. "The Question of Leadership" [Special issue]. *Journal of State Government* 60(6) (1987): 237–270.

Simon, Lucinda S., and Carl Tubbesing, eds. *A Guide to Legislative Leadership*. Denver, CO: National Conference of State Legislatures, 1981.

Smith-Lovin, Lynn, and Dawn T. Robinson. "Gender and Conversational Dynamics." In *Gender, Interaction and Inequality*, ed. Cecilia L. Ridgeway. New York: Springer-Verlag, 1992.

Squire, Peverill. "Career Opportunities and Membership Stability in Legislatures." *Legislative Studies Quarterly* 13(1) (1988): 65–82.

Squire, Peverill. "Legislative Professionalization and Membership Diversity in State Legislatures." *Legislative Studies Quarterly* 17(1) (1992): 69–79.

Stark, Steven. "*Too* Representative Government." *Atlantic* 275(5) (May 1995): 92–106.

Statham, Anne. "Women Managers: Leadership Style, Development, and Misunderstandings." In *Women and Work: Selected Papers*, ed. Knezek, Laverne. Arlington: University of Texas, Arlington, 1985.

Stewart, David W., and Prem N. Shamdasani. *Focus Groups: Theory and Practice*. Newbury Park, CA: Sage Publications, 1990.

Stivers, Camilla. *Gender Images in Public Administration*. Newbury Park, CA: Sage Publications, 1993.

Stogdill, Ralph M. *Handbook of Leadership*. New York: Free Press, 1974.

Strauss, Anselm, and Juliet Corbin. *Basics of Qualitative Research: Grounded Theory, Procedures and Techniques*. Newbury Park, CA: Sage Publications, 1990.

Straayer, John A. *The Colorado General Assembly*. Niwot: University Press of Colorado, 1990.

Suddes, Thomas. "Panorama of Ohio Politics in the Voinovich Era, 1991–." In *Ohio Politics*, ed. Alexander P. Lamis, with Mary Anne Sharkey. Kent, OH: Kent State University Press, 1994.

Thomas, Kenneth. "Conflict and Conflict Management." In *The Handbook of Industrial and Organizational Psychology*, ed. Marvin Dunnette. Chicago: Rand McNally, 1975.

Thomas, Sue. "The Effects of Race and Gender on Constituency Service." *Western Political Quarterly* 45(1) (1992): 169–180.

Thomas, Sue. *How Women Legislate*. New York: Oxford University Press, 1994.

Thomas, Sue. "The Impact of Women on State Legislative Policies." *Journal of Politics* 53(4) (November 1991): 958–976.

Thomas, Sue. 1989. "Voting Patterns in the California Assembly: The Role of Gender." *Women and Politics* 9(1) (1989): 43–53.

Thomas, Sue, and Susan Welch. "The Impact of Gender on Activities and Priorities of State Legislators." *Western Political Quarterly* 44(2) (1991): 445–456.

U.S. Bureau of the Census. "American Women: A Profile." *Statistical Brief*. Washington, DC: U.S. Department of Commerce, Economics and Statistics Administration, July 1995.

Vaill, Peter. *Managing as Performing Art: New Ideas for a World of Chaotic Change.* San Francisco: Jossey-Bass, 1989.

Verba, Sidney, Kay Lehman Schlozman, and Henry E. Brady. *Voice and Equality: Civic Voluntarism in American Politics.* Cambridge, MA: Harvard University Press, 1995.

Wahlke, John C., Heinz Eulau, William Buchanan, and LeRoy C. Ferguson. *The Legislative System.* New York: Wiley Publishers, 1962.

Weber, Max. *Essays in Sociology*, trans. H. H. Gerth and C. Wright Mills. New York: Oxford University Press. 1946.

Welch, Susan. "Are Women More Liberal Than Men in the U.S. Congress." *Legislative Studies Quarterly* 10(1) (1985): 125–134.

Welch, Susan. "Recruitment of Women to Office: A Discriminant Analysis." *Western Political Quarterly* 31(2) (1978): 372–1380.

Werner, Emmy E. "Women in State Legislatures." *Western Political Quarterly* 21(1) (1968): 40–50.

West, Candace, and Don H. Zimmerman. 1987. "Doing Gender." *Gender and Society* 1 (June 1987): 125–151.

Williams, Christine. *Gender at Work: Women and Men in Nontraditional Occupations.* Berkeley: University of California Press, 1989.

Wilson, James Q. *Bureaucracy: What Government Agencies Do and Why They Do It.* New York: Basic Books, 1989.

Woo, Lillian. "Today's Legislators: Who They Are and Why They Run." *State Legislatures* 20(4) (April 1994): 28– 33.

Yanagisako, Sylvia Junko, and Jane Fishburn Collier, eds. *Gender and Kinship: Essays toward a Unified Analysis.* Stanford, CA: Stanford University Press, 1987.

Yoder, Janice D. "Looking beyond Numbers: The Effects of Gender Status, Job Prestige, and Occupational Gender Typing on Tokenism Processes." *Social Psychology Quarterly* 57(2) (1994): 150–159

Yoder, Janice D. "Rethinking Tokenism: Looking Beyond Numbers." *Gender and Society* 5 (June 1991): 178–192.

Yoder, Janice D. "Women at West Point: Lessons for women in Male-Dominated occupations." In *Women: A Feminist Perspective*, 4th ed., ed. Jo Freeman. Mountain View, CA: Mayfield, 1989.

Yoder, Janice D., and Arnold S. Kahn. "Toward a Feminist Understanding of Women and Power." *Psychology of Women Quarterly* 16(4) (December 1992): 381–388.

Yukl, Gary. *Leadership in Organizations*, 2nd ed. Englewood Cliffs, NJ: Prentice-Hall. 1989.

Zimmerman, D. H., and C. West. "Sex Roles, Interruptions and Silences in Conversation." In *Language and Sex: Difference and Dominance*, ed. B. Thorne and N. Henley. Rowley, MA: Newbury House, 1975.

Zink, Laurie. "Three Decades of Elite Participation: Women in Oregon State Politics 1960–1990." Paper presented at the annual meeting of the Western Political Science Association, Albuquerque, NM, 1994.

# Index

abortion, as issue in Ohio legislature, 127–129, 210–211n.68
accommodation, 67, 90
accommodators, 23
Acker, Joan, 5, 181nn.9, 10
Adams, Abigail, 161
Adams, John, 6, 161
Adkins, Jeanne, 140, 153
aggregative leadership, 5, 18–19, 26, 28, 52, 55, 70, 159, 181n.11; institutional factors affecting, 97; in the Ohio legislature, 131–132, 133, 135; in the Oklahoma legislature, 112; traits of, 57–58. *See also* distributive leadership
Anderson, Irv, 92
Anderson, Norma, 138, 140, 150, 151, 154
Armitage, Susan H., 216n.23
Aronoff, Stanley, 118, 121, 124, 125, 126
Asher, Herbert, 201n.15
assimilation, 109–110
Austin, Nancy, 185n.11
avoidance, 67

*Baker v. Carr*, 208n.6
Bales, Robert F., 187n.58
Barber, James David, 215n.8
bargaining, legislative, 37, 61–62, 191n.36

Barker, Jim, 100, 103, 104, 146
Barnard, Kate, 97, 98
Baruch, Lucy, 182n.25
Bass, Bernard M., 185n.20
Bassett, Mabel, 98
Batchelder, William, 128
Baum, Lawrence, 123, 209n.28
Bayes, Jane, 196n.50
Bebitch, Sherry Jeffe, 166
Bednar, Nancy L., 206n.35
Bellah, Robert N., 164, 216n.15
Bellmon, Henry, 101, 103
Benjamin, Ann Womer, 129
Berman, Maxine, 51, 159
Bernay, Toni, 8, 183n.34
Berry, Chuck, 146, 152
Blair, Diane D., 194n.13
Blake, R., 185n.12, 187n.48
Blalock, Hubert, 189n.97
Blanchard, Kenneth T., 185n.13
Blau, Peter M., 31, 80–81, 184n.61
Bledsoe, Carl "Bev," 146, 152
Bliss, Ray, 122
Blue, Virginia Neal, 137
Bolman, Lee G., 185n.18
Bowman, Ann O'M., 203n.58
Boyd, Betty, 99

233

Boyer, E., 217n.12
Brady, David W., 84, 164, 202n.50
Brady, Henry E., 42, 192n.58
*Breaking the Glass Ceiling* (Morrison, White, and Van Velsen), 84, 94
Brewer, Margaret, 204n.3
Brooks, Becky, 150
Brown, Wendy, 187n.43
Buchanan, William, 201n.15
Buhle, Mari Jo, 216n.23
Burford, Bob, 144
Burgess, J., 195n.29
Burns, James MacGregor, 5, 18, 21, 80, 157, 164–165, 181n.7, 186nn.37, 41
Bushardt, Stephen M., 200n.100

California legislature, 37, 77–79, 166
Campbell, Ben Nighthorse, 142
Campbell, Jane, 39, 120
Cannon, Dr. Martha Hughes, 7
Canon, David T., 183n.45
Cantor, Dorothy W., 8, 183n.34
Caraway, Hattie Wyatt, 7, 8
Carroll, Susan J., 182nn.21, 22, 184n.56, 186n.39, 191n.25
Center for the American Woman and Politics (CAWP), 8
Chodorow, Nancy, 26–27, 188n.61
Church, Foster, 194n.8
Clark, Janet, 190n.1
Clay, Judy, 204n.3
Clinton, Hillary Rodham, 30
clonal effect, 82–83
Cohen, Jacob, 196n.39
Coke, James G., 209n.19
collaboration, 67, 69–70, 86, 87, 90, 128, 158
Collier, Jane Fishburn, 187n.60
Colorado: governor's power in, 213n.54; partisan politics in, 142–143; political culture of, 141–143; women in politics in, 138–141
Colorado General Assembly, 15, 17, 37, 39; committee chairs in, 138, 147, 148, 149–151, 153–158; committee system in, 145, 147–148; first women in, 7, 137; institutional factors affecting, 144–146; partisan politics in, 143; women in, 137–138, 139–141, 151–158, 163

committee chairs, legislative: in the Colorado legislature, 138, 147, 148, 149–151, 153–158; gender differences among, 51–53, 58–71, 130–134, 161–163; leadership behaviors of, 66–71; leadership traits of, 62–66; men as, 39, 42, 43; mentoring as factor among, 71–74, 199n.91; motivations of, 58–62; in the Ohio legislature, 130–134; in the Oklahoma legislature, 111–115; women as, 10–12, 13, 14, 17, 29, 31, 32–33, 37–53, 55–56, 75–76, 161–163, 166, 189n.84
committees, legislative: differences between states, 79–80, 193n.67; gender behavior in, 25; leadership styles in, 23–24
community benchmarking, 55
competing, 67
compromising, 67
conflict resolution, styles of, 23, 24, 66, 67–71, 87, 113, 115
congressional leadership, 8, 84, 164
Conoley, Jane Close, 216n.3
Constantini, Edmond, 191n.31
Cooper, Joseph, 84, 164, 202n.50
Copeland, Gary W., 206n.54
Corbin, Juliet, 216n.9
Coveny, Regina, 200n.100
Cox, Elizabeth C., 182n.23
Cox, George "Boss," 122
Craig, Minnie, 8
Cressingham, Clara, 7, 139
Cronin, Thomas E., 212n.5
Cummins, A. Gaye, 195n.22
Czitrom, Daniel, 216n.23

*Daily Oklahoman*, 101, 104
Darcy, Robert, 98, 189n.84, 190n.1, 204n.3
Davidson, Jo Ann, 65, 114, 118, 119, 124, 126, 127–130, 135–136, 164, 165
Deal, Terrence E., 185n.18
Deatherage, Cleta, 99, 108, 205n.18
DeGette, Dianne, 138
DeGregorio, Christine, 23–24, 187nn.49, 51, 53

Delaware House of Representatives, 32–33

Democratic party: in Colorado, 140, 142, 143, 144, 145, 146; in Ohio, 119, 120, 122–124, 136; in Oklahoma, 101, 102

Denver, Colo., 141, 142

Deutchman, I. E., 195n.22

Diamond, Irene, 36, 190n.4

Dillman, Don A., 216n.4

DiStefano, Christine, 22–23, 187n.43

distributive leadership, 22–26, 134, 160, 186n.41. *See also* aggregative leadership

Dix, Nancy Chiles, 121

Dodson, Debra L., 182n.21

Dolan, Kathleen, 34, 35, 36, 190n.4

Downs, Anthony, 201n.17

Drake, Grace, 117, 120–121

Draper, Dan, 99

Drucker, Peter, 20, 160, 164, 185n.21, 216n.20

Duerst-Lahti, Georgia, 20, 23, 29, 31, 81, 181n.8, 186n.28, 188–189n.82, 189n.91, 196n.50

Duke, Lois Lovelace, 35, 190n.17

Durham, Steve, 144

Eagly, Alice H., 8, 57, 58, 181n.13, 195nn.26, 27

Eckstein, Harry, 184n.63

education: as factor in legislators' backgrounds, 34–35, 40–41

Ehrenhalt, Alan, 48, 144 145, 193n.77, 206n.46

Elazar, Daniel, 15, 84–85, 100, 123, 141, 184n.58, 203n.58

Elshtain, Jean Bethke, 52, 194n.92

England, Robert E., 204n.1

Epstein, Cynthia Fuchs, 29, 162, 189n.87, 215n.12

Equal Rights Amendment, 139

Eulau, Heinz, 182n.17, 201n.15

Evans, Beverly, 77–79, 95

Fallin, Mary, 98

Faragher, John Mack, 216n.23

Felton, Rebecca Latimer, 7

femininity, as learned behavior, 26–27

Fenno, Richard, 181n.3, 217n.11

Fenton, John, 123

Fiedler, Fred, 28, 63, 185n.13, 188n.79, 197n.55

Fiorina, Morris, 184n.2

Fiske, Marjorie, 184n.57

Follett, Mary Parker, 21, 160, 186n.33

Ford, Lynne E., 34, 35, 36, 190n.4

Fowler, Aubrey, 200n.100

Francis, Wayne, 103, 148, 193n.67

Frankovic, Kathleen A., 194n.14

Furney, Linda, 120

Gamson, William A., 216n.8

Garcia, Joseph E., 197n.55

Gargan, John J., 209n.19

Garrett, Sandy, 98, 108

GAVEL amendment (Give a Vote to Every Legislator), 143, 145, 148

Gehlen, Freida, 194n.14

gender: differences among committee chairs, 51–53, 58–71, 130–134, 161–163; differences in conflict resolution, 67–71; differences as learned behavior, 26–27, 187n.59; differences in power, 28–31, 88–93, 195n.22; as factor in leadership styles, 22–31, 52, 79, 86–87, 159–167; as factor in organizations, 181n.9; as factor in state legislatures, 4–6, 12–14, 37–53, 79, 80–82, 161–167; stereotyping based on, 30–31, 109 110, 119–120, 151–153; and the workplace, 27–28. *See also* tokenism; women legislators

Gherardi, Silvia, 181n.9

Gilligan, Carol, 27, 56, 59, 188n.62

Gillmor, Karen, 121

Githens, Marianne, 36, 190nn.1, 6

Gluck, Hazel Frank, 183n.33

Goble, Danney, 205n.31

Goodchilds, J., 65, 197–198n.61

Goodman, Ellen, 95

Gorsuch, Anne, 144, 151

Greenleaf, Robert K., 21, 186n.32

Greiling, Mindy, 92

Gryski, Gerard S., 204n.11

Guy, Mary Ellen, 35, 184n.64, 189n.90, 190n.17, 196n.50

Hale, Mary M., 71, 188n.76, 195n.29, 196n.50
Hall, Elaine, 27, 188nn.70, 72
Hamm, Keith E., 193n.67
Haney, Kelly, 107
Hanna, Mark, 122
Hansen, Karen, 200n.1
Hargrove, Erwin C., 186n.41
Hausman, Alice, 92
Hawkesworth, Mary, 6–7, 164, 182n.20
Hebert, F. Ted, 201n.15
Heclo, Hugh, 201n.17
Hedlund, Ronald D., 193n.67
Heider, John, 186n.29
Helgesen, Sally, 182n.13
Henderson, Dee W., 199n.90
Hennig, Margaret, 181n.13
Henry, Claudette, 98
Hersey, Paul, 185n.13
Hertzke, Allen D., 206n.35
Hill, Anita, 30
Himmerich, Elizabeth, 205n.22
Hinckley, Barbara, 201n.15
Hochschild, Arlie, 27, 41, 188n.67, 192n.42
Hollister, Nancy P., 119
Holly, Carrie Clyde, 7, 139
Huberman, A. Michael, 216n.9
Hughes, Charles, 137
Humphreys, George G., 204n.1

Idaho legislature, 7
individualistic subculture, 84; in Ohio, 123; in Oklahoma, 100
integrative leadership, 5, 23, 25, 70, 78, 121, 181n.11; behaviors, 58; in the Colorado legislature, 138, 153–158; defined, 19–22; effects of context on, 85–95; as exemplified by Vera Katz, 54–55; and mentoring, 72; motherhood as training ground for, 39, 161; motivations for, 56–57; in the Ohio legislature, 130–135; in the Oklahoma legislature, 114–115; promise of, 159–160; traits of, 57–58; and women, 26–28, 161–163
intrusiveness theory, 30–31, 81, 92, 100, 121, 189n.97
Isabella, Lynn A., 199n.90

Jamieson, Kathleen Hall, 184n.54
Jardim, A., 181n.13
Jewell, Malcolm, 9, 10, 58, 183nn.35, 39, 43
Johnson, Blair T., 8, 58, 181n.13
Johnson, Cathy, 186n.28, 196n.50
Johnson, Glen, 100, 106
Johnson, Marilyn, 191n.25
Johnson, Paula, 23, 187n.45
Joint Budget Committee (Colorado General Assembly), 137, 145
Jones, D. C., 195n.22
Jones, Woodrow, 191n.21
Josefowitz, Natasha, 82–83, 186n.27

Kahn, Arnold S., 195n.22
Kanter, Rosabeth Moss, 29, 30, 80–81, 82, 89, 90, 106–107, 108–109, 110, 119, 121, 152, 184n.60, 189n.93, 202n.32, 203n.62
Karau, S. J., 195n.26
Kasputis, Edward, 127–128
Kassebaum, Nancy L., 8
Kates, Nancy D., 194n.1
Kathlene, Lyn, 25, 153, 187n.55, 195n.16
Katz, Vera, 54–55, 57, 61, 74, 183n.33, 194n.4
Kaufman, Herbert, 202n.37
Kawar, A., 196n.50
Kearney, Richard, 203n.58
Kearns, Merle, 117, 120
Keating, Frank, 103–104
Kelly, Patricia "Tish," 8
Kelly, Rita Mae, 20, 23, 29, 31, 57, 81, 181n.8, 188n.76, 188–189n.82, 195n.29, 196n.50, 202n.41
Kelman, Steven, 186n.41
Kendall, Patricia L., 184n.57
Kenney, Sally, 12, 13, 14, 181n.9
Kerns, Peggy, 39, 150
King, Cheryl Simrell, 186n.26
Kirkpatrick, Jeane, 34, 36, 159, 190n.2
Kirkpatrick, Samuel A., 103, 205n.32
Kleeman, Kathy, 182n.25
Klock, Frances S., 7, 139
Knepper, George, 209n.18
Korenblit, Lynn, 191n.25
Kosmin, Barry A., 202n.53
Kram, Kathy E., 199n.90

Kramer, Jack J., 216n.3
Kuhn, Thomas S., 187n.42
Kunin, Madeleine, 183n.33
Kurfess, Charles, 124
Kurtz, Karl, 191n.38

Lachman, Seymour P., 202n.53
Lacy, Elsie, 137
Ladner, Mildred, 204n.4
Lamm, Richard, 143, 144
Lao-Tzu, 21, 166–167, 186n.29
Larason, Linda, 99
Lasswell, Harold, 18, 184n.1
Laws, Judith Long, 30, 189n.98
Leader, Shelah, 194–195n.14
leadership: behaviors, 58; context as
    factor in, 85–95; definitions of, 20;
    feminization of, 55, 75; gender as
    factor in, 22–31, 160; influences on,
    188–189n.82; masculinism in, 20;
    through mentoring, 71–74;
    motivations for, 56–57; place as
    constraint upon, 80–85; traits of, 57–
    58. *See also* committee chairs,
    legislative
leadership styles: aggregative, 18–19, 26,
    28, 52, 55, 57–58, 70, 97, 112, 131–132,
    133, 135; in the Colorado legislature,
    138, 146, 147, 153–158; and
    congressional committees, 23–24;
    cultural influences on, 84–85, 95; of
    Jo Ann Davidson, 128–130;
    distributive, 18, 22–26, 134, 160,
    186n.41; gender differences in, 16, 58,
    58–71, 74–75, 86–87, 159–167;
    integrative, 19–22, 23, 25, 26, 27, 39,
    54–55, 56–58, 70, 72, 78, 85–95, 114–
    115, 121, 159–167; in the Ohio
    legislature, 118, 130–135; in the
    Oklahoma legislature, 114–115;
    political culture as influence on, 29,
    79–80, 84–85, 88, 93–94, 95;
    transactional, 18, 157, 160, 165;
    transformational, 157, 186n.37; types
    of, 23–24; of women, 4, 7, 8–10, 16–17,
    26–28, 52, 55–56, 76
"least preferred coworker" instrument,
    63, 197n.56, 198n.62
Lee, Marcia M., 191n.23

legislators, state. *See* state legislators
legislators, women. *See* women legislators
legislatures, state. *See* state legislatures
Levinson, Arlene, 216n.24
Likert, Rensis, 185n.12
listening skills: of women legislators, 70,
    114–115, 154–155
Loden, Marilyn, 56–57, 182n.13
Loevy, Robert D., 212n.5
Loughead, Nettie, 119
Louisiana legislature, 7
Luebbers, Jerome, 129
Lunneborg, Patricia, 57, 182n.13

Machung, Anne, 192n.42
Madsen, Richard, 216n.15
Main, Eleanor C., 204n.11
Mandel, Ruth, 16, 182n.25, 184n.65
Mansbridge, Jane J., 187n.41
March, James G., 18, 21, 181n.11
Maroney, Jane, 32–33
Martin, Patricia Yancey, 188n.65
masculinism: in leadership, 20–21
masculinity: as learned behavior, 26
Matthews, Donald, 201n.15
Mayhew, David, 184n.2
McClelland, David, 28, 62, 188n.78
McDiarmid, Hugh C., 209n.18
McIver, John P., 212n.29
McLemore, Lelan E., 201n.15
mentoring, 71–74, 76, 199n.91
Merton, Robert K., 184n.57
methodology, 14–17, 184n.63
Meyer, Natalie, 140
Miles, Matthew B., 216n.9
Miller, Cynthia L., 195n.22
Mintzberg, Henry, 185n.15
Missouri legislature, 60
Mitchell, James V., 216n.3
Mitchell, Stephen, 186n.29
Moffat, David, 137
Montgomery, Betty, 119
moralistic subculture, 84, 88
Morgan, David L., 184n.57
Morgan, David R., 204n.1
Morrison, Ann M., 195n.28
motherhood: as training ground, 39, 161
Mouton, J. S., 185n.12, 187n.48
Mueller, Carol, 194n.13

Nechemias, Carol, 184n.52
Nelson, Albert J., 190n.1, 191n.21, 203n.56
Netzley, Robert, 126
Neustadt, Richard E., 185n.17
New Deal, 122
New Hampshire House: Donna Sytek as speaker of, 3–4, 41
New Hampshire legislature, 37
Newman, Jody, 215n.6
Newman, Meredith Ann, 189n.89
Nicholson, Samuel, 137
Nineteenth Amendment, 97
Noe, R. A., 199n.88
Norton, Gale, 140
Norton, Noelle, 189n.88
Norton, Tom, 146, 153

Ohio: political culture of, 121–124, 134–136
Ohio General Assembly, 15, 17, 39; committee chairs in, 117, 130–134; commitee process in, 124–127, 135; Jo Ann Davidson as speaker of, 127–130; leadership styles in, 130–135; term limits, 126–127, 136; women in, 118–121, 127–134, 135–136, 208n.6
Oklahoma: political culture of, 100–102; women in politics in, 97–100
Oklahoma legislature, 15, 17, 37, 115–116; committee chairs in, 111–115; committee system in, 104–106, 148; composition of, 96–97, 98–100; institutional factors affecting, 102–104; term limits, 104; tokenism in, 97, 104, 106–111; women in, 96–97, 98–100, 106–111, 114–115
*Oklahoma Observer*, 108
Olsen, Johan P., 18, 21, 181n.11
organizations: effects on behavior, 28–29, 80, 84, 196n.51; leaders in, 28–29; professions as a form of, 82–83; sex composition of, 79, 80–82

paradigm, 22
Parsons, Talcott, 26, 187n.58
Paschall, Mark, 150–151
Patterson, S., 183n.43
Patterson, Samuel C., 123, 124, 125, 209n.35

Paulson, Chris, 158
Paulus, Norma, 183n.33
Peabody, Robert L., 183n.38
Penn, John, 6
Perlman, Ellen, 194n.6
Peters, Ronald M., Jr., 164, 185n.17, 186n.41, 189n.82, 205n.22
Peters, Tom, 185n.11
Petty, Janice, 183n.44
Pfeffer, Jeffrey, 185n.15
Pitkin, Hanna Fenichel, 6, 182n.15
political culture: in Colorado, 141–143; as influence on leadership style, 29, 79–80, 84–85, 88, 93–94, 95; in Ohio, 121–124, 134–136; in Oklahoma, 100–102; in organizations, 81–82
Populist Party, 139
power, 202n.32; gender differences in, 28–31, 88–93, 195n.22; as motivation, 56–57, 60–61, 62, 65, 66
pragmatists, 23
Prestage, Jewel, 36, 190n.6
Progressivism, 122
promoters, 23
Putnam, Robert, 42, 192n.54

Quinn, Robert E., 58, 185n.18

Ragins, Belle Rose, 196n.43, 199n.90
Rankin, Jeannette, 7
Rausch, John David, Jr., 206n.54
Reagan, Ronald, 144
Reingold, Beth, 195n.15
Reneau, Brenda, 98
representation: concept of, 6–7, 182n.16
Republican party: in Colorado, 139, 140–141, 142, 143, 144, 145, 146; in Ohio, 118, 119, 120–121, 122–124; in Oklahoma, 101, 102
*Reynolds v. Sims*, 144
Rhodes, James, 123
Rieselbach, Leroy, 10, 183n.41
Riffe, Vernal G., 118, 123, 124, 125, 126, 128, 131, 134, 135, 146
Rix, Sara E., 190n.12
Robertson, Alice Mary, 97, 204n.4
Roche, Gerald R., 199n.90
*Roe v. Wade*, 210–211n.68
Rosener, Judy, 28, 181n.13

Rosenthal, Alan, 183n.43, 191n.38, 193n.67, 202n.33
Rosenthal, Cindy Simon, 192nn.57, 60, 197n.60, 203n.57, 205n.34
Routt, John, 137

Saint-Germain, Michelle A., 194n.10
Sapiro, Virginia, 194n.9
Scales, James R., 205n.31
Schapiro, Beth S., 204n.11
Schein, Edgar, 185n.16
Schlozman, Kay Lehman, 42, 192n.58
Schoettler, Gail, 140
Schroeder, Patricia, 140
Schwartz, Nancy, 182nn.14, 16
Scott, Anne Firor, 98, 204n.10
Selznick, Philip, 202n.37
servant leadership, 21, 186nn.32, 40
sex composition of organizations, 79, 80–82, 88–89. *See also* tokenism
Shaheen, Jeanne, 4
Shamdasani, Prem N., 184n.57
Sharkansky, Ira, 202n.52
Shedrick, Bernice, 107, 108
"shell" bills, 105, 206n.62
Shin, Kwang Shik, 202–203n.55
Simon, A., 217n.12
Simon, Lucinda S., 183n.43
Sorenson, Liane, 32–33
Squire, Peverill, 192n.59
Stanley, Jean R., 194n.13, 196n.50
Stanwyck, Kathy, 191n.25
Stark, Steven, 216n.24
state legislators. ages of, 34, 39, 192n.60; ambition of, 36, 47–48; careerism, 202n.33; in citizen legislatures, 42–43; as committee chairs, 37–53; educational backgrounds, 34–35, 40–41; family backgrounds, 35, 41–42; mentoring, 71–74; in professionalized legislatures, 42–43, 204n.71; work ethic of, 48–51. *See also* committee chairs, legislative; women legislators
state legislatures: ambition in, 47–48; citizen, 37, 163, 192n.41; differences among, 42–44; gender as factor in, 4–6, 12–14, 80–82, 161–167; hybrid, 37, 191–192n.40; institutionalized, 82–83; professional, 37, 79, 83, 86, 87–88,

163, 191n.39, 202n.33, 204n.71; types of, 37, 191n.39, 191–192n.40, 192n.41; women as committee chairs in, 10–12, 13, 14, 17, 29, 31, 32–33, 37–53, 55–56, 75–76, 161–163; women in, 4–6, 7–10, 12–14, 33–37, 172, 190n.1, 203n.56. *See also* Colorado General Assembly; Ohio General Assembly; Oklahoma legislature; state legislators; women legislators
Statham, Anne, 200n.100
Stein, Beverly, 55
Steinmetz, Kaye, 60
Stewart, David W., 184n.57
Stivers, Camilla, 20, 83, 94, 185n.23
Stockton, Ruth, 137
Stoess, Jean, 183n.34
Stogdill, Ralph M., 185n.10
Stone, Walter J., 212n.29
Straayer, John A., 212n.27
Strahle, Ron, 144
Strauss, Anselm, 216n.9
Strickland, Ted, 146
Suddes, Thomas, 209n.34
Sullivan, William M., 216n.15
Sundstrom, Eric, 196n.43
Swidler, Ann, 216n.15
Sytek, Donna: as speaker of the New Hampshire House, 3–4, 41

Taylor, Ella, 182n.21
Taylor, Stratton, 100
term limits: in the Ohio legislature, 126–127, 136; in the Oklahoma legislature, 104
Thomas, Clarence, 30
Thomas, Kenneth, 23, 24, 67, 187nn.47, 48
Thomas, Sue, 10, 35, 51, 182n.21, 194n.12, 195n.14
Thomas-Kilmann Conflict Mode Instrument, 67, 198n.76
Thompson, Carolyn, 108
tokenism, 30–31, 80, 81, 162–163; in the Colorado legislature, 151–152; in the Ohio legislature, 119–120; in the Oklahoma legislature, 97, 104, 106–111
traditionalistic subculture, 84; in Oklahoma, 98, 100–101

transactional leadership, 5, 18, 157, 160, 165
transformational leadership, 157,
    186n.37
Troy, Frosty, 108
Truman, Harry, 111
Tubbesing, Carl, 183n.43

U.S. House of Representatives: women
    in, 7
U.S. Senate: women in, 7
Utah legislature, 7, 77–79

Vaill, Peter, 185n.18
Van Velson, Ellen, 195n.28
Verba, Sidney, 42, 192n.58
Verstegen, Dayna, 189n.91
Vogt, Jana, 192n.57
Voinovich, George V., 127
volunteer work: as background for
    legislative service, 41–42, 43, 129, 130,
    161

Wahlke, John C., 201n.15
Waitt, Maude, 119
Watson, Diane, 77–79, 95, 201n.11
Weber, Max, 185n.14
Welch, Susan, 190nn.1, 6, 195n.14
Wells, Jeff, 146
Werner, Emmy E., 190n.6
West, Candace, 28, 188n.72
Wham, Dottie, 140, 152, 156–157
Whicker, Marcia, 9, 10, 58, 183nn.35, 39
White, Randall P., 195n.28
Williams, Christine, 188nn.65, 71
Wilson, James Q., 201n.17
Winkler, Cheryl, 117
Wolcott, Edward, 137
women's suffrage: in Colorado, 139; in
    Oklahoma, 97
Women Elected Democrat Officials of
    Ohio (WEDO), 120, 124
women legislators, 4–6, 7–10, 12–14,
33–37, 203n.56, 212n.3; African
American, 77–79; ages of, 34, 39,
192n.60; ambitions of, 36, 47–48;
backgrounds of, 34–37, 41–42, 43, 129,
130, 161; behavioral differences of, 25;
in business, 28; in the Colorado
legislature, 137–138, 139–141, 151–158;
as committee chairs, 10–12, 13, 14, 17,
29, 31, 32–33, 37–53, 55–56, 75–76, 161–
163, 166, 189n.84; cultural influences
on, 84–85, 95; educational and
professional backgrounds, 34–35, 40–
41; family backgrounds, 35, 41–42;
impact of institutional norms on, 83–
84; and integrative leadership, 26–28;
issues of concern to, 75–76, 99; in
leadership roles, 5–6, 26–28; leadership
styles of, 4, 7, 8–10, 16–17, 26–28, 52,
55–56; legislative careers of, 44–53;
listening skills of, 114–115, 154–155;
mentoring, 71–74; in the Ohio
legislature, 118–121, 127–134, 135–136,
208n.6; in the Oklahoma legislature,
96–97, 98–100, 106–111, 114–115; power
as influenced by numbers of, 10,
15–16, 30–31, 79, 81–82, 88–93, 121,
162–163; power as motivation for, 57,
60–61, 62, 195n.22; strategies used by,
109–111; in the U.S. House and
Senate, 7; work ethic of, 48–51. *See
also* gender; state legislators
Woo, Lillian, 216n.6
Wright, Ruth, 146

Yanagisako, Sylvia Junko, 187n.60
Yoder, Janice, 30–31, 81, 90, 92, 95, 100,
    121, 184n.62, 189nn.96, 97, 195n.22
Yukl, Gary, 185n.19

Zerilli, Linda M. G., 182n.22, 184n.56
Zimmerman, Don, 28, 188n.72
Zink, Laurie, 190n.9